BLACK&DECKER®

THE COMPLETE GUIDE TO

DVD INCLUDED

KITCHENS

Do-It-Yourself and Save

- **3rd Edition**
- **Design & Planning**
- **Quick Updates**
- **Custom Cabinetry**
- **Remodeling Projects On Budget**

Creative Publishing
international

MINNEAPOLIS, MINNESOTA
www.creativepub.com

**Creative Publishing
international**

Copyright © 2009
Creative Publishing international, Inc.
400 First Avenue North, Suite 300
Minneapolis, Minnesota 55401
1-800-328-0590
www.creativepub.com
All rights reserved

Printed in China

10 9 8 7 6 5 4 3 2

Library of Congress Cataloging-in-Publication Data

The complete guide to kitchens : with DVD : do-it-yourself and
save, design & planning, quick updates, custom cabinetry, major
remodeling projects. -- 3rd edl.
    p. cm.
 At head of title: Black & Decker.
 Includes index.
 Summary: "Includes information on installing and updating all
areas of a kitchen, including cabinets, countertops, flooring, lighting
and appliances"--Provided by publisher.
 ISBN-13: 978-1-58923-480-2 (soft cover)
 ISBN-10: 1-58923-480-4 (soft cover)
 1. Kitchens--Remodeling--Amateurs' manuals. I. Title.

TH4816.3.K58C655 2009
643'.3--dc22

2009020710

The Complete Guide to Kitchens
Created by: The Editors of Creative Publishing international, Inc. in cooperation with Black & Decker.
Black & Decker® is a trademark of The Black & Decker Corporation and is used under license.

President/CEO: Ken Fund

Home Improvement Group

Publisher: Bryan Trandem
Managing Editor: Tracy Stanley
Senior Editor: Mark Johanson
Editor: Jennifer Gehlhar

Creative Director: Michele Lanci-Altomare
Senior Design Managers: Brad Springer, Jon Simpson
Design Manager: James Kegley

Lead Photographer: Joel Schnell
Photo Coordinator: Cesar Fernandez Rodriquez
Production Managers: Linda Halls, Laura Hokkanen

Contributing Writer: Karen Ruth
Page Layout Artist: Shanda Nelson
Shop Help: Charles Boldt

Cover Photography Credit: Todd Caverly

Contents

Introduction

In recent years, kitchens have received an enormous amount of attention from high-end design magazines, television home décor shows, and even manufacturers of expensive appliances. Without question, the trendsetters in the industry have concocted some amazing rooms with jaw-dropping features. In fact, the kitchens we see featured in most media today are primarily room sets built purely to showcase an impressive style rather than pleasing, efficient rooms from which we feed our families and carry on those "kitchen table discussions" politicians are always talking about. That's okay: everyone loves to dream about surrounding themselves with beauty, opulence, and state-of-the-art living accessories. But if, like most of us, your goal is to find a few practical ways to make your kitchen better meet your needs (and maybe show off just a little bit), then you need a guide that features rooms that look something like your house. *The Complete Guide to Kitchens* is exactly that kind of book.

In this freshly updated edition, we show you dozens of instant-payback projects that make your kitchen brighter and easier to use—from painting the walls to updating the lighting, childproofing cabinets and appliances, or installing pull-out shelves to convert a broom closet into an efficient pantry. We also cover some more involved kitchen improvements, such as installing all-new cabinets and countertops or replacing the flooring. These are all projects that can be done by most do-it-yourselfers with moderate skills. And for the most part they require more elbow grease than capital. Because so much activity in kitchens centers around major household appliances, we show you how to hook up and maintain your refrigerator, stove, icemaker, water filter, and more. By doing it yourself you can save money, but you'll also build the skills to be prepared for an appliance emergency. Plus, you can do the work on your own schedule—no setting aside a full day just so you can wait for a delivery or a repair call. For the truly ambitious homeowner who has more advanced carpentry skills, we even show you how to build your own custom cabinets yourself—the ultimate "luxury you can afford". *The Complete Guide to Kitchens* reflects the most current design thinking on relevant issues that matter today. Throughout this book, you'll find pointers about eco-friendly options, shopping tips to clue you in on features to look for, and notes on Universal Design, which creates accessibility for a wide range of people. After all, if your kitchen doesn't meet your needs, it doesn't work—no matter how fancy it may look. The kitchen is the most frequently remodeled room in the house. From modest makeovers to down-to-the-studs re-dos, planning and know-how are the variables that make the difference between creating a kitchen that really meets your long-term needs versus one that you'll be remodeling again in a couple of years. *The Complete Guide to Kitchens* is the best tool you'll buy to ensure that your kitchen project has real staying power.

Planning & Design

The initial step for any home improvement project is to assess the space you already have and to develop a firm concept for the ideal appearance and function. Although most of us have a fair idea which styles (traditional, contemporary, etc.) we generally gravitate toward, today's vast selection of materials, appliances, and upgrades has complicated the process of choosing products and materials. With so many customizable options—from cabinet hardware to floor tiles—the possibilities can seem endless. Whether you're looking for a dramatic transformation or simply an easy update, however, you should consider these vast selections to be opportunities for making your kitchen project a success—perhaps in ways you hadn't imagined.

In this chapter you'll find a portfolio of kitchens and kitchen details that display a wide range of achievable ideas. These well-selected images represent a good starting point, but with just a little exploring you'll find a small universe of additional shots from other sources, including magazines, television shows, design groups, design centers, or trade association websites (see Resources, page 282). Following the gallery of ideas section, you'll find some helpful, highly practical information on kitchen design and the fundamental strategies for devising a remodeling plan.

This chapter shows:

- Gallery of Kitchen Ideas
- Design Standards
- Remodeling Plans
- Budget & Finance

Gallery of Kitchen Ideas

The Shaker style cabinetry and colonial colors in this kitchen combine with knotty wood flooring for an old-fashioned yet completely fresh look.

Glass lites add interest and gleam to a kitchen, but if you are not a stickler for cabinet organization look for multi-lite doors with frosted or textured glass.

Simple, geometric lines, warm wood tones, and natural stone countertops can be found in kitchens of just about any style. But this kitchen makes clever use of a couple of additional details to pull a feeling of rustic appeal from these raw elements. Specifically, the tile backsplash and the framed cabinets.

This classic look carries on the long-standing tradition of painted cabinetry in the kitchen. Darker countertops and shades soften the room. Subway tile and a fireclay sink add extra reflection.

Although its visual effect is minimized by the wood panel door coverings and trimwork, a large side-by-side refrigerator is a hallmark of a restaurant-inspired kitchen. Other giveaways include massive amounts of countertop and island work surface.

Even a galley kitchen can be laid out to create efficient workflow. In a two-sided galley, the main issues are to leave enough space between opposing sides and to locate the sink and stove close together.

Homework has become yet another function of the kitchen. A spacious breakfast bar offers a comfortable, supervised space where kids can finish up school work while dinner is being prepared.

Kitchens invite conviviality, so why not plan for it? By creating dedicated seating and eating areas adjacent to the kitchen, a chef who enjoys entertaining can insert himself or herself into the fun without creating obstacles that can threaten the delicate timing of a gourmet meal.

Air drying dishes uses zero energy and does not spread bacteria or other contaminants as cloth-drying can. These wall-hung metal shelves function as drying racks because they are positioned directly over the integral drainboard that's cast into the countertop.

Living in an apartment or small townhome with a modest kitchen can mean you need to incorporate other elements into the room's function. Choose appliances that blend with your décor and use cabinetry to tie it all together visually.

Flow is as important for the eye as it is for the feet. If you direct the feet to move toward an eye-catching feature, like this picture window with a stunning skyline view, the eye tends to keep going after the feet stop.

A minimalist's dream, this contemporary kitchen makes a dramatic design statement mostly by virtue of what it leaves out. A concrete countertop and matching backsplash work with the clean lines of the bamboo drawer and door fronts to create a soothing effect. What else do you really need?

Counter space can double as an eating space in many kitchens. Provide approximately 24" per seated diner.

Streamlined details make small kitchens appear larger. Here, contemporary flat-front cabinets with sleek handles allow the furnishings and décor to be the room's focus.

Fitted pieces create the appearance of furniture rather than cabinets. Choosing pieces with legs and eliminating toe kicks helps emphasize this custom look.

Elements of a commercial kitchen include a stainless steel side-by-side refrigerator and specialty appliances. The sink and faucet also elevate the appearance of this residential kitchen. The multi-lite cabinet doors offset the commercial look just enough to keep the room from feeling too institutional.

Fun colors, playful shapes, and unusual textures don't cost any more than ordinary ones, but they can create a delightful and unexpected kitchen environment.

Freestanding kitchen furnishings offer convenience, ease of installation, and excellent portability—you may end up liking them so much that you take them with you when you move.

Traditional materials don't have to be dull. Here, old-world clay tile makes a lively backsplash and the painted wood cabinets topped with butcher block countertop are on-trend in any modern kitchen.

Black and white never go out of style. If you'd rather not revamp your kitchen every couple of years to keep up with the latest trends, you can't go wrong with this classic combo.

Glass mirrors and stainless steel create a repeating theme of reflection and brightness in kitchens.

An apron sink and plantation shutters add rustic, rural charm to this kitchen. The wall-mounted faucet set and cut-marble countertop complete the effect.

This semicircular raised eating area echoes the shape of the range hood, softening the room's dynamic lines.

Glass doors brighten the cabinets above this sink, relieving shadows in corners.

Modern results can come from the most ancient materials. This ultra-contemporary backsplash is fashioned with edge-glued strips of bamboo—just about the oldest building material known to man.

Open shelving adds visual interest to this contemporary setting.

Bamboo makes an exceptionally beautiful and durable cabinet material and is commonly available with blond (natural) and various darker colors.

An undermount sink and a single-body faucet make up a one-two punch that is a current favorite among kitchen designers. The combination is also highly practical because it is easy to clean and thoroughly hygienic.

Design Standards

While you may imagine that the answer to every cramped kitchen is to knock down walls and add more space, that's often not the easiest or best solution. One alternative to tearing down the walls is to install windows for light. An extra door or even a pass-through window—from the kitchen to an adjacent room—can also help make the space feel more airy. In short, the cramped feeling may only be one of perception.

Most kitchens fall into one of four categories: Galley, L-shaped, U-shaped, and Open Plan. Whether they are small or large, old or new, these floor plans have proven to be popular models for efficient kitchens, though that doesn't mean they'll necessarily be the most efficient for your needs.

Galley: In small homes or city apartments, the galley kitchen is a space-saving choice that is ideal for one or two users. The components may all be lined up along one wall or divided between two parallel walls. For this floor plan to work best, the central galley space should be large enough to allow all appliances to be open at the same time, with enough space remaining for someone to walk through the middle.

L-shape: This corner kitchen layout can feel roomier than it is in reality, because of the L-shape floor plan. However, the two "arms" might also create an awkward workstation, with little room to set items down midway through a meal. Consider taking advantage of the lost central space with a counter-height dining table that can double as a prep station or even a freestanding central island.

U-shape: This layout takes the benefits of a galley kitchen—space-saving solution plus accessibility for one user—and adds a third wall to create the ultimate triangular floor plan. In a compact space, placing the sink at the far end with the refrigerator and range on opposing walls creates a simple workstation. On a larger scale, a sizable island can anchor the center of the room and provide more storage.

Open Plan: Whether the kitchen is located in the middle of a larger great room or off to one side, an open plan layout works best with the addition of a central island or a dividing counter of some type. Perfect for family kitchens or entertaining spaces where the cooks can easily visit with guests, it's important for this floor plan to be well organized so that all necessities are close at hand.

Whichever layout plan you opt for, the most fundamental principle that you don't want to violate is to maintain plenty of free area between appliances, sinks, and other elements of the work triangle. In a galley kitchen like the one seen here, the corridor between kitchen walls should be at least 4 ft. wide, and preferably wider.

Common Kitchen Layouts

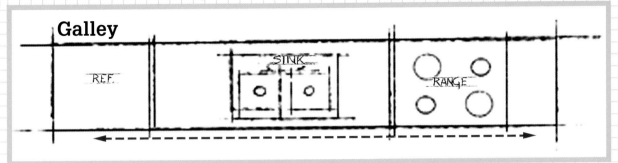

Galley

REF.

SINK

RANGE

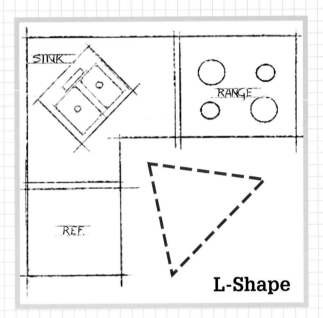

SINK

RANGE

REF.

L-Shape

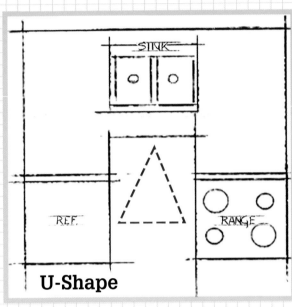

SINK

REF.

RANGE

U-Shape

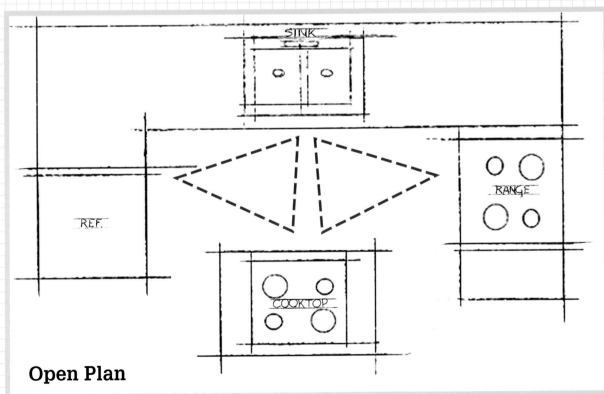

SINK

REF.

RANGE

COOKTOP

Open Plan

Whether you are doing the work yourself or hiring others, once you have a good idea of the features you want in your new kitchen, it's time to create detailed plan drawings. Good planning drawings will help you in several phases of the planning process:

- Selecting cabinets and appliances to fit your kitchen layout;
- Soliciting accurate work bids when negotiating with plumbers, electricians, and other subcontractors;
- Obtaining a building permit at your local Building inspections office;
- Scheduling the stages of a remodeling project;
- Evaluating the work of contractors. If a carpenter or cabinetmaker fails to meet your expectations, your plan drawings serve as proof that the contractor did not complete the work as agreed.

Codes & Standards

Creating plans for a kitchen can seem like an overwhelming challenge, but fortunately there are guidelines available to help you. Some of these guidelines are legal regulations specified by your local building code and must be followed exactly. Most codes have very specific rules for basic construction, as well as for plumbing and electrical installations.

Another set of guidelines, known as standards, are informal recommendations developed over time by kitchen designers, cabinetmakers, and appliance manufacturers. These design standards suggest parameters for good kitchen layout and following them helps ensure that your kitchen is comfortable and convenient to use.

Guidelines for Layout

The goal of any kitchen layout is to make the cook's work easier and, where possible, to allow other people to enjoy the same space without getting in the way. Understanding the accepted design standards can help you determine whether your present layout is sufficient or if your kitchen needs a more radical layout change or expansion. A classic kitchen design concept, the work triangle theory, proposes that the sink, range, and refrigerator be arranged in a triangular layout according to the following guidelines:

- Position of the triangle should be such that traffic flow will not disrupt the main functions of the kitchen;
- Total distance between the corners of the triangle should be no more than 26 feet and no less than 12 feet;
- Each side of the triangle should be between 4 feet and 9 feet in length.

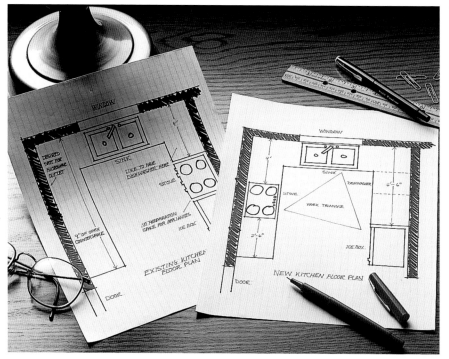

The work triangle is a layout concept that lets you develop a convenient arrangement of the range, sink, and refrigerator in the kitchen.

If two people frequently work in the kitchen simultaneously, the layout should include two work triangles. In a two-triangle kitchen, the triangles may share one side, but they should not cross one another.

Don't fret too much if you can't make the triangle layout work perfectly. Some kitchens, for example, may have four workstations instead of three, and others may not have enough space to accommodate the classic triangle.

For general traffic design, it is recommended to leave 4-feet "corridors" between all stationary items for walking comfort. Some designers will allow this standard to be reduced to 3 feet in smaller kitchens.

Industry Standards ▶

Standard Appliance Dimensions

Appliance	Standard Dimensions (width)	Minimum Countertop space	Comments
Refrigerator	30" to 36"	15" on latch side	12 cu. ft. for family of four; 2 cu. ft. for each additional person
Sink	27" single 36" double	24" on one side 18" on other side	Minimum of 3" of countertop space between sink and edge of base cabinet
Range	30", 36"	15" on one side 9" on other side	
Cooktop	30", 36", 42", 48"	15" on one side 9" on other side	If a window is positioned above a cooking appliance, the bottom edge of the window casing must be at least 24" above the cooking surface
Wall oven	24", 27", 30"	15" on either side	Oven bottom should be between 24" and 48" above the floor
Microwave	19", 24", 30"	15" on either side	When built in, place low in wall cabinets or just under counter

Eating Surface Standards

Height of Eating Surface	30"	36"	42"
Min. width for each seated diner	30"	24"	24"
Min. depth for each seated diner	19"	15"	12"
Minimum knee space	19"	15"	12"

Cabinet Standards

Recommended Minimum For Size of Kitchen		
	Less than 150 sq. ft.	More than 150 sq. ft.
Base cabinets	13 lin. ft.	16 lin. ft.
Wall cabinets	12 lin. ft.	15.5 lin. ft.
Roll-out shelving	10 lin. ft.	13.75 lin. ft.

The sizes of base cabinets and wall cabinets are fairly uniform among manufacturers, and unless you have them custom-built in unusual sizes, they will conform to the following standards:

- **Base cabinets:** height 34½"; depth 23 to 24"; width 9 to 48", in 3" increments.
- **Wall cabinets:** height 12", 15", 18", 24", 30", 33", 42"; depth 12"; width 24", 30", 33", 36", 42", 48".
- **Oven cabinets:** height 84", 96"; depth 24"; width 27", 30", 33".
- **Utility cabinets:** height 84"; depth 12", 24"; width 18", 24", 36".

Not every manufacturer will offer all these sizes and styles, so it's a good idea to obtain product catalogs when planning the layout of cabinets. Some other tips:

- Use functional corner cabinets rather than "blind" cabinets that provide no access to the corner area;
- Include at least five storage/organizing units, such as swing-out pantry units, appliance garages, and specialized drawers or shelves.

Eating areas. Kitchen tabletops and countertops used for dining are generally positioned 30", 36", or 42" above the floor, and the recommended space for each person varies according to the height of the surface.

Islands. A kitchen island should be positioned so there is at least 36" of clear space between the edges of its countertop and surrounding walls or cabinets.

▌Guidelines for Basic Construction

Plans for a major remodeling project that involves moving or adding walls or building a new room addition must accurately show the locations and dimensions of the new walls and all doors and windows. This will allow the construction carpenter to give you an accurate bid on the work and will allow him to obtain the necessary building permits. If you will be moving walls or adding windows or doors, you must identify load-bearing walls and provide appropriate support during removal and rebuilding.

▌Window Guidelines

Most building codes require that kitchens have at least one window with at least 10 sq. feet of glass area. Some local building codes, however, will allow windowless kitchens, so long as they have proper venting. Obviously, if your kitchen does not have an exterior wall it cannot have a window (although a skylight is a great solution if it makes sense structurally). Kitchen designers recommend that kitchens have windows, doors, or skylights that together have a total glass surface area equal to at least 25 percent of the total floor area.

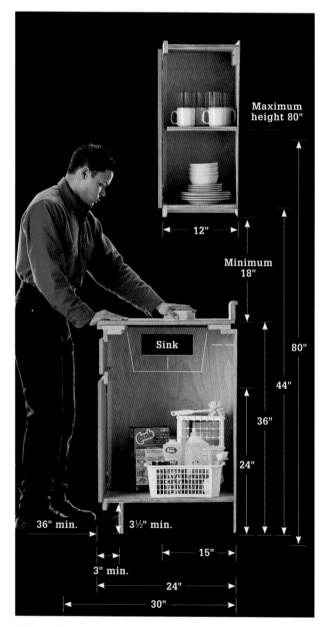

Dimensions and positions of cabinets follow accepted design standards, as shown here.

Door Guidelines

Exterior entry doors should be at least 36 inches wide and 80 inches high. Interior passage doors between rooms must be at least 30 inches wide. A kitchen must have at least two points of entry, arranged so traffic patterns don't intrude on work areas.

Guidelines for Electrical Service & Lighting

Most major kitchen-remodeling projects require some upgrading of the electrical service. While your old kitchen may be served by a single 120-volt circuit, it's not uncommon for a large modern kitchen to require as many as seven individual circuits, including a pair of dedicated 20-amp small-appliance circuits. In a few cases, the extra demands of the new kitchen may require that the main electrical service for your entire house be upgraded by an electrician. By comparing the electrical service in your present kitchen with the requirements described below, you'll get an idea of how extensive your electrical service improvements will need to be. Your plan drawings should indicate the locations of all the outlets, lighting fixtures, and electrical appliances in your new kitchen.

Many areas enforce kitchen codes that are based on the National Electric Code (NEC) standards. Among the more important NEC requirements are:

- Two small-appliance circuits (120-volt, 20-amp) to supply power for the refrigerator and plug-in countertop appliances;
- Wall outlets spaced no more than 12 ft. apart;
- Countertop outlets spaced no more than 4 ft. apart;
- GFCI (ground-fault circuit interrupter) protected receptacles installed in any general use outlet, whether above the counter or at floor level, including receptacles that are mounted inside cabinets;
- Dedicated circuits for each major appliance. Install a 20-amp, 120-volt circuit for a built-in microwave, a 15-amp circuit for the dishwasher and food disposer. An electric range, cooktop, or wall oven generally requires a dedicated circuit with service ratings of at least 50 amps and 240 volts.

The electric code only requires that a kitchen have some form of lighting controlled by a wall switch, but kitchen designers have additional recommendations:

- A general lighting circuit (120-volt, 15-amp) that operates independently from plug-in outlets;
- Plentiful task lighting, usually mounted under wall cabinets or soffits, to illuminate each work area;
- Decorative lighting fixtures to highlight attractive cabinets or other features of the kitchen.

Plumbing Guidelines

Minimum plumbing requirements for kitchens are enforced by your local code agency and many times are based on the Uniform Plumbing Codes (UPC). Like the NEC, the UPC is updated every three years, so make sure you are working with current information (the best way to assure this is to involve your local building inspector). Most codes relate to the size and material of water supply lines, the amount of pitch on branch drain lines, and venting of drain lines. The types of fittings and transitions that may be used also are closely watched by inspectors. For example, old-style saddle valves that pierce supply lines to feed an auxiliary fixture, such as an icemaker, have been disallowed by virtually every municipality.

Heating, Ventilation & Air-conditioning Guidelines

Detailed plan drawings should show the locations of heating/air-conditioning registers or fixtures in your kitchen. If you're planning a cosmetic makeover or a simple layout change, there is a pretty good chance you can get by with the same registers, radiators, or heaters found in your present kitchen. But if your new kitchen will be substantially larger than it is now or if the ratio of wall space filled by glass windows and doors will be greater, it's possible that you'll need to expand its heating and cooling capacity. Unless you happen to be a mechanical engineer, you'll need to consult a professional to evaluate your heating/ventilation/air-conditioning (HVAC) system. The code requirements for room heating are quite simple, but the methods used to calculate required energy needs of a room are fairly complex.

Finally, your cooktop should be equipped with an electric vent hood to exhaust cooking fumes, smoke, and moisture from the kitchen. The minimum volume of air moved by a vent fan is specified by code, so you should always check with a building inspector before selecting a vent hood (but don't assume that more

Remodeling Plans

Now the fun starts. Armed with a vision of the features you want to include in your new kitchen and equipped with an understanding of the code requirements and design standards, you're ready to put pencil to paper and begin to develop plan drawings—the next important step in transforming your dream kitchen into reality.

The key to success when developing plan drawings is to take as much time as you need and to remain flexible. A professional kitchen designer might take 30 to 80 hours to come up with precise floor plans and elevation drawings, so it's not unreasonable to allow yourself several weeks if you're doing this work yourself. You will almost certainly revise your plans several times before you settle on a layout that feels right to you. And it's not uncommon for kitchen plans to undergo changes as you make decisions about appliances and other materials. As you begin to research the price of cabinets and appliances and receive bids from contractors, you may well decide that it's prudent to scale back for the sake of your bank account, and these changes may require you to revise your plan drawings.

The process of creating finished plans for a kitchen project takes time and is done in three phases. First, you'll be drawing a floor plan of your present kitchen, providing a reference on which to base your new design. Next, you'll be experimenting with various layout options to find a design that best suits your needs, a process that can take several days, or even weeks. Finally, you'll be creating precise, finished floor plans and elevation drawings, which you will use when you begin interviewing contractors to do the work.

Most kitchen remodeling projects should have a plan drawing. A fully developed drawing includes elevations, floor plans, (you'll need these to get your construction permit), and any other visual details that are of use, such as the style of the cabinets and the sizes of the new appliances you plan to buy. Lighting and plumbing illustrations also are helpful.

Literature from manufacturers provides key information that you'll need for planning and for making your plan drawings. Stock cabinetry suppliers, in particular, produce very useful materials that you can use to identify and represent precisely the exact size and style of cabinets you want.

A floor plan is a scaled drawing made from an overhead perspective, showing the exact room dimensions, as well as the location of windows, doors, cabinets, appliances, electrical and plumbing fixtures. Elevation drawings are plans depicting a wall surface as if viewed from the side. For clarity, use an architectural template to show the position of appliances and fixtures in your kitchen plans. These templates are available at drafting and office supply stores, or you can photocopy the examples on pages 28 and 29. Carpenters, electricians, plumbers, and other contractors will understand exactly what you want if your plan drawings speak their language.

Once you've completed floor plans and elevation drawings of your kitchen-to-be, you're ready to begin choosing the appliances, cabinets, and other materials for your new kitchen. Create a detailed shopping list that includes dimensions and specifications for each item you'll be buying.

Now would be a good time to enlist the aid of an interior designer to help you select colors and patterns for flooring, countertops, and wall materials. Many installation contractors can also help you with design decisions.

Creating Kitchen Plans ▸

Although some homeowners have the artist's eye needed to draw accurate plans, others find this difficult, if not impossible. If you fall into the latter category, don't be afraid to seek help. Home centers and cabinet manufacturers often have designers on staff who can help you draw up plans if you agree to buy materials from them. In addition, there are computer software programs that can help you develop accurate plans that can be printed out. And, of course, there are professional kitchen designers and architects who specialize in creating kitchen plans.

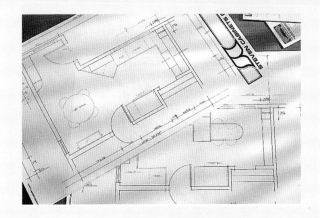

Detailed Plan Drawings ▸

Whether you are doing the work yourself or hiring others, once you have a good idea of the features you want in your new kitchen, it's time to create detailed plan drawings. Good plan drawings will help you in several phases of the planning process:

- Selecting cabinets and appliances to fit your kitchen layout;
- Soliciting accurate work bids when negotiating with plumbers, electricians and other subcontractors;
- Obtaining a building permit at your local Building Inspections office;
- Scheduling the stages of a remodeling project;
- Evaluating the work of contractors. If a carpenter or cabinetmaker fails to meet your expectations, your plan drawings serve as proof that the contractor did not complete the work as agreed.

How to Create Floor Plans & Elevation Drawings

Measure each wall in your kitchen as it now exists. Take accurate measurements of the position and size of every feature, including doors, windows, cabinets, countertops, and appliances. Also note the locations of all light fixtures and electrical outlets. Using graph paper, create a scaled floor plan of your present kitchen, using a scale of ½" equals 1 ft. Indicate doors, windows, interior, and exterior walls. Add the cabinets, appliances, countertops, electrical outlets and lights, plumbing fixtures and HVAC registers. In the margins, mark the exact dimensions of all elements.

Using tracing paper overlaid on your kitchen drawing, begin sketching possible layouts for your new kitchen, again using a scale of ½" equals 1 ft. As you develop your kitchen plan, refer often to your wish list of kitchen features and the kitchen standards and Code requirements listed earlier in this section. The goal is to create a kitchen that meets all your needs with the minimum possible impact on the present kitchen, because this will reduce the overall cost of your project.

If simple rearrangement of kitchen elements doesn't do the trick, explore the possibility of expanding your kitchen, either by enlarging the kitchen into an adjoining room or by building a room addition. A kitchen designer or architect can help with this task.

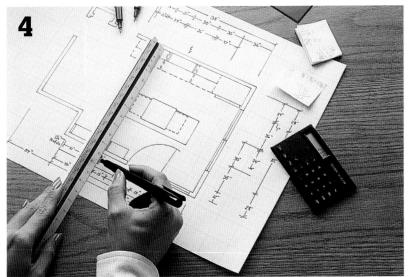

Once you settle on a layout, use graph paper to draw a very detailed floor plan of your new kitchen. Use dotted lines to fill in the base cabinets and appliances, and use solid lines to show the wall cabinets and countertops. (For straight runs of cabinets, leave a margin of about 3" to allow for adjustments during cabinet installation.) In the margins around the wall outline, indicate dimensions of kitchen elements and the distances between them.

Use colored pencils to mark the locations of plumbing fixtures, electrical outlets, and lighting fixtures; also show the locations of the heating registers, radiators, or fixtures.

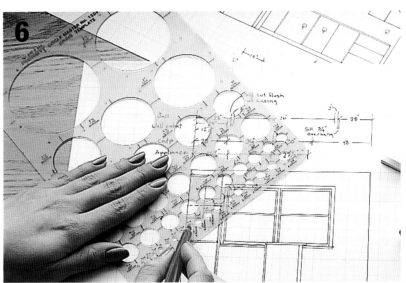

Draw a detailed, precise front elevation for each wall of your kitchen, using a scale of ½" equals 1 ft. Mark the vertical and horizontal measurements of all features, including doors, windows, wood moldings, cabinets, countertops, appliances, and soffits. Draw a side elevation of each wall of the kitchen, complete with all measurements. When satisfied with the elevation drawings, add the locations for plumbing pipes, electrical outlets, and lighting fixtures. Create close-up detailed drawings of problem spots, such as the areas where appliances butt against window frames.

Create Your Drawings

Use the icons shown here and ¼" graph paper to create drawings for your new kitchen. Use a scale of ½"= 1 ft. (1 square = 6") when drawing your plans; the icons are drawn to match this scale.

Plan view (overhead) templates for 24"-deep base cabinets

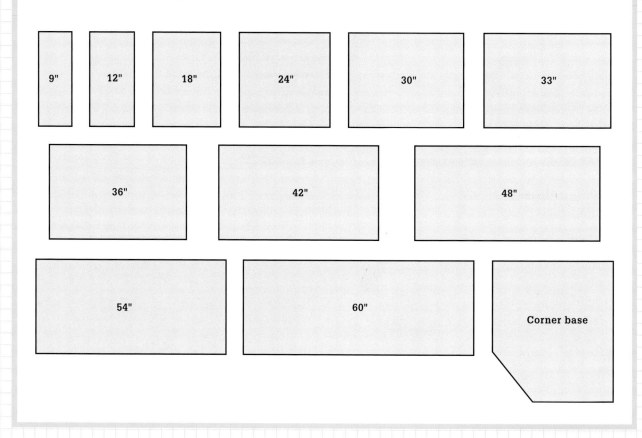

Plan view (overhead) templates for 12"-deep wall cabinets

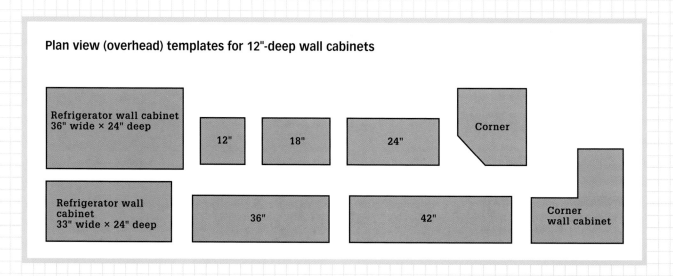

Basic construction symbols (not to scale)

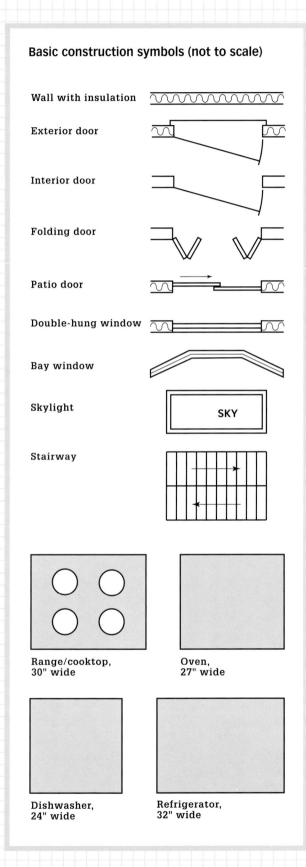

Wall with insulation

Exterior door

Interior door

Folding door

Patio door

Double-hung window

Bay window

Skylight

SKY

Stairway

Range/cooktop,
30" wide

Oven,
27" wide

Dishwasher,
24" wide

Refrigerator,
32" wide

Electrical symbols

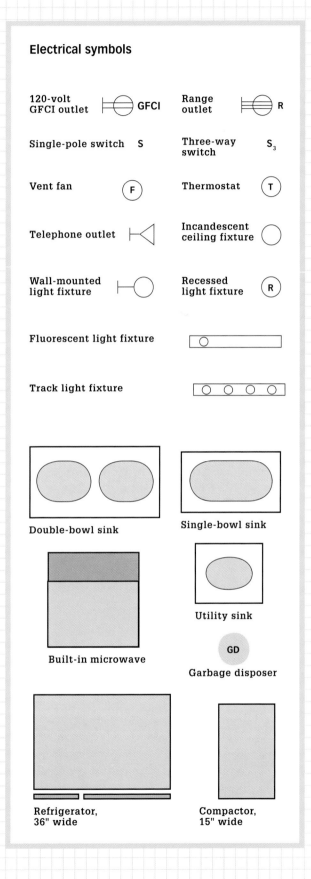

120-volt
GFCI outlet — GFCI

Range
outlet — R

Single-pole switch S

Three-way
switch S₃

Vent fan F

Thermostat T

Telephone outlet

Incandescent
ceiling fixture

Wall-mounted
light fixture

Recessed
light fixture R

Fluorescent light fixture

Track light fixture

Double-bowl sink

Single-bowl sink

Utility sink

Built-in microwave

GD
Garbage disposer

Refrigerator,
36" wide

Compactor,
15" wide

Budget & Finance

Any successful kitchen remodel starts with dreams and becomes reality. Which means that at some point, after you've spent time wishing and dreaming, you'll have to figure out where reality lies for you. Dream kitchens can be very expensive, in some cases. But before you panic, take a deep breath and read this section. You'll discover many practical ways to control costs and reduce the financial sting of remodeling.

Although you probably have an idea of how much you'd like to spend on your dream kitchen, you're likely to find that the figure is too small to cover everything you want. To avoid disappointment later, you might as well know upfront: when budgeting for a kitchen remodel, you need to be prepared to pay a bit more than you've planned and be willing to settle for a bit less than you've dreamed. Compromise is inevitable in the remodeling process, but with perseverance and a bit of luck, you can spend reasonably and still end up with a beautiful new kitchen that you'll love to use.

Determining a budget depends primarily on the extent of remodeling needed in your kitchen. When budgeting for a kitchen remodel, you must also consider how much an updated kitchen will add to the value of your home. Kitchen remodels have the highest rate of return over every other room in the home, so that you can expect to recoup up to 80 or 90 percent of your investment in added real estate value. Something to consider when shopping for a loan to finance a kitchen renovation is that if you choose to take out a home equity loan, the interest may be tax deductible.

Whatever your projected budget, comparison-shopping can help keep you within your budget. Be sure to get three to four estimates for any work you hire out, and ask that the estimates be broken down by materials and labor costs. The same goes for appliances; a simple online search can help you determine the lowest rates for standard appliances, which will often be honored by any subsequent seller you find. A visit to your local supplier allows you to touch and feel the products before buying. Be sure to quote the lowest rate for the same model and style, to see if they can match it.

As a guide, here are a few of the projected prices for standard kitchen appliances and fixtures in brand-new condition. This does not account for top-of-the-line imported models available at the luxury end of the spectrum or bargain-basement discontinued models at the lowest end.

Dream kitchens, even modest ones like this, can be shockingly expensive. Realistic decision-making, comparison shopping, and strict budgeting can feel like they're dampening your dream kitchen at times, but they are important aspects of turning your dreams into a real kitchen.

Budgeting

Establishing a budget is an important step in the remodeling process, and it involves more than determining how much money you have, or want, to spend. Additional factors, including the current value of your home and how long you plan to stay there, should have bearing on your budgeting decisions because they will help you set a sensible budget goal.

Setting a Budget Goal

How much should you spend on your kitchen project? Real estate professionals offer the following rough guidelines, based on the market value of your home before the remodel and the complexity of your project.

- For a full, down-to-the-wall-studs kitchen remodeling job with a general contractor and all new materials and fixtures, plan to spend 10 percent to 20 percent of your home's value ($15,000 to $30,000 for a $150,000 home);
- For a full remodel that includes an addition to your house, plan to spend up to 35 percent of your home's value ($52,500 for a $150,000 home);
- For a simple cosmetic makeover, plan to spend at least 2 percent of your home's value ($3,000 for a $150,000 home).

Do these sound like huge sums of money? There are good reasons to invest in a new kitchen. A remodeled kitchen is one of the few home improvements that translates directly into a higher market value for your home. Even if you plan to sell in the near future, you'll enjoy the improvements until that time, and the kitchen's new look may help make the sale when the time comes. However, it's probably wise to scale back on the project if you plan to sell immediately. If you'll be keeping your home for many years, the investment risk of the project lies in your enjoyment of the new kitchen. But with thoughtful planning and careful selection of appliances and materials, you're sure to get a great return on your investment over the years. While it may be best to pay for a remodel with disposable income—that is, accumulated savings—there are several legitimate ways to pay for an improvement project and even more ways to reduce and manage the cost of a new kitchen.

Major appliances are likely to account for a big percentage of your total kitchen remodeling budget. But unlike other aspects of the project, you have a great ability to control the costs of appliances by choosing inexpensive but dependable models. Consider, however, that expensive, high-end ranges and refrigerators are likely to last longer, both functionally and stylistically.

Appliance Costs ▶

Side-by-Side Refrigerator: $900 to $5,000
Self-cleaning Range: $800 to $2,000
Gas Cooktop: $400 to $6,000
Convection Oven: $1,000 to $4,000
Range Hood: $100 to $2,500
Dishwasher: $200 to $1,500
Double-basin sink: $300 to $2,000
Faucet with Sprayer: $100 to $400

Estimating Costs

Begin your budgeting process by estimating the cost of your ideal kitchen, as you've envisioned it so far, including appliances, countertops, cabinets, flooring, lighting, and miscellaneous materials. Note that the cost figures for products and services can involve guesswork; minimize it by checking the prices in appliance stores and building centers, and ask contractors about their rates. Also add any additional labor charges you expect, such as interior design, cleanup help, and trash hauling.

Finally, total all your costs, then add a 10 percent to 20 percent contingency fund to the total. The contingency fund is essential: few remodeling projects come in exactly on budget, and it's difficult to list every expense at this stage, so keep your estimates on the high side to avoid any unpleasant surprises.

Use Your Rough Estimate

Don't panic when you see the total; your first rough estimate is simply a starting point. In addition, it can help you answer some crucial questions:

- Is your rough estimate within the recommended ratio of your home's market value? If it exceeds the range shown above, look for ways to reduce your budget.
- Should you do the work yourself or hire a contractor? The elements with the highest labor cost offer the greatest potential savings if you do the work yourself. In most cases, however, there are reasons why labor costs are high, so you should consider doing work yourself only if you're experienced and confident that you can successfully complete the job.
- Are you getting accurate bids? If a contractor submits a bid that's much higher or lower than the ranges shown, ask why.

Reducing Costs

At this point you should have a rough idea of how much your dream kitchen will cost. Are you already over your budget? If so, don't worry; the first estimate usually exceeds the budget. That's why you're figuring costs before you get started—it allows you to make carefully planned cutbacks now, which may save you from having to make drastic ones later. There are several ways to begin lowering your remodeling costs.

Comparison-Shop for Materials

If your heart is set on premium-quality materials, do some homework to make sure you're getting the best price you can. If the best price is still too high, bear in mind that good-quality materials can be just as serviceable as top-of-the-line luxury products.

Although contractors and subcontractors will purchase appliances and materials for you, this service isn't free; they typically take a markup on every item they buy. It's often cheaper to research and purchase the materials yourself.

Comparison-Shop for Contractors

While cost shouldn't be your first consideration when looking for a contractor, it's an important one for most people. If you want to reduce your total labor expense, it's better to cut back on service rather than on the contractor's experience and abilities.

Regardless of the contractor's reputation or how much he or she charges, always check references. Whenever possible, talk to several recent customers and visit some completed job sites. As the saying goes, "The best predictor of future success is past performance."

Do Some Work Yourself

Since labor is often the most expensive element of a remodeling project, you may be able to save money by doing parts of the job yourself. However, tackle only those tasks that you're confident you can complete successfully.

Bargain hunting is a very practical way to control remodeling costs that many homeowners actually enjoy (but many others despise). Do bear in mind this simple bit of advice however: Don't buy junk.

Financing Options ▸

Once you've reduced the cost estimate to a realistic amount, it's time to consider where the money will come from. The following are six of the most common methods of financing a major remodeling project. Some methods of financing involve considerable paperwork that can take several weeks to process, so the sooner you start, the better.

Out-of-Pocket Funds

The ideal way to pay for a remodeling project is to use accumulated savings. The advantage of this method is that you don't have to pay any loan interest, which can mean a savings of thousands of dollars. For example, when you borrow $25,000 at 10% interest and pay it off over 10 years, you actually end up paying over $39,000—the cost of the loan plus over $14,000 in interest. Although paying out-of-pocket is cheaper in the long run, it has one significant drawback: If the actual costs far exceed your estimates, you could end up in a pay-as-you-go situation, and the project would take a lot longer to complete. A sizable kitchen remodel could easily take many months to complete if you're paying for it by squeezing a little bit from each paycheck.

Revolving Credit

If you're thinking of using credit cards to pay the bills for your new kitchen, think again. Unless it's absolutely unavoidable, resist all temptations to pull out the plastic when remodeling your kitchen. The interest rates on credit cards, which typically range from 12% to 25%, are far higher than other financing options. This will add thousands of dollars to the cost of your project, and none of the interest is tax-deductible.

Government-Backed Loans

There are a number of programs that you may be able to turn to for help through the FHA (Federal Housing Administration). To find qualified lenders, contact your local HUD (Housing & Urban Development) field office. The interest rates and payback schedules for these government-backed loans are about the same as conventional mortgages, but obtaining them often has income-based eligibility requirements.

Mortgage Refinancing

Converting an old mortgage to a new loan is a common way to finance a new kitchen. This option is especially advisable if current interest rates are 1% or more below the rate of your old mortgage, and you have a sizable amount of equity in your home. Refinancing is also a good choice if you're doing a costly project that will add considerably to the market value of your home. One potential benefit of refinancing your current mortgage is that you may be able to take a tax deduction on the interest you pay on the loan. Ask a mortgage company or bank about the current tax laws regarding mortgage loans; then consult your tax advisor.

Home Equity Loans

If you prefer not to refinance your existing mortgage, you can opt to borrow money against your home equity—the difference between your home's market value and the amount you owe on your mortgage. For example, if your home is worth $150,000 and your remaining mortgage balance is $100,000, you have $50,000 in home equity; you can use much of this money to serve as collateral for a loan. Find out the outstanding balance on your mortgage by calling your lender. There are two types of home equity loans. The first is a simple second mortgage, in which you borrow a lump sum at a fixed interest rate and pay it back in regular installments over a period of 15 years or more. The second is an equity line of credit. Equity credit lines operate like revolving credit card accounts, in which you borrow money when you need it and pay interest on the outstanding balance. The interest rates on these loans vary with the market rates, so your payments may change from month to month. Like credit cards, equity credit accounts can be dangerous if you aren't a disciplined borrower.

Home Improvement Loans

This is the standard, everyday bank loan—the same type of loan you would use to buy a car. Any full-service bank or credit union can process a home improvement loan. The advantage of a home improvement loan is that it can be processed very quickly, no appraisal is needed and little paperwork is involved, other than a quick computerized credit check. The drawback is that the interest rates are generally 2% to 5% higher than the current rates for home equity loans. Since home improvement loans are generally secured by your home, the interest may be tax-deductible. Ask your lender about the tax laws specific to your loan.

Practical Planning Tips

There are plenty of practical things to consider before starting a kitchen remodel, but some of the most important involve timing and preparation. In short, the more planning you can do before even touching a tool, the better you will be able to handle the inevitable setbacks. As long as you make sure that it doesn't coincide with major holidays or extended houseguests, a do-it-yourself kitchen remodel doesn't have to take over your life.

The first tip is to be generous when creating a timeline. You never know when ordered parts will be delayed or paint will take twice as long to dry as you estimated. For the most part, the simplest remodel can be completed within a week with more extensive remodels—that involve new cabinets, floors, and professionally installed countertops—taking up to three months to complete. Even if it's a small-scale project, be prepared to not have access to your kitchen while work is being done, since even paint fumes can disrupt daily life for a day or two. One smart solution is to create a temporary kitchen elsewhere in your home where you can plug in a coffeemaker or microwave, or even a mini refrigerator.

Another thing to consider is the need for permits from your local building authority. Familiarize yourself with local codes before you alter anything electrical or structural. For plumbing projects, you'll want to look into the requirements in your area or determine the need for a new line before you get started. As for changes that involve ventilation, you'll want to refer to some of the building codes and guidelines we've included earlier in the book.

Like successful stand-up comedy, successful kitchen remodeling requires impeccable timing. Dedicate a calendar to the projects and be sure to keep it updated. Planning the timing is the only way to keep the amount of time you'll be without a functioning kitchen to a bare minimum, and it will let contractors and tradespeople work more efficiently.

The most important lesson of any DIY project is to know when to call in the professionals. While many of the how-to projects in this book are simply completed by someone with little construction experience, some projects will be more involved than they first appear. For instance, replacing a resilient tile floor may seem like an easy enough project, but the plot thickens when the subfloor is revealed to be in terrible shape and must be torn out and rebuilt. Another time to call in expert assistance is when plumbing or electrical systems are more than twenty years old. Though wires and pipes are meant to last over fifty years, some conditions will cause them to deteriorate, making it tricky to remove them safely. And while many hobbyists can pull off the replacement of upper cabinets with the help of a friend, there are plenty of us who would require a team of carpenters to help hang and install new cabinets.

The how-to lessons in this book have been carefully broken down into step-by-step manuals for each project. Whether you need assistance or have lots of experience at DIY home improvement, the right tools and smart safety precautions make it possible for anyone to achieve dream-kitchen status.

Flextime: Your Little Secret ▸

For added security, it's a good idea to add at least 25 percent more time to your best guess when determining the overall schedule for your remodeling project. Building in a few flex days as a safeguard against unforeseen problems is also a good idea. However, keep this information to yourself.

If contractors know that your schedule is padded, they may feel free to bump your project for a day or two to squeeze in a smaller rush job for another client. To ensure that your contractors stay on schedule, mark your flex days "cleanup" or "out of town"—don't tell them you've built some extra time into the schedule.

Talk to Building Inspectors ▸

Although building inspectors aren't paid consultants, they can be an excellent design and planning resource. They are your community's field representatives, and their job is to inspect the work done on your project to ensure that it meets building code requirements.

As experts in their respective fields, the building inspector, electrical inspector, and plumbing inspector can give you sound advice on designing your kitchen. Not all inspectors have the time or the willingness to answer a lot of design questions, so make your questions short and specific, and be sure to describe your situation clearly. Also ask if the inspections office provides a pamphlet that summarizes the local code requirements for kitchens.

Cabinets

Years ago the built-in kitchen cabinet was relatively rare. Food was stored in pantries and in freestanding cupboards, such as Hoosier cabinets, most of which are now considered antiques. Plates and silver resided in chests or in boxes stacked on open shelves. Today, you rarely see an American kitchen that doesn't dwell in the shadow of large banks of built-in cabinets spanning floor to ceiling. But just as the kitchen furnishings have evolved, the cabinets themselves continue to change, mostly to reflect changes in style and design. It is also true that many cabinets installed in the last twenty or thirty years were, simply put, cheap.

If your cabinets are dated or marred (or just plain ugly) but still structurally sound, you may be able to get by with painting them or replacing the cabinet doors. But in most cases, the inescapable conclusion you'll draw when you evaluate your cabinets is that it is time for them to go. Installing cabinets yourself is easy. If you just want to modify your existing cabinets, you'll find quick-fix projects in this chapter.

In This Chapter

- Cabinet Selection
- New Cabinet Prep
- Cabinet Installation
- Freestanding Cabinets
- Cabinet Upgrades
- Slide-out Storage
- Pull-down Shelves
- Customizing Cabinets
- Vertical Divider
- Custom Cabinets
- Kitchen Cabinet Paint

Cabinet Selection

When purchasing cabinets, you have a number of decisions to make. First, you need to decide if you want to go with stock, semi-custom, or custom cabinets. Then you need to choose between face-frame or frameless styles. Materials, door and drawer styles, hardware and finishes must also be decided.

Cabinets comprise three categories: stock, semi-custom, and custom. Stock cabinets and some semi-custom cabinets are available for homeowners to install themselves; custom cabinets usually are installed by the cabinetmaker. There's a growing trend in "unfitted" kitchen systems, too. Seen most frequently in European kitchens, the cabinets and shelves are modular—like pieces of storage furniture—rather than built-in or fitted.

Stock

Stock cabinets are available as either ready-to-assemble (RTA) or ready-to-install. Ready-to-assemble cabinets, also referred to as knockdown or flat-pack, are shipped as flat components that the consumer puts together using connecting hardware. In other words, in addition to installing the cabinets, you have to assemble them. Your options will be somewhat limited if you choose RTA cabinets, but you will be able to achieve a slightly different look from ready-to-install cabinets. Although some RTA cabinets are made with low-quality materials, not all are poorly constructed. Carefully inspect samples of assembled cabinets to check material quality and engineering quality. If possible, also look at assembly directions to check for clarity.

Ready-to-install cabinets are purchased already assembled. They tend to be lower on the quality level, but typical utility units are suitable for a workshop or a weekend home. Larger building centers typically carry a single style of stock kitchen cabinets made from a relatively economical species of wood, such as red oak.

Semi-Custom

Semi-custom cabinets are also factory-made to standard sizes, but they offer far more options in finish, size, features, and materials than stock cabinets. These are typically sold through higher-end design showrooms, with prices much higher than

stock cabinets but still less than custom cabinets. Semi-custom is the best choice for homeowners who want better-quality cabinets with some special features and a custom appearance, but at a lower price than custom cabinets. You should allow at least three to eight weeks of lead time when ordering semi-custom cabinets.

Custom

Custom cabinets offer the most in terms of options. These cabinets are designed, built, and installed to fit a unique space. It is wise to shop around before settling on a custom cabinetmaker, as price, quality, and availability will vary widely. The minimum lead time for custom cabinet construction is six weeks in most markets. When you get bids, find out if the lead time is from acceptance of the bid or from when the condition of the kitchen allows the cabinetmaker to take accurate measurements. Remember that exotic or difficult-to-machine materials and intricate custom designs will end up costing you more.

Standard Cabinet Sizes ▶

Base cabinets (without countertop)

Height	34½"
Depth	24"
Width	6" to 42", in 3" increments

Wall cabinets

Height	12", 15", 18", 24", 30", 36"
Depth	12"
Width	6" to 36", in 3" increments

Oven cabinets

Height	83", 95"
Depth	24"
Width	30", 33"

Pantry cabinets

Height	83", 95"
Depth	24"
Width	18", 24"

Once you have decided whether you will be purchasing factory-made or custom cabinets, you need to decide which type of cabinet: face-frame or frameless.

Face-frame cabinets have frames made of solid wood around the front of the cabinet box. Because the frame extends into cabinet space, the door openings will be reduced and a certain amount of "dead" space exists within the cabinet behind the frames. The hinges for doors on face-frame cabinets mount on the frame. The door itself may be flush within the frame or raised above it. Flush-fitting doors were common on older cabinets, but because they require a precise fit, which means more time and craftsmanship, they will be more expensive and more difficult to find.

Frameless cabinets are often referred to as "Eurostyle." These cabinets do not have a face-frame and the doors and drawers span the entire width of the carcass, which allows easier access and a bit more storage space. The doors are mounted using cup hinges that are invisible when the doors are closed. Frameless cabinets have a streamlined look that makes them feel more contemporary in style. One drawback of frameless cabinets is that they do not have the added strength of the face frame, so it is critical that they are solidly constructed and properly installed.

Face-frame cabinets have openings that are completely surrounded by face frames made of vertical stiles and horizontal rails. They give kitchens a traditional look.

Frameless cabinets, sometimes called "European-style," are more contemporary. Because they have no face frames, frameless cabinets offer slightly more storage space than framed cabinets. The doors and drawers on frameless cabinets cover the entire unit.

Cabinets & Universal Design

When considering a design for kitchen cabinets, the issue of accessibility should be a priority. Cabinets that require constant bending down would be inappropriate for someone with a bad back.

Shelves so high you need a step stool are not the safest bet for someone who is elderly. Considering the needs of users—and future users—is a smart way to start planning for a new kitchen.

Accessible Cabinets ▸

Making a kitchen accessible to wheelchair users involves incorporating open, roll-in space in the base cabinets so that sink, cooktop, and countertops are within reach. Roll-in cabinets have no bottom or toe kick. The roll-in space can be concealed with a fold-away door. All other base cabinets should be modified to have an 8" toe kick. If upper cabinets are used, they need to have pull-down shelving. Base cabinets with pull-out shelves and pantries with lazy Susans are the best storage options.

Pull-out shelves for upper and lower cabinets offer the ultimate in easy access, not just for operators with restricted movement. If someone in your household requires a wheelchair, design your new cabinets so they have a full 8"-tall toe-kick area, not just the standard 2½ to 3".

Universal Design

Design your kitchen around a clear, circular space of at least 5 ft. in diameter to provide room for a wheelchair. If your kitchen doesn't have 60" of clear space, allow 48" for pathways. Plan for 30 to 48" of clear approach space in front of all appliances and workstations.

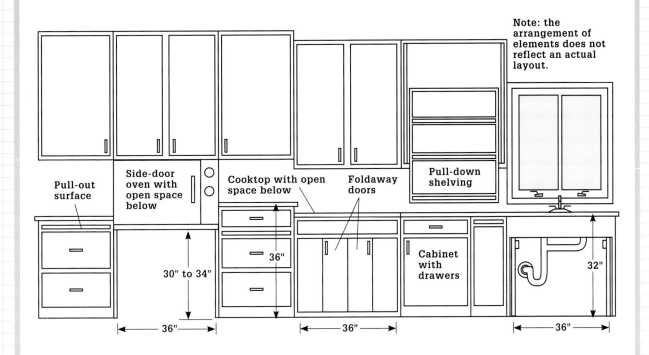

Note: the arrangement of elements does not reflect an actual layout.

Pull-out surface

Side-door oven with open space below

Cooktop with open space below

Foldaway doors

Pull-down shelving

30" to 34"

36"

Cabinet with drawers

32"

36"

36"

36"

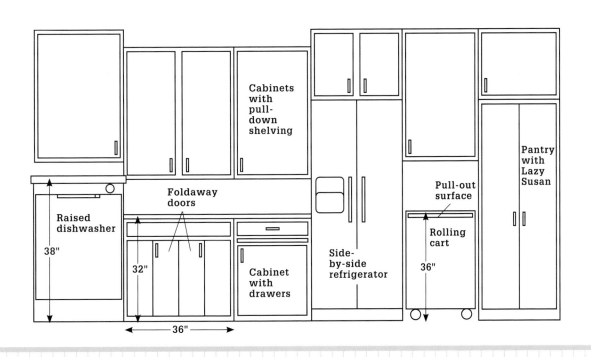

Raised dishwasher

38"

Foldaway doors

Cabinets with pull-down shelving

Cabinet with drawers

32"

36"

Side-by-side refrigerator

Pull-out surface

Rolling cart

36"

Pantry with Lazy Susan

New Cabinet Prep

Installing new cabinets is easiest if the kitchen is completely empty. Disconnect the plumbing and wiring, and temporarily remove the appliances. To remove old cabinets and countertops, see pages 44 to 45. If the new kitchen requires plumbing or electrical changes, now is the time to have this work done. If the kitchen flooring is to be replaced, finish it before beginning the layout and the installation of cabinets.

Cabinets must be installed plumb and level. Using a level as a guide, draw reference lines on the walls to indicate cabinet location. If the kitchen floor is uneven, find the highest point of the floor area that will be covered by base cabinets. Measure up from this point to draw reference lines.

Tools & Materials ▸

Stud finder	Marking pencil
Pry bar	Tape measure
Trowel	1 × 3 boards
Putty knife	Straight 6- to 8-ft.-long
Screwdriver	2 × 4
Straightedge	Wallboard compound
Level	2½" wallboard screws

Filled-in low area

Stud locations

1 × 3 ledger

Reference line

Removing Old Cabinets

Old cabinets can be salvaged fairly easily if they are modular units that were installed with screws, and some custom built-in cabinets can be removed in one piece. If you're not planning to salvage the cabinets, they should be cut into pieces or otherwise broken down and discarded. If you're demolishing your old cabinets, the main danger is causing collateral damage in the room, especially to the plumbing, so work with care.

Tools & Materials ▸

Tape measure
Pry bar
Putty knife
Cordless screwdriver
Sander
Stud finder
Taping knife
Level
Laser level

Reciprocating saw
Hammer
Eye protection
Scrap wood
2 × 4
Wallboard compound
1 × 3 lumber
2½" wallboard screws

Remove trim moldings at the edges and tops of the cabinets with a flat pry bar or putty knife.

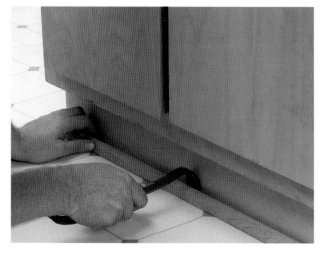

Remove base shoe from cabinet base if the molding is attached to the floor.

Remove baseboards and other trim moldings with a pry bar. Protect wall surfaces with scraps of wood. Label the trim boards on the back side so you can replace them correctly.

Remove valances above cabinets. Some valances are attached to the cabinets or soffits with screws. Others are nailed and must be pried loose.

How to Remove Cabinets

Remove doors and drawers to make it easier to get at interior spaces. You may need to scrape away old paint to expose hinge screws.

At the backs of cabinets, remove any screws holding the cabinet to the wall. Cabinets can be removed as a group or can be disassembled.

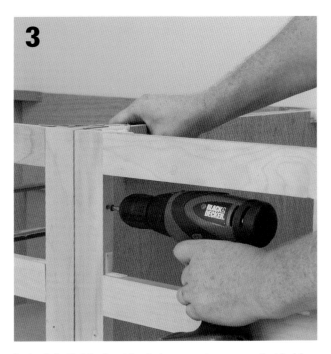

Detach individual cabinets by removing screws that hold face frames together.

Countertops are usually not salvageable. Cut them into manageable pieces with a reciprocating saw, or take them apart, piece by piece, with a hammer and pry bar.

How to Prepare Walls

1

Find high and low spots on wall surfaces using a long, straight 2 × 4. Sand down any high spots.

2

Fill in low spots in the wall by applying wallboard compound with a taping knife. Let the compound dry, and then sand it lightly.

3

Locate and mark wall studs using an electronic stud finder. Cabinets normally will be hung by driving screws into the studs through the back of the cabinets.

4

Find the highest point along the floor that will be covered by base cabinets. Place a level on a long, straight 2 × 4, and move the board across the floor to determine if the floor is uneven. Mark the wall at the high point.

Measure up 34½" from the high-point mark (for standard cabinets). Use a level (a laser level is perfect) to mark a reference line on the walls. Base cabinets will be installed with top edges flush against this line.

Measure up 84" from the high-point mark and draw a second reference line. Wall cabinets will be installed with their top edges flush against this line.

Measure down 30" from the wall-cabinet reference line and draw another level line where the bottoms of the cabinets will be. Temporary ledgers will be installed against this line.

Install 1 × 3 temporary ledgers with top edges flush against the reference lines. Attach ledgers with 2½" wallboard screws driven into every other wall stud. Mark stud locations on the ledgers. Cabinets will rest temporarily on ledgers during installation (the ledgers alone will not support them, however).

Cabinet Installation

Cabinets must be firmly anchored to wall studs, and they must be plumb and level when installed. The best way to ensure this is by attaching a ledger board to the wall to assist in the installation. As a general rule, install the upper cabinets first so your access is not impeded by the base cabinets. (Although some pros prefer to install the base cabinets first so they can be used to support the uppers during installation.) It's also best to begin in a corner and work outward from there.

Tools & Materials ▸

Handscrew clamps	Toe-kick molding
Level	Filler strips
Hammer	Valance
Utility knife	6d finish nails
Nail set	Finish washers
Clamps	2½", 4" wood screws
Drill	2½" cabinet screws or
Counterbore drill bit	flathead wood screws
Phillips screwdriver	Sheet metal screws
Jigsaw	#8 panhead wood screws
1 × 3 lumber	3" drywall screws
Cabinets	Shims
Trim molding	

Stock cabinets are sold in boxes that are keyed to door and drawer packs (you need to buy these separately). It is important that you realize this when you are estimating your project costs at the building center (often a door pack will cost as much or more than the cabinet). Also allow plenty of time for assembling the cabinets out of the box. It can take an hour or more to put some more complex cabinets together.

How to Fit a Corner Cabinet ▸

Before installation, test-fit the corner and adjoining cabinets to make sure doors and handles will not interfere with each other. If necessary, increase the clearance by pulling the corner cabinet away from the side wall by no more than 4". To maintain even spacing between the edges of the doors and the cabinet corner, cut a filler strip and attach it to the corner cabinet or the adjoining cabinet. Filler strips should be made from material that matches the cabinet doors and face frames.

How to Install Wall Cabinets

Position a corner upper cabinet on a ledger and hold it in place, making sure it is resting cleanly on the ledger. Drill ³⁄₁₆" pilot holes into the wall studs through the hanging strips at the top rear of the cabinet. Attach the cabinet to the wall with 2½" screws. Do not tighten fully until all cabinets are hung.

Filler strip

Attach a filler strip to the front edge of the cabinet, if needed (see page 48). Clamp the filler in place and drill counterbored pilot holes through the cabinet face frame near hinge locations. Attach filler to cabinet with 2½" cabinet screws or flathead wood screws.

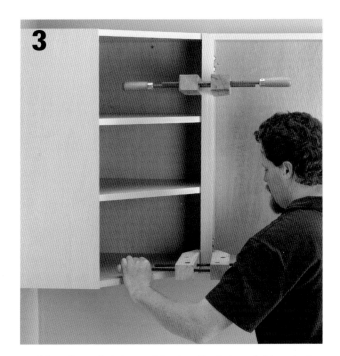

Position the adjoining cabinet on the ledger, tight against the corner cabinet or filler strip. Clamp the corner cabinet and the adjoining cabinet together at the top and bottom. Handscrew clamps will not damage wood face frames.

Check the front cabinet edges or face frames for plumb. Drill ³⁄₁₆" pilot holes into the wall studs through the hanging strips in the rear of the cabinet. Attach the cabinet with 2½" screws. Do not tighten the wall screws fully until all the cabinets are hung.

(continued)

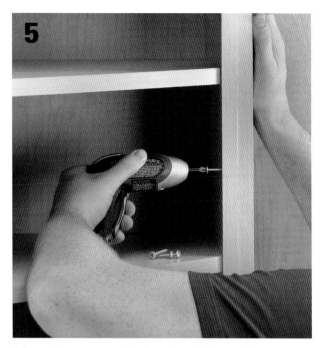

5

Attach the corner cabinet to the adjoining cabinet. From the inside corner cabinet, drill pilot holes through the face frame. Join the cabinets with sheet-metal screws.

6

Position and attach each additional cabinet. Clamp frames together, and drill counterbored pilot holes through the side of the face frame. Join the cabinets with wood screws. Drill ³⁄₁₆" pilot holes in the hanging strips, and attach the cabinet to the studs with wood screws.

7

Join the frameless cabinets with #8 × 1¼" panhead wood screws or wood screws with decorative washers. Each pair of cabinets should be joined by at least four screws.

8

Fill the gaps between the cabinet and wall or neighboring appliance with a filler strip. Cut the filler strip to fit the space, then wedge wood shims between the filler and the wall to create a friction fit that holds it in place temporarily. Drill counterbored pilot holes through the side of the cabinet (or the edge of the face frame) and attach filler with screws.

9

Remove the temporary ledger. Check the cabinet run for plumb, and adjust if necessary by placing wood shims behind the cabinet, near the stud locations. Tighten the wall screws completely. Cut off the shims with a utility knife.

10

Use trim moldings to cover any gaps between the cabinets and the walls. Stain the moldings to match the cabinet finish.

11

Attach decorative valance above the sink. Clamp the valance to the edge of cabinet frames and drill counterbored pilot holes through the cabinet frames and into the end of the valance. Attach with sheet-metal screws.

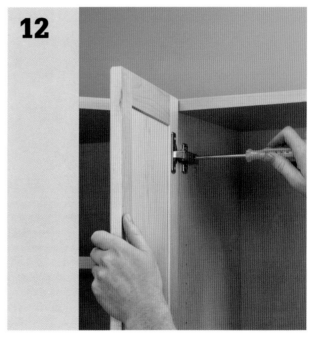

12

Install the cabinet doors. If necessary, adjust the hinges so that the doors are straight and plumb.

How to Install Base Cabinets

Begin the installation with a corner cabinet. Draw plumb lines that intersect the 34½" reference line (measured from the high point of the floor—see page 46) at the locations for the cabinet sides.

Place the cabinet in the corner. Make sure the cabinet is plumb and level. If necessary, adjust by driving wood shims under the cabinet base. Be careful not to damage the flooring. Drill ³⁄₁₆" pilot holes through the hanging strip and into the wall studs. Tack the cabinet to the wall with wood screws or wallboard screws.

Clamp the adjoining cabinet to the corner cabinet. Make sure the new cabinet is plumb, then drill counterbored pilot holes through the cabinet sides or the face frame and filler strip. Screw the cabinets together. Drill ³⁄₁₆" pilot holes through the hanging strips and into the wall studs. Tack the cabinets loosely to the wall studs with wood screws or wallboard screws.

Use a jigsaw to cut any cabinet openings needed in the cabinet backs (for example, in the sink base seen here) for plumbing, wiring, or heating ducts.

Position and attach additional cabinets, making sure the frames are aligned and the cabinet tops are level. Clamp cabinets together, then attach the face frames or cabinet sides with screws driven into pilot holes. Tack the cabinets to the wall studs, but don't drive screws too tight—you may need to make adjustments once the entire bank is installed.

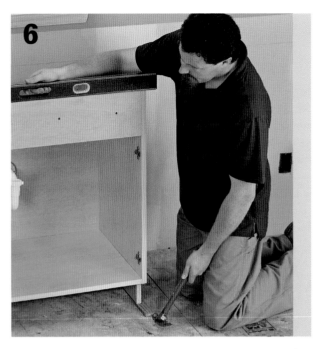

Make sure all the cabinets are level. If necessary, adjust by driving shims underneath the cabinets. Place the shims behind the cabinets near the stud locations to fill any gaps. Tighten the wall screws. Cut off the shims with a utility knife.

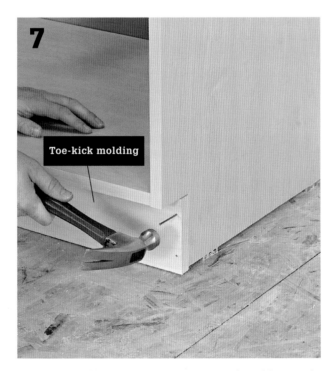

Toe-kick molding

Use trim moldings to cover gaps between the cabinets and the wall or floor. The toe-kick area is often covered with a strip of wood finished to match the cabinets or painted black.

Hang the cabinet doors and mount the drawer fronts, then test to make sure they close smoothly and the doors fit evenly and flush. Self-closing cabinet hinges (by far the most common type installed today) have adjustment screws that allow you to make minor changes to the hardware to correct any problems.

Variation: Installing Face-Frame Cabinets

The more traditional-looking face-frame cabinets differ only slightly from frameless cabinets in terms of installation. The opening of the cabinet is surrounded by vertical and horizontal frames called "stiles" and "rails." The face frame typically overhangs the cabinet case on the outside by $\frac{1}{16}$" to $\frac{1}{8}$". Because of this overhang, the frames must be the connection point rather than the cabinet case. Use $2\frac{1}{2}$" No.10 wood screws to connect the frames (or use special $2\frac{1}{2}$"- or 3"-long cabinet screws). Do not screw the cabinet sides together at any other point than the face frame, as this will skew the cabinets and create structural stress.

Most face-frame cabinets use overlay doors. The hinges for these doors simply attach to the back of the door and to the side or face of the cabinet face-frame with screws. They are called "overlay wrap" or "partial wrap" hinges if they attach to the side of the face frame, and they are called "semi-concealed" if they attach to the front of the face-frame. Cup or Euro-style hinges are available for face-frame cabinets, but are somewhat more difficult to install if the doors have not been predrilled for this hinge style. The best way to attach the door hardware uniformly is to use a drilling template. You can usually purchase one where you purchase the cabinets or hardware.

Tools & Materials ▸

Drill	Filler strip (if needed)
No. 10 counterbore bit	¾" finish-grade plywood
⁵⁄₆₄" self-centering vix bit	Finish materials
Cabinet screws (or 2½" No. 10 screws)	Drilling template

To join face-frame cabinets, set the cabinets in position, aligned with the frame faces flush and the frame tops flush. Clamp the frames together at the top and bottom. Using a drill with a No.10 counterbore bit, drill two pilot holes through the sides of the frame into the adjoining frame. Attach the frames with cabinet screws or 2½" No. 10 screws.

Start at the corner when installing a bank of cabinets that includes a blind corner cabinet. Attach the cabinet adjoining the corner by driving screws through the face frame (see photo at the top of this page). If a filler strip is necessary to fill a gap between the two cabinets, attach the filler strip to the base cabinet first and then run screws through the corner cabinet face frame and into the filler strip only after the adjoining cabinet is positioned and shimmed.

To install partial wrap overlay hinges, use a template to mark the hinge locations on the back of the door. Drill ⁵⁄₆₄"-dia. pilot holes no more than ⅜" deep using a self-centering vix bit. Screw the hinge to the door back. Place the hinge against the face frame and mark the screw holes. Drill ⁵⁄₆₄" pilot holes. Drive all the screws for both hinges partially, then tighten all.

Adjusting European Hinges ▸

European hinges (also called cup hinges) are the standard hinges used on frameless cabinets and some face-frame cabinets. One advantage of these hinges is their adjustability. This adjustability means that you will need some patience to tackle this project.

At first glance, European hinges appear to need a Phillips screwdriver to be adjusted, but you will have more success if you use a Pozidrive #2 screwdriver. This looks like a Phillips driver, but it is engineered with extra blade tips for reduced slippage. Never use a power screwdriver for hinge adjustments.

European hinges have three adjustment screws that secure the hinge to the door and cabinet while moving the door in and out, up and down, or right to left. If you own face-frame cabinets, the hinges may be more compact than frameless cabinet hinges. Some of the most compact hinges have unique adjustment systems, so you may have more trial and error in installing them.

Before making any adjustments, try tightening the anchoring screw or the vertical adjustment screws. Often these screws have worked loose over time and are affecting the door alignment and function.

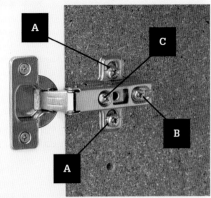

Long-arm European hinges. The standard long-arm European hinge has four adjustment screws. The first pair (A) attach the mounting plate to the side of the cabinet. Loosen these screws slightly on both hinges to move the cabinet up and down vertically. Retighten the screws when you have the hinge aligned as desired. The third adjustment screw (B) attaches the hinge to the mounting plate. If this screw is loose, the door will move in and out and seem floppy. This screw should be in the same relative position in its slot as the B screw on the other hinge, and they should both always be tight. The fourth screw (C) adjusts the door left and right horizontally. Adjust one hinge at a time in small increments by turning the screw. Check the adjustment results frequently by closing the door.

European hinges. Cabinet doors with European hinges can be adjusted in three dimensions: vertical (up and down) (A); depth (in and out) (B); and horizontal (right and left) (C). If your cabinets are slightly out of alignment, begin door installation with the center cabinet and work your way out to one side and then the other.

Compact European hinges. The compact European hinge for overlay doors on face-frame cabinets has three adjustment screws. The first pair (A) attach the mounting clip to the side or front of the face frame. Screws B and C attach the hinge to the mounting plate and serve as the left and right adjustment. Loosen all the A screws slightly to adjust the door up or down, then tighten. Loosen or tighten one B or C screw in small increments to move the door left or right. Check the adjustment results frequently by closing the door.

Freestanding Cabinets

Recently, some large retailers and catalog sellers have introduced another kitchen cabinetry option that's fairly new to North America but has been around for a long time in Europe: the freestanding cabinet. Boasting a contemporary appearance and ease of installation, these cabinets have the added benefits of portability and interchangeability (sink base cabinets being a notable exception). Most freestanding bases come in an assortment of materials, colors, and sizes with matching upper cabinets. The upper cabinets are hung nontraditionally, usually mounting directly onto a rail that is attached to the wall and can also support shelves and organizer bins.

Freestanding cabinets, like their permanently installed counterparts, are usually shipped and sold in flat packs. Because they are ready to assemble (RTA), you won't get out of work completely by choosing freestanding cabinets. You will have the additional step of assembling the cabinets before installing them. It is best to start your assembly with a basic, small cabinet. That way, you can get the knack of the process without wrestling with large pieces. Installing a freestanding kitchen cabinet system is similar to most other wall cabinet installations. You need to begin with level wall surfaces. The cabinets are hung on a suspension rail and then bolted to this bar. The bolts, in the upper inside corners of the cabinets, are then covered with plastic caps. If you install the suspension rail properly, this type of installation ensures that your cabinets will be level. If you add toe-kick panels to your base cabinets, they will be virtually indistinguishable from fully installed base cabinets. Or, you can create a European look by installing attractive legs and leaving the toe-kick covers off. When opting for this look, cut the ledger board 5" to 6" short, and install a third leg on the exposed end cabinets so the ledger board will not be visible. When creating an island with base cabinets, you must attach the legs to the floor to prevent movement. A sink base cabinet also must be secured to prevent movement.

Freestanding base cabinets really have more in common with furniture—including ease of installation—than cabinetry, but they serve the same important function as fully installed cabinets.

Nontraditional materials make visual sense with European-style freestanding base cabinets. Metals and colorful laminates are two options you can find fairly easily.

Tips for Installing Freestanding Cabinets ▸

- Carefully unpack each carton and double-check hardware contents with instruction sheets.
- Use blue painters' tape to tape hardware packets and instructions to their respective parts.
- Check nooks and crannies of packing materials. Hardware bags are often encased in packing materials.
- Parts may be grouped—for example, the ledger boards are packed with the toe kicks.
- If you are assembling large cabinets in another room, make sure you have the space to move them to the kitchen when fully assembled.
- Make sure you have the proper side of the cabinet back facing the inside of the cabinet.
- Check that drawers are right side up before drilling handle holes.
- Fiberboard material is very heavy. You should have at least one helper when installing.

Freestanding base cabinets share design similarities within a family of options so they can retain a cohesive, uniform appearance.

Cabinet Upgrades

Customize your kitchen storage with swing-up, glide-out, and pull-down shelves. Incorporate heavy-duty, swing-up shelves to bring base-cabinet items like stand mixers to the countertop. Build your own full-extension, glide-out shelves to divide larger spaces into two or more shelves and reduce bending and reaching for wheelchair users and people with back problems. Choose pull-down shelf accessories to bring upper-cabinet items like spices within reach. When purchasing specialized hardware accessories, check load ratings, locking mechanisms, arc swings, and clearance heights to be sure they can support the items you want to store, and they will fit in the intended location.

Installing Swing-up Shelves

Swing-up shelves are perfect for storing heavy appliances beneath the counter. Most swing arms are sold without the shelf surface, which must be purchased separately and cut to fit.

Take accurate measurements of your cabinet's interior dimensions, noting any objects that protrude into the interior. Purchase a swing-up unit that is compatible with your cabinetry. Frameless cabinets often have fully concealed hinges that can interfere with swing mechanisms. Framed cabinets have a front perimeter face frame and may have hinges that interfere with lifting hardware.

Refer to the manufacturer's recommendations for the proper length of the shelf to ensure it will fit into the cabinet when the assembly is locked down and the door is closed. Cut the shelf from ¾"-thick plywood, MDF, or melamine-coated particleboard. If the shelf is bare wood, finish all sides with a washable paint or varnish. For melamine-coated board, cover the cut edges with melamine tape to prevent water from damaging the wood core.

Tools & Materials ▶

Circular saw	Shelving
Tape measure	1 × 3 lumber
Screwdriver	#8 machine screws

Swing-up shelves are used most often to store stand mixers and other heavy small appliances so they're always at the ready.

How to Install Swing-Up Shelves

1

2

Carefully trigger the locking mechanism on each swing arm, and set the arm in its fully extended position. Hold each arm against the inside face of the cabinet side and make sure the arm will clear the door hinge and/or the cabinet face frame. If the arms do not clear, you'll need to use wood spacers to allow the arms to clear the hinges or frames by at least ½". In most cases, one 1 × 3 spacer for each arm will provide enough clearance. Cut the spacers so they match the length of the mounting plate on the swing arms.

Mark the locations of the swing arm mounting plates onto the inside cabinet faces. Mount a swing arm on each side of the cabinet opening, using screws. Unlock and rotate both swing arms so they are fully extended.

3

4

Determine the width of the shelf by measuring between the outer edges of the shelf-mounting flanges.

Fasten each locking bar to the bottom shelf face with the provided screws and plastic spacers to ensure the bars will slide smoothly. Test the locking bars' operation with the shelf in the extended and retracted positions, and make any necessary adjustments.

Slide-out Storage

A base cabinet with slide-out trays or shelves is one of those great modern conveniences that has become standard in new kitchen design. Not only do slide-out trays make reaching stored items easier than with standard cabinet spaces—no more crouching and diving into the deep recesses of cavernous low shelves—they also store more items far more efficiently. With a few shallow trays, a standard base cabinet can hold dozens of food cans and still leave room for tall items like cereal boxes and bags of flour or even deep pots and countertop appliances.

To get the most from your new slide-out system, think carefully about how you will use each tray. Measure the items you're most likely to store together, and let the items dictate the spacing of the trays. Most standard base cabinets are suitable for trays. Wide cabinets (24" or wider) without a center partition (middle stile) are best in terms of space usage, but trays in narrow (18"-wide) cabinets are just as handy. If you have a wide cabinet with a middle stile, you can add trays along one or both sides of the stile. For economy and simplicity, the trays in this project are made with ¾"-thick plywood parts joined with glue and finish nails. If you prefer a more finished look (not that there's anything wrong with the look of nice plywood), you can use 1 × 4 hardwood stock for the tray sides and set a ⅜"-thick plywood bottom panel into dadoes milled into the side pieces. Another option is to assemble plywood tray pieces using pocket screws so the screw heads don't show on the front pieces of the trays.

Tools & Materials ▸

Circular saw with straightedge guide or table saw
Drill
Wood screws
Drawer slides (1 set per tray)
1 × 2 hardwood stock
¾" finish-grade plywood
Wood glue
6d finish nails
Finish materials
Tape measure
Varnish or polyurethane

Slide-out trays eliminate the everyday problem of hard-to-reach and hard-to-see spaces in standard base cabinets. Better still, you can install your trays to accommodate the stuff you use most often.

Drawer Slides

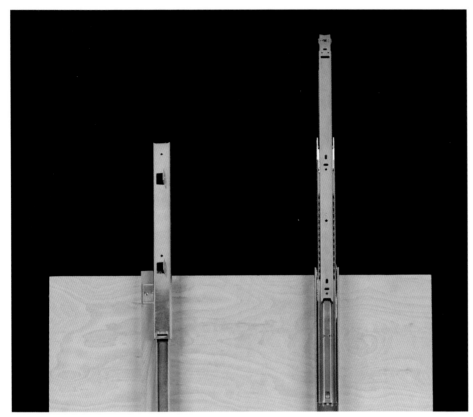

Drawer slides suitable for pullout shelves are commonly available in both standard (left) and full extension (right) styles. Standard slides are less expensive and good enough for most applications. They allow the tray to be pulled out most of the way. Full extension slides are a little pricier than standard slides but they allow the tray to be pulled completely out of the cabinet box for easy access to items in the back.

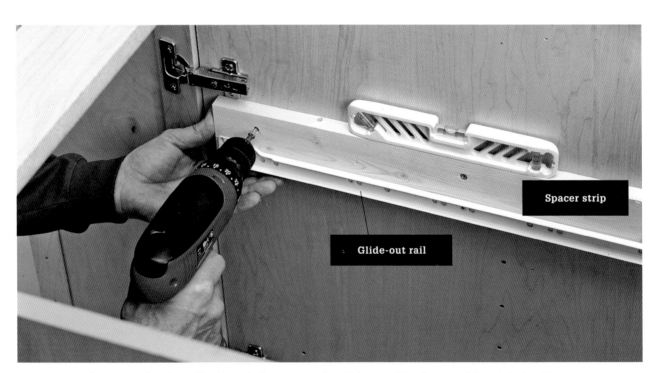

Spacer strip

Glide-out rail

Spacers must be mounted to the wall cabinets before you can install drawer slides for your slide-out shelves. They are necessary for the drawers to clear the cabinet face frame and the door. For a ¾" spacer, a 1 × 3 or 1 × 4 works well. Paint or finish it to match the cabinet interior.

How to Install Slide-out Cabinet Trays

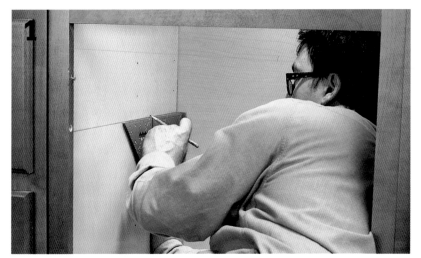

Lay out the tray positions, starting with the bottom tray. Check the drawer slides to see how much clearance you need for the bottom tray. Draw lines on the side panels of the cabinet to represent the bottom edges of the slide supports. Make sure the lines are level and are perpendicular to the cabinet front. Cut the slide supports to length from 1 × 2 hardwood stock (or any hardwood ripped to 1½" wide).

Mount the supports to the side panels of the cabinet with glue and screws driven through countersunk pilot holes. *Note: Depending on the overhang of the cabinet face frames, you may need thicker support stock to provide sufficient clearance for the trays and slide rails.*

Install the drawer slides flush with the bottom edges of the slide supports using the provided screws. Assemble the two halves of each slide, and then measure between the drawer side pieces (rails) to find the exact width of each tray.
Plan the depth of the trays based on the cabinet depth.

Cut the bottom piece for each tray from ¾" plywood 1½" smaller than the planned width and depth of the finished tray. Rip three ¾" -wide pieces for the sides, front, and back of each tray. Cut the side pieces to length, equal to the depth dimension of the bottom piece. Cut the front and back pieces 1½" longer than the width of the bottom.

Build the trays with glue and 6d finish nails or pneumatic brads. Fasten the sides flush with the bottom face and front and back edges of the bottom piece, and then add the front and back pieces. Sand any rough surfaces, and finish the trays with two or three coats of polyurethane or other durable varnish. If desired, you can stain the trays prior to finishing so they match your cabinets.

Partially mount the drawer slide rails to one of the trays, following the manufacturer's directions. Test-fit the tray in the cabinet and make any necessary adjustments before completely fastening the rails. Mount the slide rails on the remaining trays and install the trays to finish the job.

Pull-down Shelves

A pull-down shelf makes wall cabinets more user-friendly by bringing all the contents down to eye level. Because of the space taken up by the mechanism and the shelf boxes, this is not a good project for a narrow cabinet.

Before you begin this project, hold each swing arm assembly against the inside face of the cabinet side and make sure both arms will clear the door hinge and the cabinet face frame. If the arms do not clear, add custom wood spacers of plywood or solid lumber that are at least as large as the swing arm mounting plates.

Follow the manufacturer's specifications for the box dimensions, which will be based on the size of your cabinet. If the boxes are bare wood, lightly sand the edges and finish all sides with a highly washable paint or a clear varnish, such as polyurethane. For melamine-coated board, cover the cut edges with melamine tape to keep water from damaging the wood core.

Note: The springs that help raise the arms are strong and may make it difficult to lower empty shelves. When the shelves are loaded, the weight of the items makes it easier to move the shelf.

Tools & Materials ▸

Tape measure
Pencil
Circular saw
Drill
Awl
Hacksaw
Allen wrench
Swing-up shelf kit & hardware

½" MDF
Fasteners & finishing materials for shelf boxes
#8 panhead screws
Coarse-thread drywall screws
Lumber for custom spacers
Wallboard screws

Shopping Tips ▸

• Specialty hardware catalogs carry pull-down shelf hardware.

• Make sure the capacity of the mechanism you are purchasing matches the weight of the items you will be storing on the shelf.

A pull-down shelf is essentially the opposite of a swing-up shelf. Mounted in an upper wall cabinet, a pull-down shelf can be drawn out of the cabinet and lowered so the user can reach the contents more easily.

How to Install a Pull-down Shelf

Use the shelf manufacturer's paper template to determine the general positions of the swing arms, then fasten the wood spacers to the inside faces of the cabinets with coarse-thread wallboard screws. The screws should not go completely through the cabinet side.

Use the template as a reference for marking the location of the swing arm mounting plates with a scratch awl. Drill a pilot hole at each mark. Fasten the swing arms to the custom spacers or cabinet sides with #8 panhead screws (inset). The screws should not go completely through the cabinet side.

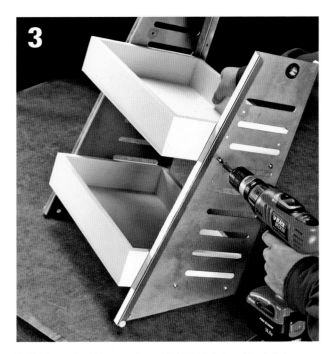

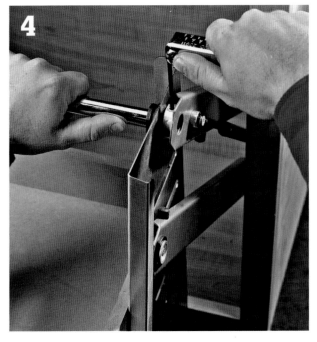

Build two shelf boxes from ½" MDF. Paint and install the boxes between the sides of the shelf unit using the predrilled holes in the side pieces. Secure the boxes with #8 panhead screws. Because the lower box can be installed in only one position, install it first. Then, find the desired position for the upper box, and secure it in place. Slide the lower handle through the holes in the side pieces.

Position the box unit in front of the cabinet, rotate the lower arms downward, and secure them to the side pieces using the bolts, washers, and nuts provided. Insert the top handle. Lower the upper arms one at a time, and insert the handle end into the arm. Secure the handle with the two setscrews in each arm using an Allen wrench.

Customizing Cabinets

Even if you don't have the time or need to pursue a complete kitchen remodel, there are some ways to easily freshen the look of your cabinets. You can raise a single wall cabinet within a bank of cabinets to create more space for countertop appliances or simply to change the look. This tactic works especially well on corner cabinets. Or, you can convert a cabinet to open shelving and create a new display area. Adding crown molding to stock cabinets will give your whole kitchen a more finished look. Another idea is to remove a cabinet door panel, replace it with a glass door, and form an enclosed display space.

Create a display cabinet. If your cabinets have removable shelves, you can transform one or more of them into a display cabinet. Begin by removing the door and hinges and removing the existing shelves and shelf supports. Fill the screw holes and finish to match the cabinet exterior. Paint the inside of the cabinet with gloss enamel. Create a template with guide holes for pin-style shelf supports. Drill the holes for the shelf supports. Measure the space and order tempered glass shelves to fit.

Raise a cabinet. To raise a cabinet, remove the contents of the cabinet and the adjoining cabinets. Remove any trim or crown molding. Remove the screws holding the face frames together or the binder bolts holding the cabinet cases together in a frameless cabinet. Remove the screws holding the cabinet to the wall. Move the cabinet up 4 to 6". It is likely it will stick from paint or age. If so, use a hammer against a padded piece of 2 × 4 to persuade it to move (you'll want a helper to steady the cabinet). Reinstall the cabinet at its new height. Refinish the cabinet sides to match.

Attach crown molding. This project is for face-frame cabinets, since frameless cabinets do not have the traditional look that crown molding complements. If your cabinets have exposed sides with a lip or edge trim, you will need to remove a portion of the lip or add a ¾" wide x ⅛" trim strip to build up the side to match the lip. To remove the lip, measure down ¾" from the top of the cabinets and mark a line on the lip. Use a fine-tooth backsaw to carefully cut down to the side of the cabinet. Use a chisel to remove the upper part of the lip. Cut the longest piece of crown molding first. Measure the cabinet run from end to end. Using a compound miter saw, cut each end at 22½°. Install the molding ¾" down from the top of the cabinets. Nail the molding in place with a finish nailer (photo). Cut the end piece to fit and nail in place.

How to Install a Glass Panel Door

Cut a recess for a glass panel in the frame. Use a router with a straight bit to cut away the lip on the rails and stiles of the door that holds the panel in place. Set the router to the depth of the lip. Clamp the door to the worksurface. Clamp guides to the worksurface. Rout out the lip. Remove the panel. Square the corners of the cutout with a chisel.

Install the glass. Measure the cutout and order a piece of tempered glass to fit. Consider the many types of glass, including frosted and pebbled glass to coordinate with the rest of the kitchen. Use glass clips (See Resources, page 282) to install the glass panel. Reattach the hardware and rehang the door.

Vertical Dividers

Most kitchen cabinets are based on a one-box-fits-all design, and this works fine for much of the stuff we need to store there. But some things just can't be conveniently stored on a horizontal shelf; namely large, flat items like platters, party trays, cutting boards, and baking sheets. These common kitchen products end up getting loaded onto shelves in heavy stacks, and when you need an item it's inevitably near the bottom of the stack.

Vertical cabinet dividers solve this common problem by letting you stow the big, flat stuff on-edge, making for easy retrieval of items. You can custom-fit the dividers for any wall or base cabinet. One of the best places to use dividers is in over-the-fridge cabinets, which are short and wide and tend to be a good fit for sheet pans and platters without wasting space. If this space is too high or too cumbersome to reach up and over the fridge, consider using the space above or below a fixed shelf in a full-height cabinet.

The following steps show two simple methods for adding vertical dividers. One version is adjustable and allows you to move dividers as needed to accommodate new storage items. The second method includes fixed dividers but retains a little more headroom in the cabinet than with the adjustable system. If necessary, a fixed divider can be moved by unscrewing and refastening its slotted cleats.

Tools & Materials ▶

Circular saw	⅜" MDF
Straightedge guide	¼" plywood
Router and ⁵⁄₁₆" straight bit	Wood screws or coarse-
Drill	thread drywall screws

Vertical storage of flat pieces means less wasted cabinet space and no more sorting through stacks when retrieving or replacing an item.

How to Install Vertical Dividers

Cut two MDF panels to fit the inside dimensions of the top and bottom of the cabinet. On one of the pieces, mark the locations of the divider slots using any spacing you like. *Note: With traditional face-frame cabinets, you may need extra MDF pieces or lumber spacers behind the slotted piece so that the slots extend below the face-frame overhang.*

Clamp the MDF pieces to a bench with their faces up and their edges aligned. Using a router and a straightedge guide, mill a 5/16"-wide × 3/16"-deep groove into both pieces at each slot location. If the cabinet has a center partition (middle stile), cut the pieces in half so you'll be able to fit them into the cabinet.

Install the top and bottom pieces into the cabinet so the slots are aligned. Fasten the top piece in place with screws. Measure vertically between the slot bottoms, then cut the divider panels 1/16" shorter than this dimension. Slide the panels into place at the desired spacing.

Variation: For a cabinet with a deep overhanging face-frame, you can save headroom by using slotted 1 × 2 or 2 × 2 cleats to hold the panels instead of solid top and bottom pieces. Mill the cleats with a router and fasten them to the cabinet with screws.

Custom Cabinets

The simple base cabinet and hanging wall cabinet shown here use the same basic construction as professionally built kitchen cabinets, but because they are custom-designed, trimmed, and finished to blend into the room, they become permanent built-in features of your home.

These basic cabinets are built with maple plywood, which gives them the look of fine custom-made cabinets, but at a much reduced cost. The base cabinet has extra-large drawers that are well suited for storing table linens.

You can use the methods shown here to build a single based cabinet with a wall cabinet above it or several cabinets side by side (for a full wall of storage or display).

Tools & Materials ▸

Electronic stud finder	Pocket screw jig
Cordless screwdriver	Wood glue
Hammer	Biscuits, splines, or dowels
Tape measure	Finish nails (1", 2", 3", 4")
Utility knife	Shims
Router with bits	Pin-style shelf supports
(¾" straight, ¼" rabbet)	¾" plywood
Drill and bits	1 × 3, 1 × 6, 2 × 4 lumber
Right-angle drill guide	1 × 3 maple
Pegboard scraps	Finishing materials
Pipe clamps	Drawer and door hardware
Level	Trim or base shoe molding
Sander	Wood putty
Circular saw	Countertop hardwood (see
Power-driver screws	page 80)
(¾", 2½", 3½")	

Building your own custom cabinets from scratch isn't necessarily a cost-savings venture, but it allows you to populate your kitchen with sturdy cabinets made of high-quality materials with the exact tone and appearance you want.

Cutting Sheet Goods ▸

A full-sized table-saw and a helper, you'll find no better combination for cutting full-sheet panels, with the possible exception of a panel saw. But if you are working alone, it is still possible to cut full panels down to size accurately and safely using a circular saw. The main difficulty beginners encounter when cutting panels with a circular saw is that they do not adequately support the waste so it falls away prematurely and ruins the cut (or causes an accident). Another common mistake is to support both ends so the area being cut binds on the saw blade as the cut is made. The solution is simply to support the entire panel along both edges with sacrificial scraps of 2 × 4. Set your saw blade to cut just slightly deeper than the thickness of the panel. The blade will score the 2 × 4s as it cuts, but they will continue to support the workpiece all the way through the cut. Be sure to use a straightedge guide for your saw, and always cut with the good face down when using a circular saw.

Overlay Doors ▸

Easy-to-build overlay doors, made with ½" finish-grade plywood panels framed with door-edge moldings, are designed to overhang the face frame by about ⅜" on each side. Semi-concealed overlay hinges, which require no mortising, are attached to the back of the door and to the edge of the face frame. This door style also can be adapted to make folding doors.

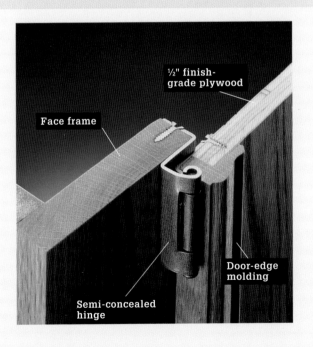

½" finish-grade plywood

Face frame

Door-edge molding

Semi-concealed hinge

Exploded View of Hanging Wall Cabinet

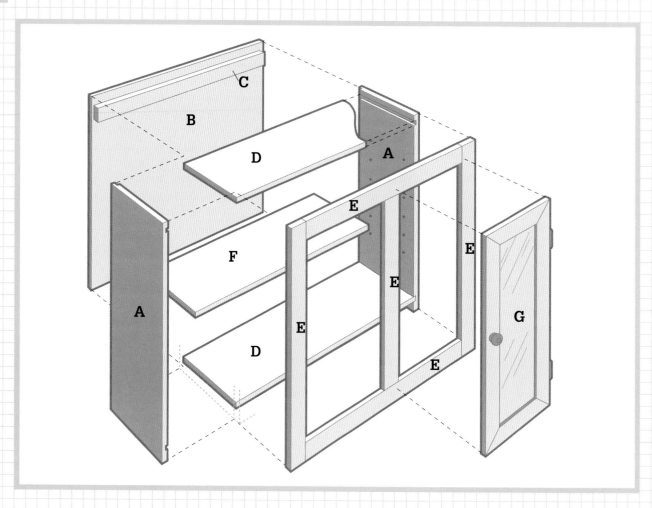

Parts List: Wall Cabinet

Project as Shown

Key	Part	Material	Pieces	Size
A	Side panels	¾" maple plywood	2	11¼" × 30"
B	Back panel	¼" maple plywood	1	30" × 35¼"
C	Nailing strip	1 × 3 maple	1	34¼"
D	Top, bottom panels	¾" maple plywood	2	35¼" × 11¼"
E	Face frame	1 × 3 maple	12 linear ft	
F	Shelves	¾" maple plywood	2	9¾ × 34¼"
G	Glass panel or overlay doors			

Exploded View of Base Cabinet

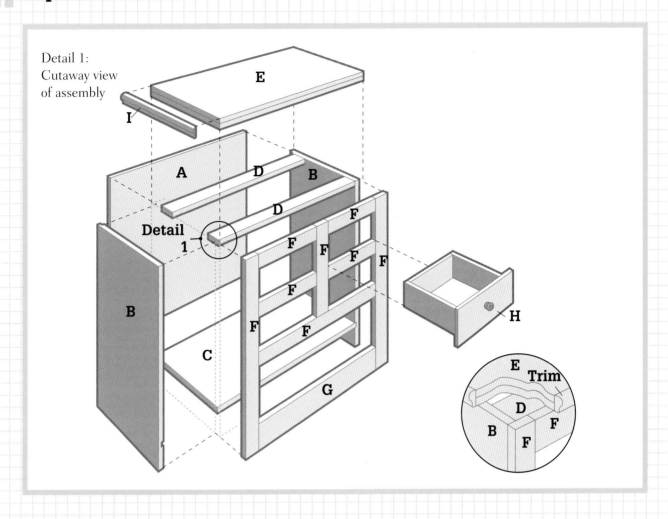

Detail 1:
Cutaway view
of assembly

E

I

A   D   B

D

Detail

1

F

F

F   F

B

F

F   F

C

F   F

H

G

E   Trim

D

B   F

F

Parts List: Base Cabinet

Project as Shown

Key	Part	Material	Pieces	Size
A	Back panel	½" maple plywood	1	34½ × 35¼"
B	Side panels	¾" maple plywood	2	34½ × 17¼"
C	Bottom panel	¾" maple plywood	1	16¾ × 35¼"
D	Supports	1 × 3 maple	2	34½"
E	Countertop	¾" plywood	2	36¼ × 18"
F	Face-frame	1 × 3 maple	15 linear ft.	
G	Bottom rail	1 × 6 maple	1	31¼"
H	Overlay drawers			
I	Trim molding	12 linear ft.		

Wall Cabinet Project Details

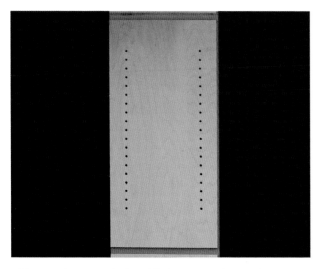

Side panels are made from ¾" plywood and have ¾"-wide, ⅜"-deep dadoes where bottom and top panels fit and ¼"-wide rabbets where the back panel fits. Rows of parallel peg holes, 1½" in from edges, hold pin-style shelf supports.

A back panel made from ¼" plywood has a 1 × 3 nailing strip mounted 1½" below the top edge of the back panel and set in ⅜" on each side. It is fastened with glue and ¾" screws driven through the back panel.

How to Build & Install a Wall Cabinet

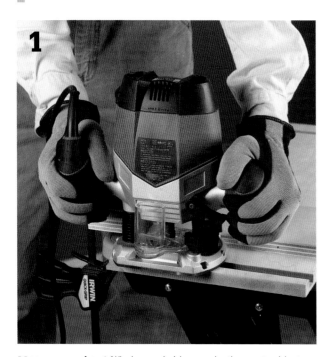

Measure and cut ¾" plywood side panels, then cut rabbets and dadoes using a router and a straightedge guide, following the dimensions in the project details (see page 72 and 73).

Drill two parallel rows of ¼"-dia. holes for pin-style shelf supports on the inside face of each side panel. Use a right-angle drill guide and a scrap of pegboard as a template to ensure that holes line up correctly. Holes should be no deeper than ⅜"—most right-angle drill guides include a depth stop.

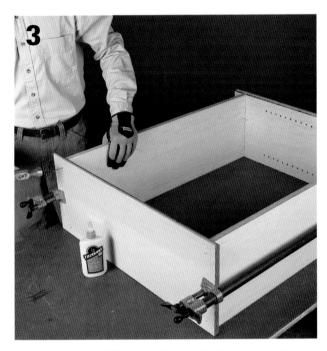

Measure and cut ¾" plywood top and bottom panels, then glue and clamp the side panels to the top and bottom panels to form dado joints. Reinforce the joints with 2" finish nails driven every 3".

Attach the back panel (see page 72 and 73) using glue and ¾" screws. Set the back panel into the rabbets at the back edges of the cabinet. Secure the back with 1½" finish nails driven into the cabinet edges.

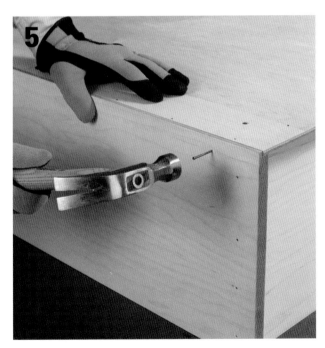

Attach a 1 × 3 nailing strip on the inside of the cabinet, about 1½" down from the top. Drive three ¾" wood screws through the back panel and into the nailing strip, and then drive a pair of 2" finish nails through the side panel and into the ends of the nailing strip.

Make the face frame. Measure the height and width of the cabinet interior and then cut 1 × 3 face-frame rails that are 4¾" shorter than the cabinet width. Cut face-frame stiles 4" longer than the height. Glue, square, and then clamp the rails between the stiles. You could use biscuits, splines, or dowels to reinforce the joints (these need to be installed before clamping). Here, pocket screws are being driven at the joints of the face frame using a pocket screw jig.

(continued)

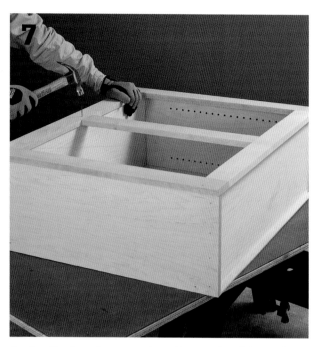

Center the face frame on the cabinet so the slight overhang on each side is equal and the top edge of the bottom rail is flush with the bottom shelf surface. Attach the face frame with glue and 2" finish nails driven through pilot holes.

Finish the cabinet. Sand all wood surfaces, and then apply wood stain (if desired) and two or three thin coats of polyurethane or other topcoat material. Use tinted wood putty that matches the color of the stained wood to fill nail holes.

Mark a level reference line on the wall where the bottom edge of the cabinet will be located—54" above the floor is a standard height. Locate the wall studs and mark their locations beneath the reference line.

Attach a temporary ledger strip to the wall studs so the top edge is flush with the reference line using screws.

Install the cabinet by setting it onto the temporary ledge, and then brace it in position with a 2 × 4 wedged between the cabinet and the floor below (or the base cabinet, if present). Drill countersunk pilot holes in the nailing strip at the top of the cabinet, and drive 3" screws into the wall studs.

Use a level to make sure the cabinet is plumb. If not, loosen the screws slightly and insert shims behind the cabinet to adjust it to plumb. Tighten the screws completely, score shims with a utility knife, and break off excess.

Build or buy cabinet doors. A simple overlay door can be made from ½" plywood that matches the cabinet and door-edge molding that is mitered at the corners to frame the plywood panel. Hang the cabinet doors with hinges.

Build and install shelves. Here, shelves are made from ¾"-thick plywood with a ¼ × ¾" hardwood strip nosing on the front edge. Set the finished shelves on shelf pins inserted in the pin-holes drilled in the cabinet side.

Base Cabinet Project Details

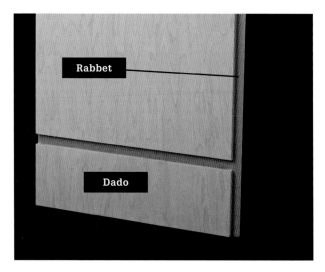

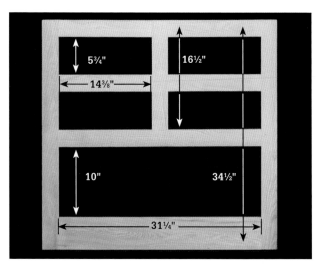

Side panels made from ¾" plywood have ¾"-wide, ⅜"-deep dadoes to hold the bottom panel and ½"-wide, ⅜"-deep rabbets where the back panel will fit. The bottom dado is raised so the bottom drawer will be at a comfortable height.

The face frame includes 1 × 6 bottom rails and 1 × 3s for the stiles and other rails. Cut and assemble the face frame, following the dimensions shown in the photo above. Use biscuits, splines, or dowels to reinforce the joints. Alternately, drive pocket screws after the parts are glued and clamped.

How to Build & Install a Base Cabinet

Assemble cabinet panels. Cut the side and bottom panels from ¾" plywood (cabinet-grade maple is seen here), and cut the ½" plywood back panel. Use a router and piloted rabbet bit to create ⅜ × ½" rabbets in the side panels for the back panel. Cut dadoes for the bottom panel into the side panels using a router, straight bit, and straightedge guide. Install the bottom panel between the side panels. Glue, clamp, and then drive finish nails through the side panels and into the ends of the bottom panel.

Install two 1 × 3 spreaders between the side panels at the top of the cabinet. Clamp the spreaders in position and attach them with glue and 2" finish nails driven through the side panels.

3

Build the face-frame from 1 × 3 maple (actual sizes ¾ × 2½" and ¾ × 5¼"). The glued joints can be reinforced with biscuits, splines, or dowels prior to assembly, or they can be glued, clamped, and reinforced with pocket screws, as seen here.

4

Attach the face frame to the cabinet with glue and 2" finish nails driven through pilot holes. The face-frame should be flush with the cabinet tops, slightly above the cabinet bottoms, and overhanging the sides equally by a small amount. Sand and finish the cabinet as desired.

5

Install the cabinet. Mark the locations of the wall studs in the project area, and then set the cabinet in place. Check with a level and shim under the cabinet, if necessary, to level it. Toenail the side panels to the floor at shim locations using 2" finish nails. Score shims, and break off excess.

6

Anchor the cabinet by driving 3½" screws through the back panel and into wall studs just below the top of the cabinet.

(continued)

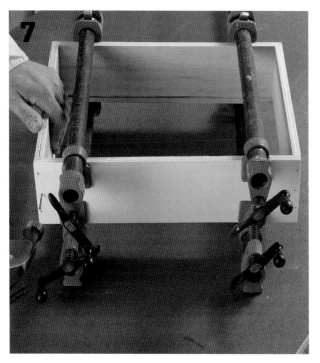

Build or purchase drawers. Simple overlay drawers are easy to make from ½" plywood and a false front made of hardwood. Refer to the information on page 81 for construction details and guidance on sizing drawers.

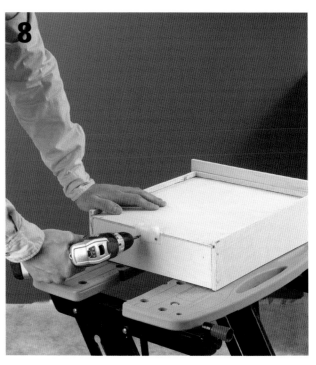

Install drawer slide hardware on the drawer. Slides may be center-mounted, as seen here, or side-mounted in pairs. Typically, side-mounted slides are rated for higher weight capacity.

Mount drawer slide hardware in the cabinet interior according to the manufacturer's instructions. Install the drawers and test the fit. Add drawer pull hardware.

Add the countertop of your choice. See pages 86 to 89 for information on choosing a countertop type and building it yourself. If you are building just a single base cabinet, consider a higher end material such as solid surfacing or granite. The small scale will let you introduce an expensive material without spending a fortune.

Building Overlay Drawers ▸

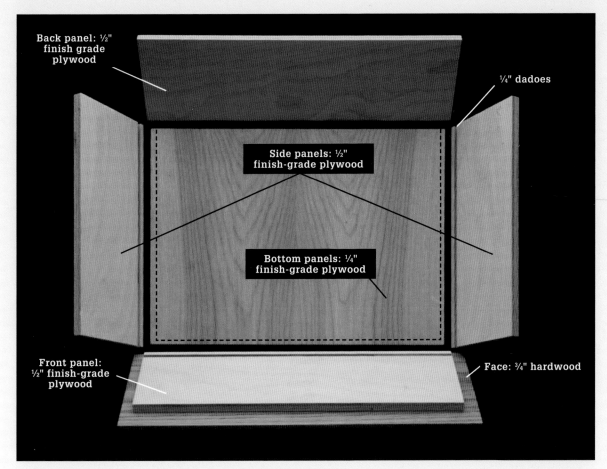

Back panel: ½"
finish grade
plywood

¼" dadoes

Side panels: ½"
finish-grade plywood

Bottom panels: ¼"
finish-grade plywood

Front panel:
½" finish-grade
plywood

Face: ¾" hardwood

Anatomy of an overlay drawer: The basic drawer box is made using ½" plywood for the front, back, and side panels with a ¼" plywood bottom panel. The bottom panel fits into ¼" dadoes cut near the bottom of the front and side panels and is nailed to the bottom edge of the back panel. The hardwood drawer face is screwed to the drawer front from the inside, and it is sized to overhang the face frame by ½" on all sides. *Note: This drawer is designed to be mounted with a center-mounted drawer slide attached to the bottom of the drawer. If you use different hardware, like side-mounted drawer slides, you will need to alter this design according to slide manufacturer's directions.*

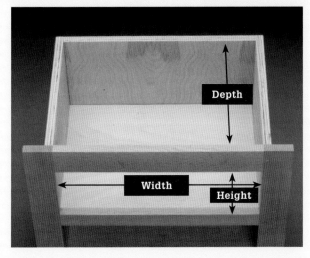

Depth

Width

Height

Part		Measurement
Sides	Length	Depth of opening, minus 3"
Sides	Height	Height of opening, minus ½"
Front	Length	Width of opening, minus 1½"
Front	Height	Height of opening, minus ½"
Back	Length	Width of opening, minus 1½"
Back	Height	Height of opening, minus 1"
Bottom	Width	Width of opening, minus 1"
Bottom	Depth	Depth of opening, minus 2¾"
Face	Length	Width of opening, plus 1"
Face	Height	Height of opening, plus 1"

Kitchen Cabinet Paint

Painting the cabinets can brighten any drab and dreary kitchen. Doing the job properly does require a substantial amount of work, however, but the payoff is large. As with most painting jobs, preparation is crucial to success. Kitchen cabinets have been exposed to years of grease and water damage, so thorough cleaning and sanding is necessary. Before sanding previously painted kitchen cabinets, test the existing paint for lead. Do not sand lead-based paint. It is toxic.

If veneer layers have bubbled from water damage, slice away the loose veneer, fill the area with wood filler, and then sand smooth when dry. *Note: Nonwood cabinets, such as melamine-coated, are difficult to repaint due to the impenetrable nature of the surface.* There are specialty paints available, however, that bond reasonably well to these slick, nonwood surfaces. Many of them are oil-based, which creates more fumes and makes cleanup more difficult. The steps for painting melamine are the same as for painting wood. Metal cabinets can also be repainted. The best results for metal are obtained using spray paint.

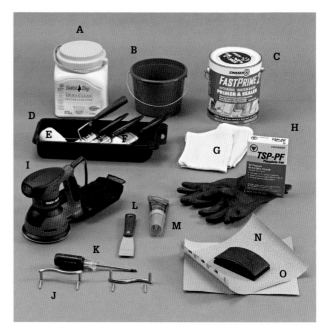

Tools and materials for painting wood cabinets include: (A) Semigloss or gloss enamel paint; (B) wash bucket; (C) primer; (D) roller tray; (E) roller sleeve (3"); (F) paintbrushes; (G) rags; (H) TSP cleaner and rubber gloves; (I) palm sander; (J) new cabinet hardware (optional); (K) screwdriver; (L) putty knife; (M) wood filler; (N) sandpaper (100- and 150-grit) and (O) sanding block.

Painting cabinets is an easy and inexpensive way to brighten up your kitchen. Painted cabinets also happen to be popular in current design trends.

How to Paint Cabinets

Begin painting by labeling each door and its cabinet bay with a number printed on painters' tape. This will help you replace the doors and drawers. Remove all the doors, drawers, and hardware. Clean all surfaces—front, back, top, bottom, inside, outside, edges—with a grease-cutting cleaner such as synthetic trisodium phosphate (TSP). Follow the directions carefully.

Sand all surfaces with 100-grit sandpaper. Fill all screw holes and nicks and dents with wood filler, and then sand smooth when dry. If you are reusing the same hardware, you do not need to fill the screw holes.

Prime the surfaces. Use a synthetic brush to paint all surfaces with a coat of high-quality, sandable acrylic primer. Allow the primer to dry. Sand with 150-grit sandpaper to remove brush marks and drips.

Apply a coat of latex enamel paint using 3"-wide short nap rollers. Make sure to smooth out any drips. Allow the paint to dry completely. Apply a second coat. Allow to dry thoroughly. Install the hardware and rehang the doors.

Countertops

Your countertops play an important role in your kitchen. They must be sturdy and durable enough to withstand the daily pounding and chopping that goes on in most kitchens. They should resist staining and heat and be easy to clean. And because they command so much visible area, they have a great impact on the appearance of the kitchen. In short, if you don't like the look of your countertops, you won't like your kitchen.

While you will find a wide range of countertop types in the marketplace, just a handful of them are truly well suited for DIY installation. Among these are postform (probably the easiest to work with) and plastic laminate countertops. Installing tiled countertops remains a very popular DIY project, with traditional ceramic floor tiles still the leading product. Newer variations are increasing in popularity, however, including tiles that are made from natural stone such as granite. Poured concrete countertops are another option that has seen strong growth in popularity and is a manageable DIY project if you have some concrete experience and plenty of patience.

Although it is possible to get around the restrictions if you're a creative type, manufacturers of solid surfacing and quartz countertop materials generally insist that only licensed technicians do the installations. Natural stone countertops are simply too heavy for most homeowners to install. Stainless steel countertops are popular now, too, but they require a lot of skill and some expensive fabricating equipment to be installed correctly.

This chapter shows:

- Countertop Selection
- Post-form Countertop
- Butcher Block Countertop
- Laminate Countertop
- Tile Countertop
- Granite Countertop
- Tile Backsplash

Countertop Selection

More than simply a worksurface, a kitchen countertop can dazzle with the look-at-me drama of mottled granite or bring together a country theme with honed soapstone and butcher block. But durability and maintenance (and cost of course) are generally the primary concerns when it comes to countertops.

Some materials, like granite, can withstand the heat of pots and pans, so they are better suited for heavy-duty cooks. Others, including laminate, are affordable options that come in a wide variety of modern colors. There are many choices in countertops, from the less-expensive laminate, through ceramic and stone tile, to concrete and wood, to high-end granite and marble.

Countertop options for your kitchen depend on how much you are willing to spend, whether you will be doing it yourself or contracting it out, and what look you want to achieve. When choosing countertops, remember that you do not need to have a uniform countertop. Many people choose to use more expensive countertop materials as accents or for islands rather than for the entire kitchen. And last, but not least, if you are inclined toward green remodeling practices, you may find some surprises when you compare countertop materials (see page 87).

Fabricated countertop material like quartz and solid-surface is virtually impenetrable to water. If it becomes scratched, minor damage can easily be buffed out.

Laminate & Post-form

Laminate countertops are formed from layers of resin-saturated paper and plastic that are bonded under pressure, then given a protective coating. The laminate is bonded to a substrate to create the countertop. Also available is through-color laminate, in which the surface color runs all the way through. This product doesn't have the dark edge of standard laminate and does not show surface damage as easily, but it is two to three times more expensive.

The cheapest laminate countertop is ready-made post-form. A post-form countertop comprises a backsplash, counter, and bullnose front apron formed into one seamless piece. Home centers carry post-form countertop options in various lengths and in a few stock colors. You can also have a custom post-form countertop made, which will be slightly more expensive.

One limitation of laminate countertops is that sinks must be drop-in, not undermounted. Though the laminate itself is waterproof, the particleboard or plywood it is attached to will swell if it gets wet. Laminate is also not as heat-proof or scratch-proof as other countertop materials.

Tile

Whether they are ceramic or natural stone, tile countertops are popular, mid-priced options. If you like the look of granite but don't want to pay the price, granite tile can create a similar look for substantially less, especially if you do the installation yourself. When selecting tiles for countertops, make sure they are floor tiles—wall tiles will not stand up to the wear and tear of countertop use.

Two major drawbacks of ceramic or stone tile are hardness and grout lines. Glassware and pottery will break and chip readily when knocked or dropped against this surface. Grout lines make the surface uneven and difficult to keep clean, so choose larger tiles to minimize grout lines. Using tiles for a backsplash is an excellent way to get the look of tile near the countertop.

Plastic laminate is bonded to a particleboard subbase with contact cement.

Post-form countertops have a laminate surface that is applied at the factory.

Tiles are set into a bed of thinset mortar troweled onto a cementboard or tilebacker subbase.

Solid Surface

Solid-surface countertops, commonly described by the common brand name Corian™, are popular but more expensive options. With solid color throughout, the pieces are joined with a bonding compound that leaves no visible seam line. Solid-surface countertops can be shaped and inlaid, it comes in many colors and patterns, it is durable, and light damage like scratches can be repaired easily. Solid-surface should not be used as a cutting board, however, and hot pans cannot be placed directly on the surface. Most spills are easily cleaned with soap and water.

Though solid-surface materials are easily worked with standard hand tools, do-it-yourselfers may have difficulty purchasing the materials and bonding agents. If a non-licensed installer installs one of those countertops, the manufacturer will not honor any product warranties.

Solid-surface countertops can be installed on islands or as accents if you don't have the budget to put them everywhere in your kitchen.

Quartz Surfaces

Quartz countertops resemble solid-surface countertops in many ways, but they have a higher percentage of mineral material versus plastic resins and binders. Quartz surfaces are manufactured from 93 percent quartz and 7 percent pigments, resins, and binders. Because all quartz surfaces are manufactured using essentially the same equipment and formulas, any difference in appearance among products is due to the type of quartz used.

The quartz surface is unscratchable, non-porous, non-staining, does not need to be sealed, and will not scorch or mar from high heat. Although it is as hard as granite, quartz has more inherent flexibility, so surface cracking does not occur. The surface is cool to the touch, like granite and marble.

Quartz countertops are almost solid granulated and reconstituted quartz (the most common mineral on earth).

Stainless Steel

Although it is slightly more expensive than solid surface or quartz on a per-square-foot basis, stainless steel is a popular countertop material in home kitchens as well as in commercial kitchens. That's because it is an impervious material that doesn't stain, can handle hot pots, and can be fabricated into seamless countertops and sinks. Stainless steel countertops for residential use are usually bonded to plywood or particleboard to quiet the noise and prevent denting. Sinks can either be fabricated as part of the countertop, or, more likely, welded in. Either way, it is a seamless application. The biggest downside is that stainless steel shows fingerprints and watermarks, especially on a polished surface, so it's best to get a matte or satin surface.

Stainless steel countertops normally are bonded to a plywood subbase in residential applications.

Butcher Block & Wood

Advancing technology in wood finishes and sealants have made wood countertops a viable option for kitchen applications. Historically, the amount of water splashed around a sink would ruin a wood surface. The best of the wood options is butcher block, which can be ordered and installed as a relatively easy DIY project. Butcher block is made up of small pieces of wood glued together into a slab. It's generally categorized as either end grain, which is composed of vertical pieces of wood, or edge grain, made of long strips of wood. The thickness of stock slabs can vary, from 1½" for the standard countertop to 4" for an island or small-section installation. Many people assume that butcher block is convenient because you no longer need cutting boards, but it's a poor idea to use them as direct cutting surfaces. Every nick and cut will collect dirt and will darken differently when the surface is reoiled. Wood, no matter how well it is sealed, expands and contracts in relation to humidity levels, so installation of a wood countertop requires special considerations (see pages 96 to 101).

Butcher block material is sold in standard countertop width and thickness and in varying lengths.

Concrete Countertops

Concrete has become a very popular, exceptionally dramatic countertop choice. It is a custom option, but is not as expensive as granite. It can be cast in place under certain conditions, but as a moderate to difficult DIY project, it should be created off-site where the dust and chemicals can be easily managed. Concrete can be dyed or stained in many different colors and will accept a virtually unlimited number of finishes. Drainboards can be cast in and ornamental objects can be embedded in the concrete for added functionality or just to make it more unique. Concrete needs to be resealed regularly, or it will permanently stain.

Acidic foods will etch the surface. Like ceramic tile and stone surfaces, it has no give, so expect a greater number of broken glasses and plates. Custom concrete sinks as part of the counter are also possible.

Concrete countertops are cast in forms in a well-ventilated work area and then transported to the cabinets after they are machined and polished.

Stone

Soapstone, slate, marble, and granite are all types of natural stone that are used for countertops. Although they are all quarried stone and are all fairly expensive, they have numerous differences. Soapstone has been used for kitchen countertops and sinks for hundreds of years. Though the stone itself is easily workable with nonspecialized tools, its surface is nonabsorbent and unaffected by either acids or alkalis. The surface will age to a glossy patina, or it can be oiled to achieve this finish. Slate for countertops is durable, hard, and dense. Scratches can be rubbed out, its surface is nonabsorbing and it does not require sealing. Slate comes in shades of green, purple, gray, and black, with a rare red available at a higher cost.

The beauty of marble comes from its veining patterns—unfortunately these are mini fault lines along which the stone will easily break, especially if improperly installed. Some marble is as hard as granite, but most is fairly soft and scratches easily. Granite is the hardest of the stone countertops. It comes in an ever-increasing array of colors—ranging from whites and blacks to pinks, reds, yellows, and greens—as more countries begin exporting their local granites. The main drawback is that it must be sealed to prevent staining.

A big slab of beautiful, natural stone makes an incomparable countertop that is normally at the top of the cost range.

Comparing Countertop Materials ▸

Material	Description	Making it Greener
Plastic Laminate	Paper and resin laminate glued to particle board (or MDF) substrate. Resistant to stains, scratches, and moisture; easy to clean; inexpensive. Surface susceptible to chipping and burning; damage cannot be repaired.	Use formaldehyde-free, recycled-wood substrate and low-VOC adhesive; laminate should be made with recycled paper and water-based resins, if possible.
Paper-resin	Solid slab of paper and resin. Highly workable for custom applications; solid color and same durability throughout slab; resistant to stains and heat. May need periodic cleaning and finishing treatments.	Choose product with high recycled content; purchase from local or regional supplier/fabricator to minimize shipping.
Tile	Ceramic, porcelain, or glass tiles glued to cementboard and wood substrate. Durable and highly heat-resistant; tiles are highly washable; versatile material for custom applications. Grout between tiles is prone to staining and must be sealed periodically.	Use tiles with recycled content or locally produced tiles. Use marine plywood and/or seal plywood to reduce formaldehyde offgassing; set tiles with low-VOC adhesive. Seal grout and tiles (if necessary) with formaldehyde-free, low-VOC sealer.
Glass Composite	Solid slab of glass and resin binder. Durable; unique appearance; heat- and scratch-resistant. May require periodic cleaning and/or sealing treatments.	Choose product with high recycled content. Purchase from local or regional fabricator to minimize shipping.
Butcher Block	Solid-wood strips laminated to form a slab. Natural, renewable material; good surface for cutting; can be refinished. Must be oiled and sealed periodically to maintain appearance.	Choose only FSC-certified wood. Treat surface with food-safe finishes and sealers.
Stainless Steel	Alloy of steel, nickel, and chromium; often glued to wood substrate. Highly durable, rustproof, and easy to clean. Can be scratched and dented.	Recycle the metal if you replace the countertops. Use formaldehyde-free substrate.
Natural Stone	Solid quarried stone slabs or tiles glued to substrate. Durable; heatproof and waterproof. Can chip and crack; some varieties will stain; dark colors make cleaning problematic.	Look for salvaged slabs or buy stone from local quarry.
Engineered Stone	Composite of quartz or other stone, pigments, and polyester resin. Same color and durability throughout slab; doesn't require sealing.	Purchase from a manufacturer in your region and use a local fabricator.
Solid-surface	Composite of petrochemical-based resins (polyester, acrylic) and bauxite. Color and durability consistent throughout material; highly workable and customizable.	Green options are limited; perhaps minimize quantity of countertop.
Concrete	Available in various forms, including poured-in-place concrete, cast concrete, and fiber cement composite materials. Versatile material is highly customizable; durable and heat-resistant. Can be very heavy; prone to cracking, chipping, and staining; must be sealed regularly.	Look for products with high recycled content, such as fly ash (to replace high-embodied energy and aggregates cement). Color material with natural, nontoxic pigments added to concrete mix instead of stains applied to surface.

Post-form Countertop

Post-form laminate countertops are available in stock and custom colors. Pre-mitered sections are available for two- or three-piece countertops that continue around corners. If the countertop has an exposed end, you will need an endcap kit that contains a pre-shaped strip of matching laminate. Post-form countertops have either a waterfall edge or a no-drip edge. Stock colors are typically available in 4-, 6-, 8-, 10-, and 12-foot straight lengths and 6- and 8-foot mitered lengths.

Post-form countertops are among the easiest and cheapest to install. They are a good choice for beginning DIYers, but the design and color options are fairly limited.

Tools & Materials ▸

Tape measure
Framing square
Pencil
Straightedge
C-clamps
Hammer
Level
Caulking gun
Jigsaw
Compass
Adjustable wrench

Belt sander
Drill and spade bit
Cordless screwdriver
Post-form countertop
Wood shims
Take-up bolts
Drywall screws
Wire brads
Endcap laminate
Silicone caulk
Wood glue

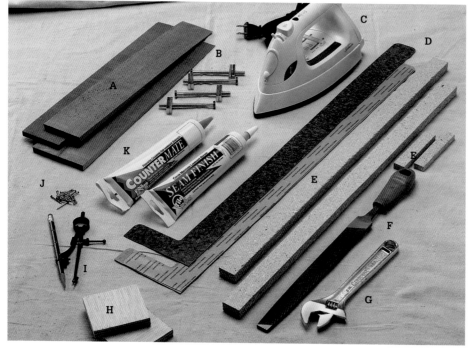

The following tools and materials will be used in this project: wood for shimming (A); take-up bolts for drawing miters together (B); household iron (C); endcap laminate to match countertop (D); endcap battens (E); file (F); adjustable wrench (G); buildup blocks (H); compass (I); fasteners (J); silicone caulk and sealer (K).

How to Install a Post-form Countertop

1

OPTION: Use a jigsaw fitted with a downstroke blade to cut post-form. If you are unable to locate a downstroke blade, you can try applying tape over the cutting lines, but you are still likely to get tear-out from a normal upstroke jigsaw blade.

2

Use a framing square to mark a cutting line on the bottom surface of the countertop. Cut off the countertop with a jigsaw using a clamped straightedge as a guide.

3

Attach the battens from the endcap kit to the edge of the countertop using carpenter's glue and small brads. Sand out any unevenness with a belt sander.

(continued)

4

Hold the endcap laminate against the end, slightly overlapping the edges. Activate adhesive by pressing an iron set at medium heat against the endcap. Cool with a wet cloth, then file the endcap laminate flush with the edges of the countertop.

5

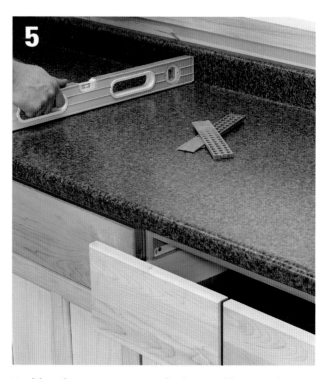

Position the countertop on the base cabinets. Make sure the front edge of the countertop is parallel to the cabinet faces. Check the countertop for level. Make sure that drawers and doors open and close freely. If needed, adjust the countertop with shims.

6

Because walls are usually uneven, use a compass to trace the wall outline onto the backsplash. Set the compass arms to match the widest gap, then move the compass along the length of the wall to transfer the outline to the top of the backsplash. Apply painter's tape to the top edge of the backsplash, following the scribe line (inset).

7

Remove the countertop. Use a belt sander to grind the backsplash to the scribe line.

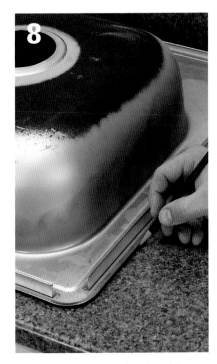

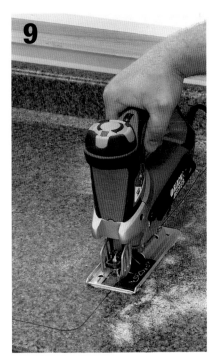

Mark cutout for self-rimming sink. Position the sink upside down on the countertop and trace its outline. Remove the sink and draw a cutting line ⅝" inside the sink outline.

Drill a starter hole just inside the cutting line. Make sink cutouts with a jigsaw. Support the cutout area from below so that the falling cutout does not damage the cabinet.

Apply a bead of silicone caulk to the edges of the mitered countertop sections. Force the countertop pieces tightly together.

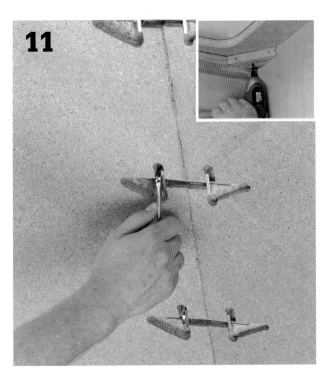

From underneath the countertop, install and tighten miter take-up bolts. Position the countertop tightly against the wall and fasten it to the cabinets by driving wallboard screws up through the corner brackets and into the countertop (inset). Screws should be long enough to provide maximum holding power, but not long enough to puncture the laminate surface.

Seal the seam between the backsplash and the wall with silicone caulk. Smooth the bead with a wet fingertip. Wipe away excess caulk.

Butcher Block Countertop

Butcher block slabs come in a variety of woods or— since they are made up of small pieces of wood glued together—a combination of different woods. They're available most commonly in maple or oak in end grain, which is composed of vertical pieces of wood, or edge grain and face grain, made up long strips of wood. Making butcher block can be accomplished as an advanced DIY project, but it's often more cost-effective (and always faster) to purchase pieces in stock sizes and cut it down to fit your kitchen. Since butcher block is ideal for food prep areas but can be impractical near a sink or stove, another option is to install a small section of butcher block in combination with other countertop materials.

Tools & Materials ▸

Circular saw with
  cutting guide
Carpenter's square
Drill and bits
Bolt connector
  hardware
Caulk gun and silicone
  adhesive
Clamps
Sander
Varnish

Router with piloted
  roundover bit
Wood screws with
  fender washers
Jigsaw with downstroke bit
Brush and finish material
Tape
Connector fittings
Forstner bit
Silicone adhesive
Faucet and sink

Butcher block countertops are enjoying a resurgence in popularity because of their natural beauty and warm wood tones.

Butcher block sold by the foot for countertop ranges from 1½" to 3" thick, although some end grain products, used mostly for chopping blocks, can be up to 5" thick. For residential kitchens, the 1½"-thick material is the most available and most affordable choice. Stock length varies but 6-foot and 12-foot slabs are common. You can also order the material with sink cutouts completed. Premade countertop is sold in the standard 25" depth, but wider versions (30" and 36") for islands are not difficult to find.

Butcher block countertop material comes pre-sealed, but a finish of varnish or oil, such as mineral or tung oil, is recommended. Seal cut wood around sink cutouts and on trimmed edges to keep it watertight.

A self-rimming sink is the easiest type to mount in a butcher block countertop, but undermount types can look stunning (just make sure to get a perfect seal on the end grain around the sink cutout.

End grain vs. face grain: Traditionally, butcher block countertop surfaces were made with square sections of wood (often maple) oriented with their end grain facing upward. This orientation creates a better, more durable, knife-friendly cutting surface. For economy, many of today's butcher block sections are edge-glued with exposed edge grain or face grain.

Typical countertop material is 1½" wide and 25" deep, available in a number of lengths from 4 ft. to 12 ft. long.

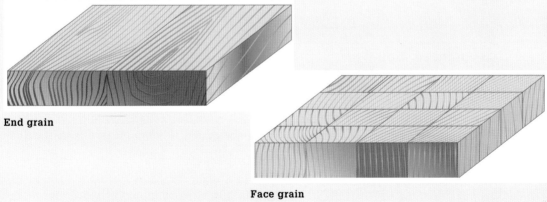

End grain

Face grain

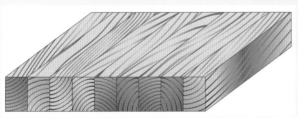

Edge grain

Butcher block that's constructed with the end grain oriented up is the most desirable, but it is relatively hard to find and fairly expensive. Material with the face grain or edge grain facing up is more common and more affordable (prefinished, it still runs around $30 a linear foot).

How to Build a Butcher Block Countertop

1

Before beginning installation, allow the butcher block to acclimate to your home's moisture level for a couple of days. Wood contracts and expands with moisture and humidity, so it may have warped or expanded during transport. Place it level on the cabinet tops and let it sit until it's settled.

2

Measure your countertop area, adding 1" to the base cabinet depth to allow for overhang. Using a circular saw, cut the piece to size if needed. Butcher block with precut miter corners and cutouts for kitchens is available, but if you're cutting the piece yourself, be sure to apply finish to each new raw edge.

3

Butcher block should be attached using wood screws that allow for some movement. Mark three points in a line on the underside of the countertop, spacing rows of drilling points at 12-inch intervals.

4

Drill pilot holes for screws at drilling points. Stick tape to the bit 1" from the point to create a depth stop.

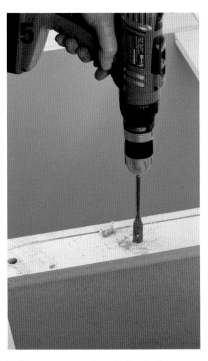

5

Drill corresponding holes in the cabinet base that are slotted or at least ⅜" larger than the screws you are using. When driven with a washer under the screw head, screws will be able to move slightly with the wood.

6

35mm Forstner bit

Bolt connectors

Bolt driver bit

7

TIP: In most cases butcher block countertops are not mitered at the corners as some other countertop types are. Instead, they are butted at the corners. You also may need to join two in-line pieces with a butt joint. In both instances, use connector fittings.

Make butt joints between countertop sections. Lay the two sections of countertop to be joined upside down on a flat worksurface in their correct orientation. Mark drilling points for the connector holes. Drill the holes with a Forstner bit.

8

9

With the countertop sections roughly in position on the cabinets and flipped right-side up, apply a bead of silicone adhesive near the top of one mating edge.

From below, insert the connector bolt so the two heads are flat in the holes and then tighten the bolt with the driver bit (supplied with bolt hardware) to draw the two sections of countertop together. Do not overtighten.

(continued)

10

Clamp a piece of scrap wood to the end of the countertop so the tops are flush. The scrap wood prevents the router bit from rounding over the corner when the edge of the countertop is profiled.

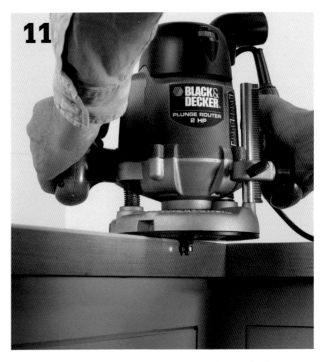

11

Pull the countertop section away from the wall a few inches, and make a roundover cut along the front edges with a piloted roundover bit.

12

Attach the countertop to the cabinet mounting strips by driving screws up through the cabinet strips and into the countertop. The screws should be ¼" shorter than the distance from the bottom of the mounting strips to the top of the countertop. Use 1" fender washers with the screws and snug them up, but do not overtighten. Because of the counterbores and the washers, the countertop will be able to move slightly as it expands and contracts.

13

If installing a sink in your countertop, start by outlining the sink in the correct position as recommended in the installation material from the sink manufacturer. Mount a downstroke blade into the jigsaw (inset), and drill a starter hole just inside the sink outline. Make the cutout, taking care to stay just inside the cutting line. If you are installing an undermount sink, smooth the cuts up to the line with a power sander.

Option: If you're installing an undermount sink, mark a centerpoint for drilling a hole to accommodate the faucet body following the recommendations of the faucet manufacturer. A 1⅜"-dia. hole is fairly standard.

Seal the edges of the sink opening with a varnish as instructed by the butcher block manufacturer or by coating it generously with pure mineral oil or tung oil for a natural finish. Let sit for 15 minutes then wipe off the excess with a clean, lint-free cloth. Let it dry for 48 hours. Repeat six times, letting it dry thoroughly between coats.

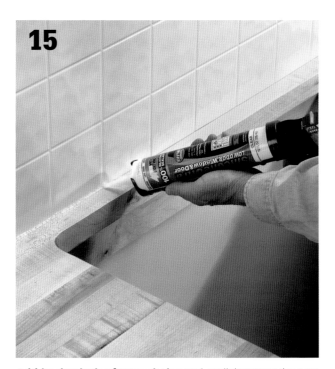

Add backsplash of your choice and caulk between the new countertop and the backsplash area with silicone caulk.

Install the faucet and sink and make the water supply and drain hookups (see pages 196 to 199).

Laminate Countertop

Building your own custom laminate countertop using sheets of plastic laminate and particleboard offers two advantages: the countertop you get will be less expensive than a custom-ordered countertop, and it will allow you more options in terms of colors and edge treatments. A countertop made with laminates also can be tailored to fit any space, unlike premade countertop material that is a standard width (usually 25").

Laminate is commonly sold in 8-ft. or 12-ft. lengths that are about ¹⁄₂₀" thick. In width, they range from 30" strips to 48" sheets. The 30" strips are sized specifically for countertops, allowing for a 25"-wide countertop, a 1½" wide front edge strip, and a short backsplash.

The plastic laminate is bonded to the particleboard or MDF substrate with contact cement, though most professional installers use products that are available only to the trades. Water-based contact cement is nonflammable and nontoxic, but solvent-based contact cement, which requires a respirator and is highly flammable, creates a much stronger, more durable bond.

Tools & Materials ▸

Tape measure	Router (with bevel cutting bit)
Framing square	½" scrap wood
Straightedge	¼" plywood
Scoring tool	1 × 4 lumber
Paint roller	¾" particleboard
Bar clamps	Sheet laminate
Caulk gun	Contact cement
J-roller	Wood glue
Miter saw (as needed)	¼" drywall screws
Compass	2" wallboard screws
Utility knife	Mineral spirits
Aviator snips	Wood filler
Circular saw	Finishing materials
Belt sander	Laminate
	Silicone caulk

Fabricating your own custom countertop from particleboard and plastic laminate is not exactly an easy DIY project, but it gives you unlimited options, and the results can be very satisfying.

Tips for Working with Laminate ▸

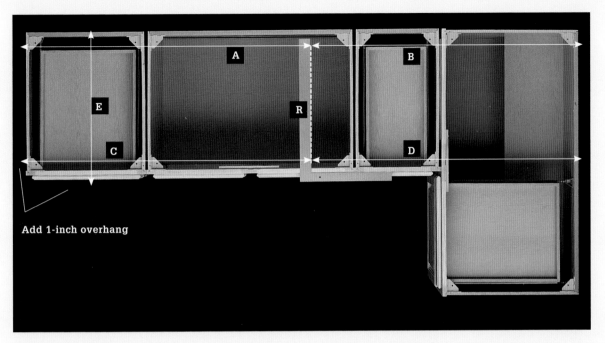

Add 1-inch overhang

Measure along the tops of the base cabinets to determine the size of the countertop. If the wall corners are not square, use a framing square to establish a reference line (R) near the middle of the base cabinets, perpendicular to the front of the cabinets. Take four measurements (A, B, C, D) from the reference line to the cabinet ends. Allow for overhangs by adding 1" to the length for each exposed end and 1" to the width (E).

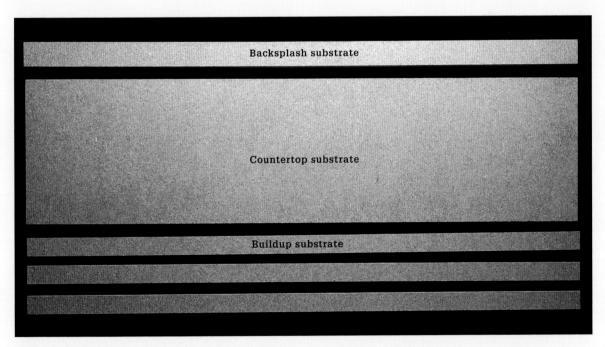

Backsplash substrate

Countertop substrate

Buildup substrate

Lay out cutting lines on the particleboard so you can rip-cut the substrate and buildup strips to size using a framing square to establish a reference line. Cut the core to size using a circular saw with a clamped straightedge as a guide. Cut 4" strips of particleboard for the backsplash and for joint support where sections of countertop core are butted together. Cut 3" strips for the edge buildups.

How to Build a Laminate Countertop

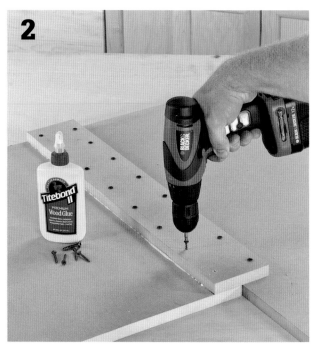

Join the countertop substrate pieces on the bottom side. Attach a 4" particleboard joint support across the seam using carpenter's glue and 1¼" wallboard screws.

Attach 3"-wide edge build up strips to the bottom of the countertop, using 1¼" wallboard screws. Fill any gaps on the outside edges with latex wood patch, and then sand the edges with a belt sander.

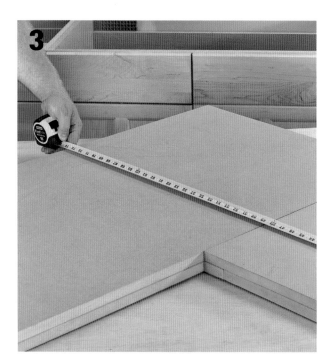

To determine the size of the laminate top, measure the countertop substrate. Laminate seams should not overlap the substrate. Add ½" trimming margin to both the length and width of each piece. Measure the laminate needed for face and edges of backsplash and for exposed edges of countertop substrate. Add ½" to each measurement.

Cut laminate by scoring and then breaking it. Draw a cutting line, and then etch along the line with a utility knife or other sharp cutting tool. Use a straightedge as a guide. Making two passes with the scoring tool will help the laminate to break cleanly.

Bend laminate toward the scored line until the sheet breaks cleanly. For better control on narrow pieces, clamp a straightedge along the scored line before bending the laminate. Wear gloves to avoid being cut by the sharp edges.

Option: Some laminate installers prefer to cut laminate with special snips that resemble aviator snips. Available from laminate suppliers, the snips are faster than scoring and snapping, and they are less likely to cause cracks or tears in the material. You'll still need to square the cut edges with a trimmer or router.

Create tight-piloted seams with plastic laminate by using a router and a straight bit to trim the edges that will butt together. Measure from the cutting edge of the bit to the edge of the router baseplate (A). Place the laminate on scrap wood and align edges. To guide the router, clamp a straightedge on the laminate at distance A plus ¼", parallel to the laminate edge. Trim the laminate.

Apply laminate to the sides of the countertop first. Using a paint roller, apply two coats of contact cement to the edge of the countertop and one coat to the back of the laminate. Let cement dry according to manufacturer's directions. Position the laminate carefully, and then press against the edge of the countertop. Bond the laminate to the countertop with a J-roller.

Use a router and a flush-cutting bit to trim the edge strip flush with top and bottom surfaces of the countertop substrate. At edges where the router cannot reach, trim the excess laminate with a file. Apply the laminate to the remaining edges, and trim with the router.

Test-fit the laminate top on the countertop substrate. Check that the laminate overhangs all the edges. At seam locations, draw a reference line on the core where the laminate edges will butt together. Remove the laminate. Make sure all the surfaces are free of dust, and then apply one coat of contact cement to the back of the laminate and two coats to the substrate. Place spacers made of ½"-thick scrap wood at 6" intervals across the countertop core. Because contact cement bonds instantly, spacers allow the laminate to be positioned accurately over the core without bonding. Align the laminate with the seam reference line. Beginning at one end, remove the spacers and press the laminate to the countertop core.

Apply contact cement to the remaining substrate and the next piece of laminate. Let the cement dry, and then position the laminate on the spacers and carefully align the butt seam. Beginning at the seam edge, remove the spacers and press the laminate to the countertop substrate.

Roll the entire surface with a J-roller to bond the laminate to the substrate. Clean off any excess contact cement with a soft cloth and mineral spirits.

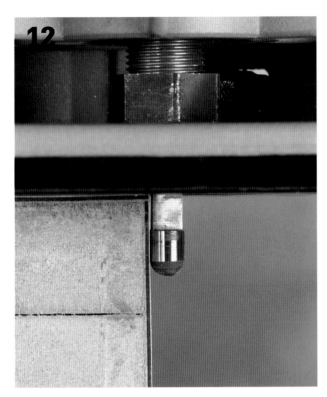

12

Remove the excess laminate with a router and a flush-cutting bit. At edges where the router cannot reach, trim the excess laminate with a file. The countertop is now ready for the final trimming with a bevel-cutting bit.

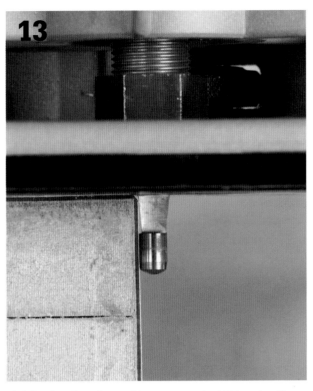

13

Finish-trim the edges with a router and a 15° bevel-cutting bit. Set the bit depth so that the bevel edge is cut only on the top laminate layer. The bit should not cut into the vertical edge surface.

Tip ▸

File all the edges smooth. Use downward file strokes to avoid chipping the laminate.

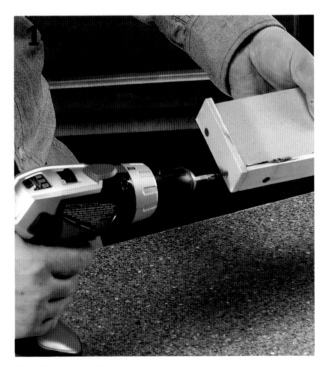

1

Cut 1¼"-wide strips of ¼" plywood to form an overhanging scribing strip for the backsplash. Attach it to the top and sides of the backsplash substrate with glue and wallboard screws. Cut laminate pieces and apply to the exposed sides, top, and front of the backsplash. Trim each piece as it is applied.

(continued)

15

Test-fit the countertop and backsplash. Because your walls may be uneven, use a compass to trace the wall outline onto the backsplash-scribing strip. Use a belt sander to grind backsplash to the scribe line (see page 94).

16

Apply a bead of silicone caulk to the bottom edge of the backsplash.

17

Position the backsplash on the countertop, and clamp it into place with bar clamps. Wipe away the excess caulk, and let it dry completely.

18

Screw 2" wallboard screws through the countertop and into the backsplash core. Make sure the screw heads are countersunk completely for a tight fit against the base cabinet. Install the countertops.

Repairing & Maintaining Laminate ▶

Laminate countertops can be found in more kitchens than any other type of countertop material. The main reason is that laminate is versatile and inexpensive. It's stain resistant, durable, sanitary, and it's the only material that requires no maintenance aside from regular cleaning (you can't say that about even the most expensive marble or stainless steel surfaces). If you like the look of laminate, its only real drawbacks are that it's susceptible to damage.

Topping the list of common laminate damage problems are knife marks, burns, delamination, and misaligned or curling seams. While damaged laminate cannot be easily repaired and scars cannot be removed, there are some simple repairs you can make to spruce up your laminate.

Did someone forget to use a cutting board? You can help hide scratches and light gouges in laminate with a commercial seam filler, available from laminate manufacturers. For chips or small holes, you can purchase a repair kit from home and hardware stores. Seam filler and repair kits consist of a plastic compound that you mix to match the color of your surface. Follow the product directions for mixing and applying the patch. Again, the repair won't be invisible, but it's better than doing nothing.

Burn marks are next on the list, as many a laminate countertop has been marred by a hot pan, a fallen cigarette, or a potholder left too close to a stovetop burner. If the burn is near a cooking area, you're in luck: you can cut out the damage and set a large tile into the surface to create a built-in trivet.

A vinyl and leather repair kit (See Resources, p. 282) can be used to make touch up repairs on laminate countertops. To use this kit, prepare the repair area with an abrasive pad, blend paints to achieve similar color, apply the paint to the repair area, cover with a clear coat, and then heat-set with a household iron after the paint dries.

Seam-filling compound is purchased pre-tinted to match common plastic laminate colors. It can be used to repair minor chips and scratches or to fill separated seams between laminate sheets.

Use a J-roller to re-bond loose or bubbled laminate to its substrate. Heat the repair area with an iron first.

Tile Countertop

Ceramic and porcelain tile remain popular choices for countertops and backsplashes for a number of reasons: it's available in a vast range of sizes, styles, and colors; it's durable and repairable; and some tile—not all—is reasonably priced. With careful planning, tile is also easy to install, making a custom countertop a good do-it-yourself project.

The best tile for most countertops is glazed ceramic or porcelain floor tile. Glazed tile is better than unglazed because of its stain resistance, and floor tile is better than wall tile because it's thicker and more durable. While glaze protects tile from stains, the grout between tiles is still vulnerable because it's so porous. To minimize staining, use a grout that contains a latex additive or mix the grout using a liquid latex additive. After the grout cures fully, apply a quality grout sealer, and reapply the sealer once a year thereafter. Choosing larger tiles reduces the number of grout lines. Although the selection is a bit limited, if you choose 13" × 13" floor tile, you can span from the front to the back edge of the countertop with a single seam.

The countertop in this project has a substrate of ¾" exterior-grade plywood that's cut to fit and fasten to the cabinets. The plywood is covered with a layer of plastic (for a moisture barrier) and a layer of ½"-thick cementboard. Cementboard is an effective backer for tile because it won't break down if water gets through the tile layer. The tile is adhered to the cementboard with thinset adhesive. The overall thickness of the finished countertop is about 1½". If you want a thicker countertop, you can fasten an additional layer of plywood (of any thickness) beneath the substrate. Two layers of ¾" exterior-grade plywood without cementboard is also an acceptable substrate. You can purchase tiles made specifically to serve as backsplashes and front edging. While the color and texture may match, these tiles usually come in only one length, making it difficult to get your grout lines to align with the field tiles. You can solve this problem by cutting your own edging and backsplash tiles from field tiles.

Tools & Materials ▸

Tape measure	Ceramic tile
Circular saw	Tile spacers
Drill	¾" exterior-grade (CDX) plywood
Utility knife	4-mil polyethylene sheeting
Straightedge	Packing tape
Stapler	½" cementboard
Drywall knife	1¼" galvanized deck screws
Framing square	Fiberglass mesh tape
Notched trowel	Thinset mortar
Tile cutter	Grout
Grout float	Silicone caulk
Sponge	Silicone grout sealer
Corner bracket	Cement board screws
Moisture barrier	Metal rule
Caulk gun	

Ceramic or porcelain tile makes a durable countertop that is heat-resistant and relatively easy for a DIYer to create. By using larger tiles, you minimize the grout lines (and the cleaning that goes with them).

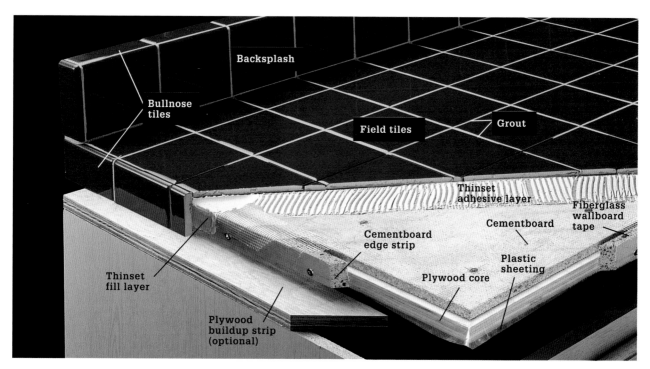

A ceramic tile countertop made with wall tile starts with a core of ¾" exterior-grade plywood that's covered with a moisture barrier of 4-mil polyethylene sheeting. Half-inch cementboard is screwed to the plywood, and the edges are capped with cementboard and finished with fiberglass mesh tape and thinset mortar. Tiles for edging and backsplashes may be bullnose or trimmed from the factory edges of field tiles.

Options for Backsplashes & Countertop Edges

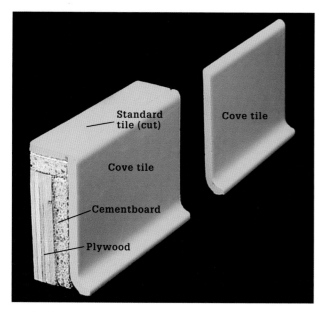

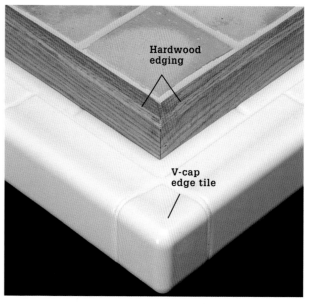

Backsplashes can be made from cove tile attached to the wall at the back of the countertop. You can use the tile alone or build a shelf-type backsplash using the same construction as for the countertop. Attach the plywood backsplash to the plywood core of the countertop. Wrap the front face and all edges of the plywood backsplash with cementboard before laying tile.

Edge options include V-cap edge tile and hardwood strip edging. V-cap tiles have raised and rounded corners that create a ridge around the countertop perimeter—good for containing spills and water. V-cap tiles must be cut with a tile saw. Hardwood strips should be prefinished with at least three coats of polyurethane finish. Attach the strips to the plywood core so the top of the wood will be flush with the faces of the tiles.

Tips for Laying Out Tile ▸

• You can lay tile over a laminate countertop that's square, level, and structurally sound. Use a belt sander with 60- or 80-grit sandpaper to rough up the surface before setting the tiles. The laminate cannot have a no-drip edge. If you're using a new substrate and need to remove your existing countertop, make sure the base cabinets are level front to back, side to side, and with adjoining cabinets. Unscrew a cabinet from the wall and use shims on the floor or against the wall to level it, if necessary.

• Installing battens along the front edge of the countertop helps ensure the first row of tile is perfectly straight. For V-cap tiles, fasten a 1 × 2 batten along the reference line using screws. The first row of field tile is placed against this batten. For bullnose tiles, fasten a batten that's the same thickness as the edging tile, plus ⅛" for mortar thickness, to the face of the countertop so the top is flush with the top of the counter. The bullnose tiles are aligned with the outside edge of the batten. For wood edge trim, fasten a 1 × 2 batten to the face of the countertop so the top edge is above the top of the counter. The tiles are installed against the batten.

• Before installing any tile, lay out the tiles in a dry run using spacers. If your counter is L-shaped, start at the corner and work outward. Otherwise, start the layout at a sink to ensure equal-sized cuts on both sides of the sink. If necessary, shift your starting point so you don't end up cutting very narrow tile segments.

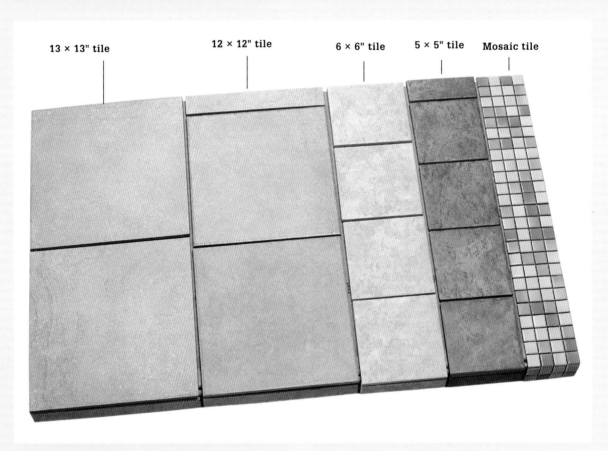

13 × 13" tile   **12 × 12" tile**   **6 × 6" tile**   **5 × 5" tile**   **Mosaic tile**

The bigger the tile the fewer, the grout lines. If you want a standard 25"-deep countertop, the only way to get there without cutting tiles is to use mosaic strips or 1" tile. With 13 × 13" tile, you need to trim 1" off the back tile but have only one grout line front to back. As you decrease tiles, the number of grout lines increases.

How to Build a Tile Countertop

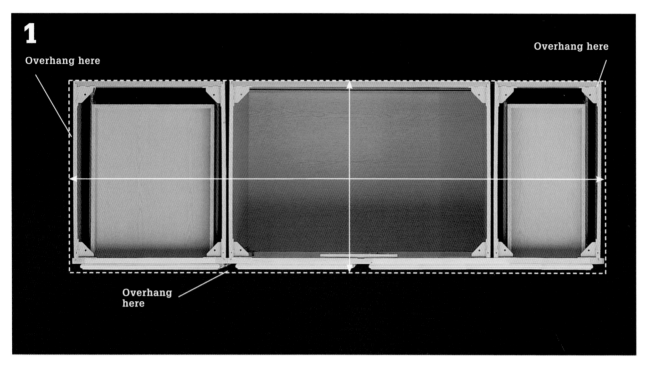

1

Overhang here

Overhang here

Overhang here

Determine the size of the plywood substrate by measuring across the top of the cabinets. The finished top should overhang the drawer fronts by at least ¼". Be sure to account for the thickness of the cementboard, adhesive, and tile when deciding how large to make the overhang. Cut the substrate to size from ¾" plywood using a circular saw. Also make any cutouts for sinks and other fixtures.

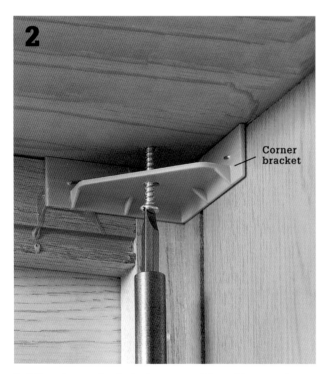

2

Corner bracket

Set the plywood substrate on top of the cabinets, and attach it with screws driven through the cabinet corner brackets. The screws should not be long enough to go through the top of the substrate.

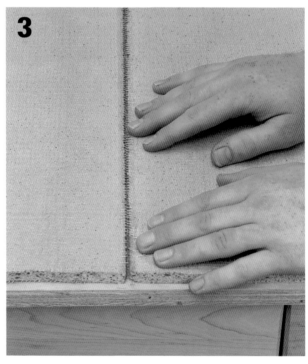

3

Cut pieces of cementboard to size, then mark and make the cutout for the sink. Dry-fit them on the plywood core with the rough sides of the panels facing up. Leave a ⅛" gap between the cementboard sheets and a ¼" gap along the perimeter.

(continued)

Option: Cut cementboard using a straightedge and utility knife or a cementboard cutter with a carbide tip. Hold the straightedge along the cutting line, and score the board several times with the knife. Bend the piece backward to break it along the scored line. Back-cut to finish.

Lay the 4-mil plastic moisture barrier over the plywood substrate, draping it over the edges. Tack it in place with a few staples. Overlap seams in the plastic by 6", and seal them with packing tape.

Lay the cementboard pieces rough-side up on the plywood and attach them with cementboard screws driven every 6". Drill pilot holes using a masonry bit, and make sure all screw heads are flush with the surface. Wrap the countertop edges with 1¼"-wide cementboard strips, and attach them to the core with cementboard screws.

Tape all cementboard joints with fiberglass mesh tape. Apply three layers of tape along the front edge where the horizontal cementboard sheets meet the cementboard edging.

7

Fill all the gaps and cover all of the tape with a layer of thinset mortar. Feather out the mortar with a drywall knife to create a smooth, flat surface.

8

Determine the required width of the edge tiles. Lay a field tile onto the tile base so it overhangs the front edge by ½". Hold a metal rule up to the underside of the tile and measure the distance from it to the bottom of the subbase. The edge tiles should be cut to this width (the gap for the grout line causes the edge tile to extend the subbase that conceals it completely).

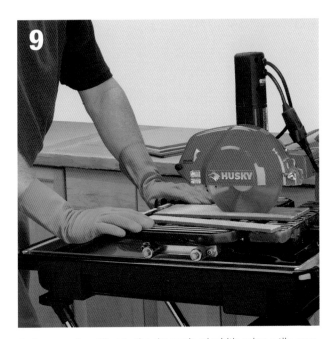

9

Cut your edge tiles to the determined width using a tile saw. It's worth renting a quality wet saw for tile if you don't own one. Floor tile is thick and difficult to cut with a hand cutter (especially porcelain tiles).

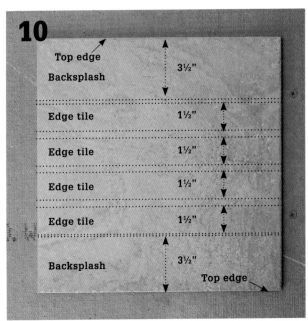

10

Top edge
Backsplash — 3½"
Edge tile — 1½"
Edge tile — 1½"
Edge tile — 1½"
Edge tile — 1½"
Backsplash — 3½"
Top edge

Cut tiles for the backsplash. The backsplash tiles (3½" wide in our project) should be cut with a factory edge on each tile that will be oriented upward when they're installed. You can make efficient use of your tiles by cutting edge tiles from the center area of the tiles you cut to make the backsplash.

(continued)

Sink cutout area

Dry-fit tiles on the countertop to find the layout that works best. Once the layout is established, make marks along the vertical and horizontal rows. Draw reference lines through the marks and use a framing square to make sure the lines are perpendicular.

Variation: Small Floor Tiles & Bullnose Edging ▶

Lay out tiles and spacers in a dry run. Adjust the starting lines, if necessary. If using battens, lay the field tile flush with the battens, then apply the edge tile. Otherwise, install the edging first. If the countertop has an inside corner, start there by installing a ready-made inside corner or by cutting a 45° miter in the edge tile to make your own inside corner.

Place the first row of field tile against the edge tile, separating the tile with spacers. Lay out the remaining rows of tile. Adjust the starting lines if necessary to create a layout using the smallest number of cut tiles.

11

Use a ⅜" square notched trowel to apply a layer of thin set adhesive to the cementboard. Apply enough for two or three tiles, starting at one end. Hold the trowel at roughly a 30° angle and try not to overwork the adhesive or remove too much.

12

Set the first tile into the adhesive. Hold a piece of the edge against the countertop edge as a guide to show you exactly how much the tile should overhang the edge.

13

Cut all the back tiles for the layout to fit (you'll need to remove about 1" of a 13 × 13" tile) before you begin the actual installation. Set the back tiles into the thin set, maintaining the gap for grout lines created by the small spacer nubs cast into the tiles. If your tiles have no spacer nubs, see the option.

Option: To maintain even grout lines, some beginning tilers insert plus-sign-shaped plastic spacers at the joints. This is less likely to be useful with large tiles like those shown here, but it is effective. Many tiles today feature built-in spacing lugs, so the spacers are of no use. Make sure to remove the spacers before the thin set sets. If you leave them in place they will corrupt your grout lines.

(continued)

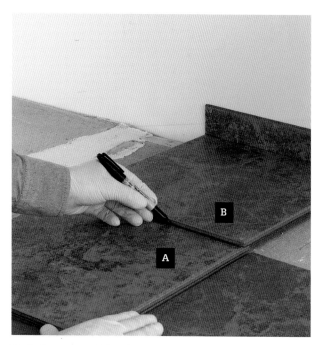

Variation: To mark border tiles for cutting, allow space for the backsplash tiles, grout, and mortar by placing a tile against the back wall. Set another tile (A) on top of the last full tile in the field, then place a third tile (B) over tile (A) and hold it against the upright tile. Mark and cut tile (A) and install it with the cut edge toward the wall. Finish filling in your field tiles.

To create a support ledge for the edge tiles, prop pieces of 2 × 4 underneath the front edge of the substrate overhang using wood scraps to prop the ledge tightly up against the substrate.

Apply a thick layer of thin set to the backside of the edge tile with your trowel. This is called "buttering" and it is easier and neater than attempting to trowel adhesive onto the countertop edge. Press the tiles into position so they are flush with the leading edges of the field tiles.

Butter each backsplash tile and press it into place, doing your best to keep all of the grout lines aligned.

17

Mix a batch of grout to complement the tile (keeping in mind that darker grout won't look dirty as soon as lighter grout). Apply the grout to the grout line areas with a grout float.

18

Let the grout dry until a light film is created on the countertop surface, then wipe the excess grout off with a sponge and warm, clean water. See grout manufacturer's instructions on drying tiles and polishing.

19

Run a bead of clear silicone caulk along the joint between the backsplash and the wall. Install your sink and faucet after the grout has dried (and before you use the sink, if possible).

20

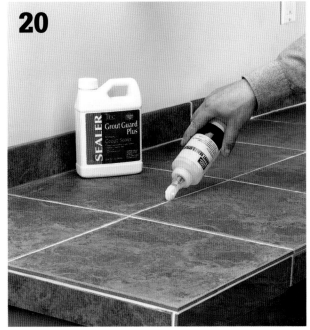

Wait at least one week and then seal the grout lines with a penetrating grout sealer. This is important to do. Sealing the tiles themselves is not a good idea unless you are using unglazed tiles (a poor choice for countertops, however).

Granite Countertop

Solid granite countertops are hugely popular in kitchen fashion today, and for good reason: they are beautiful and sturdy and natural. However, they are also expensive and virtually impossible for a do-it-yourselfer to install. There is a way for an enterprising DIYer to achieve the look and feel of natural granite, but at a fraction of the price: granite tile countertops.

You have two basic product options with granite tile. You can use the standard granite tiles, which consist of field tiles and edge tiles with square edges that are installed just like normal ceramic or porcelain tiles and finished with thin edge tiles to create the nosing; or you can use granite tiles that are installed with front tiles that feature an integral bullnose that better imitates the look of solid granite. Typically, granite tiles fit together more snugly than ceramic tiles to give you the option of grouting with grout that's the same color as the tiles for a near-seamless finished appearance.

Layout is the most important step on any tile project. If tiles need to be cut to fit, it is best to cut the tiles at the center of the installation or the sets of tiles at both ends. This creates a more uniform look. Granite tile can be installed over laminate countertop (not post-form) if you remove the nosing and backsplash first. The laminate substrate must be in good condition with no peeling or water damage.

Tools & Materials ▸

⅝" exterior grade plywood	Straightedge
¼" tile backer or cementboard	¼" notched trowel
Cementboard screws	Modified thinset
Tiles	Unsanded grout
Tile wet saw with diamond blade	Grout sealer
Honing stone	Stone sealer
Cordless drill	Sponge
Circular saw	Bucket
Jigsaw	Rubber gloves
Compass	Prybar
Utility knife	Carpeted mallet

Granite tiles are installed in much the same way as ceramic tiles, but the ultra-narrow gaps and matching grout mimic the appearance of solid polished granite.

How to Install Granite Tile Countertops

Remove the countertops. From inside the base cabinets, unscrew the screws holding the countertops to the cabinets. Unscrew take-up bolts on mitered sections of the countertop. Use a utility knife to cut through the caulk, if present. Countertops should lift off easily, but if they don't, you can use a prybar to carefully pry them away from the base cabinets. *Note: In some cases you can install these tiles over old laminate countertops (see previous page).*

Prepare and install the subbase. Measure the cabinet bank from outside edges to outside edges on all sides and cut a piece of ⅝"-thick exterior grade plywood to fit. The edges of the plywood should be flush with the outside edges of the cabinet tops. Screw the plywood to the cabinet braces from underneath.

Make the sink cutout. To create cutting lines, place the sink upside down in the desired location. Trace the edges of the sink and remove it. To create support for the drop-in sink flange, use a compass to trace new cutting lines inside the traced lines (usually ⅝"). See the manufacturer's instructions to confirm dimensions (some sinks come with a template for making the cutout. Use a jigsaw to cut out the sink opening.

Install the tile underlayment. Granite tile, like ceramic tile, requires a cementboard or denseboard underlayment layer. Cut the material (see page 114) to the same dimension as the plywood subbase and lay the cementboard over the plywood with the edges flush. From inside the sink base, trace around the sink cutout with a marker. Remove the underlayment and make the cutout with a jigsaw.

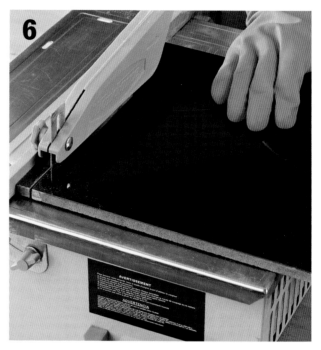

Attach the cementboard underlayment to the subbase. First, apply a ⅛"-thick layer of modified thinset to the top of the plywood using a ¼" notched trowel. Screw the cementboard to the plywood with cementboard screws. Space the screws 4" to 5" apart across the entire surface.

Cut (as needed) and lay out the tiles, beginning with an inside corner if you have one. Arrange tiles for the best color match. Tiles abut directly, with no space for grout. Cut the tiles as necessary to fit. Cut self-edged tiles edge side first. Cut the tiles with the polished side up. Use a fine honing stone to relieve the cut edge to match the manufactured edges.

▌ Variations for Corners & Angles

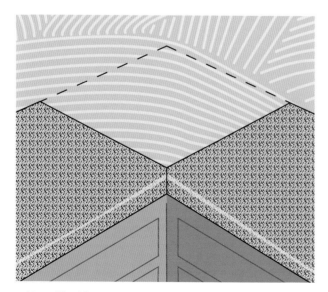

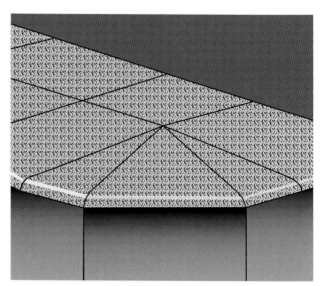

Mitered inside corners are a bit tricky to cut because the mitered point needs to align with the starting point of the bullnose edge. This has the effect of making the corner set back roughly an inch.

Kitchen islands often have corners that do not form a right angle. In such cases, you can avoid a sharp angle on the countertop by cutting a triangular bullnose piece to fill in.

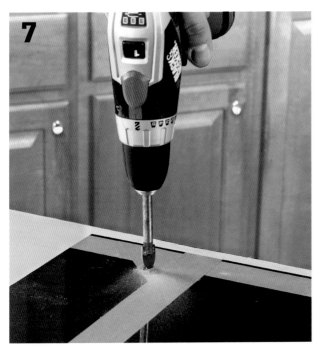

Round the inside corner cuts. Even though the flange of the sink shown here will cover the inside corners in the sink cutout, take care to make a gentle rounded corner cut by drilling at the corner with a ½" masonry bit. Perpendicular corner cuts can lead to cracking. Finish the straight legs of the cutout with a tile saw or a jigsaw with a masonry blade.

Start laying tiles. Use modified thinset and a ¼" trowel. If you have an inside corner in your countertop, begin there. Apply thin set at the inside corner, enough to place four or five tiles. Set the left and right inside corner pieces and the first 12 × 12 field tile.

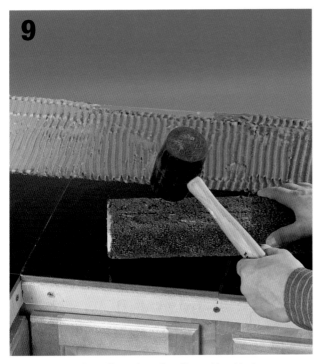

Continue setting tiles (for edge tile and backlash installation, see page 118). Apply the thin set mortar to an area big enough for two to four tiles and place the tiles. Use a 2 × 4 covered with carpeting to set the tiles. Push down on tiles to set, and also across the edges to ensure an even face.

Apply grout and seal. After the thin set has dried for at least 24 hours, grout with an unsanded grout. When the grout has dried, seal with natural stone sealer.

Tile Backsplash

There are few spaces in your home with as much potential for creativity and visual impact as the space between your kitchen countertop and your cupboards. A well-designed backsplash can transform the ordinary into the extraordinary. Tiles for the backsplash can be attached directly to wallboard or plaster and do not require backerboard. When purchasing the tile, order 10 percent extra to cover breakage and cutting. Remove the switch and receptacle coverplates and install the box extenders to make up for the extra thickness of the tile. Protect the countertop from scratches by covering it with a drop cloth.

Tools & Materials ▶

Level	Story stick
Tape measure	Straight 1 × 2
Pencil	Wall tile
Tile cutter	Tile spacers (if needed)
Rod saw	Mastic adhesive
Notched trowel	Masking tape
Rubber grout float	Grout
Beating block	Caulk
Rubber mallet	Drop cloth
Sponge	Sanded grout
Bucket	

Tip ▶

Break tiles into fragments and make a mosaic backsplash. Always use a sanded grout for joints wider than ⅛".

Contemporary glass mosaic sheets create a counter-to-cabinet backsplash for a water-proof, splash-proof wall with very high visual impact.

How to Install a Tile Backsplash

Make a story stick by marking a board at least half as long as the backsplash area to match the tile spacing.

Starting at the midpoint of the installation area, use the story stick to make layout marks along the wall. If an end piece is too small (less than half a tile), adjust the midpoint to give you larger, more attractive end pieces. Use a level to mark this point with a vertical reference line.

While it may appear straight, your countertop may not be level and therefore is not a reliable reference line. Run a level along the counter to find the lowest point on the countertop. Mark a point two tiles up from the low point and extend a level line across the entire work area.

Variation: Diagonal Layout. Mark vertical and horizontal reference lines, making sure the angle is 90°. To establish diagonal layout lines, measure out equal distances from the crosspoint, and then connect the points with a line. Additional layout lines can be extended from these as needed.

(continued)

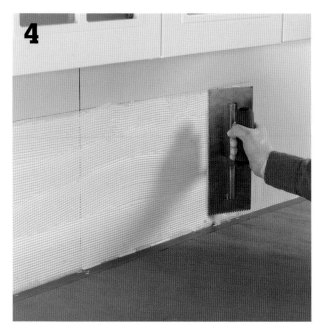

Apply mastic adhesive evenly to the area beneath the horizontal reference line using a notched trowel. Comb the adhesive horizontally with the notched edge.

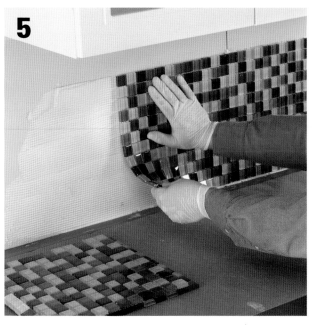

Press tiles into the adhesive with a slight twisting motion. If the tiles are not self-spacing, use plastic spacers to maintain even grout lines. If the tiles do not hang in place, use masking tape to hold them in place until the adhesive sets.

Install a whole row along the reference line, checking occasionally to make sure the tiles are level. Continue installing tiles below the first row, trimming tiles that butt against the countertop as needed.

Install an edge border if it is needed in your layout. Mosaic sheets normally do not have bullnose tiles on the edges, so if you don't wish to see the cut edges of the outer tiles, install a vertical column of edge tiles at the end of the backsplash area.

When the tiles are in place, make sure they are flat and firmly embedded by laying a beating block against the tile and rapping it lightly with a mallet. Remove the spacers. Allow the mastic to dry for at least 24 hours, or as directed by the manufacturer.

Mix the grout and apply it with a rubber grout float. Spread it over the tiles, keeping the float at a low 30° angle, pressing the grout deep into the joints. Note: *For grout joints ⅛" and smaller, be sure to use a non-sanded grout.*

Wipe off excess grout, holding the float at a right angle to the tile, working diagonally so as not to remove grout from the joints. Clean any remaining grout from the tiles with a damp sponge, working in a circular motion. Rinse the sponge thoroughly and often.

Clean excess grout with a damp sponge. When the grout has dried to a haze, buff the tile clean with a soft cloth. Apply a bead of caulk between the countertop and the tiles.

Islands

Contemporary kitchen design strives to enhance function while putting a premium on form, and the island is no exception. The kitchen island not only adds countertop space, extra cabinet storage, and sometimes an extra sink or cooktop, but it also acts as extra seating and a place for guests to relax and still converse with you while you're cooking.

In this chapter we discuss the different styles of islands being used by kitchen designers today and then we show you how to make those islands and install the necessary amenities, such as an island vent hood, to help them function at their best.

This chapter shows:

- Kitchen Island Selection
- Stock-Cabinet Island
- Two-Level Tile Island
- Concrete Countertop Island
- Island Vent Hood

Kitchen Island Selection

A traditional hardwood floor with genuine Oriental rugs makes a beautiful design statement in any room. High-quality carpets resist staining, and a well-applied finish will offer more than adequate protection for hardwood in a kitchen situation.

Natural stone countertops are heat resistant and highly durable but they can be quite expensive and they are susceptible to staining. The natural, rustic appearance is unmatched by any other countertop material.

Portable islands like this one are readily available at home centers and home furnishing stores. They often match other freestanding cabinets and amenities, such as the rolling cart shown here (inset).

Quartz countertops are similar to solid surface countertops in appearance but because they do not contain plastic resins or binders, they are much more heat resistant. Manufacturers also claim the material is completely impervious to water and moisture.

A tiled countertop is a heat-resistant surface that is good for islands because this space is often used to hold hot pans during meal preparation. On the down side, the grout lines stain easily and can crack over time. Regular maintenance is required.

Stock-Cabinet Island

Kitchen islands can be created using a whole range of methods, from repurposing an old table to fine, custom woodworking. But perhaps the easiest (and most fail-safe) way to add the conveniences and conviviality of a kitchen island is to make one from stock base cabinets. The cabinets and countertops don't have to match your kitchen cabinetry, but that is certainly an option you should consider. When designing and positioning your new island, be sure to maintain a minimum distance of 3 ft. between the island and other cabinets (4 ft. or more is better).

Tools & Materials ▸

Marker
Drill/driver
2 × 4 cleats
Pneumatic nailer
   and 2" finish nails or
   hammer and 6d
   finish nails

2 base cabinets (approx. 36"
   wide × 24" deep)
Countertop
Wallboard screws

Two base cabinets arranged back-to-back make a sturdy kitchen island base that's easy to install. When made with the same style cabinets and countertops as the rest of the kitchen, the island is a perfect match.

How to Create a Stock-Cabinet Island

Set two base cabinets back-to-back in position on the floor and outline the cabinet corners onto the flooring. Remove the cabinets and draw a new outline inside of the one you just created to allow for the thickness of the cabinet sides (usually ¾").

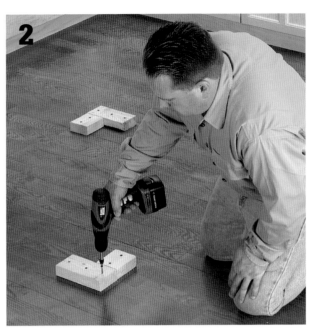

Cut 2 × 4 cleats to fit inside the inner outline to provide nailing surfaces for the cabinets. Attach the cleats to the floor with screws or nails. Tip: Create an L-shaped cleat for each inside corner.

Join the two base cabinets together by driving 1¼" wallboard screws through the nailing strips on the backs of the cabinets from each direction. Make sure the cabinet sides are flush and aligned. Lower the base cabinets over the cleats. Check the cabinets for level, and shim underneath the edges of the base if necessary.

Attach the cabinets to the floor cleats using 6d finish nails. Drill pilot holes for nails, and recess the nail heads with a nail set. Make a countertop (see pages 86 to 123) and install it on top of the cabinets.

Two-level Tile Island

Islands are one of the most requested kitchen features. People love them for many reasons, including their value as bi-level counter space. In most cases, the lower level is used as work space and the upper as casual dining space. The upper level provides a little camouflage for the work space, something that's especially welcome in open-plan kitchens where meal preparation areas can be seen from other areas.

When planning casual dining space, remember that designers suggest at least 24" per person. For the work space, remember that standard design guidelines recommend at least 36" of uninterrupted work space to the side of a sink or cooktop.

On work surfaces, mosaic and other small tile is rarely the best choice. Larger tile requires fewer grout lines, always a good idea when it comes to cleaning and maintenance. But there is no rule that all three elements of a bi-level island have to use the same material. In fact, projects like this offer wonderful opportunities to mix materials or colors or textures. Choose floor tile or tile made especially for counters and then branch out when it comes to the backsplash. Wall tile and mosaics work beautifully.

Tools & Materials ▸

Tape measure	Adhesive
Circular saw	Paint
Drill	Tile spacers
Utility knife	¾" exterior-grade (CDX) plywood
Straightedge	4-mil polyethylene sheeting
Stapler	Packing tape
Drywall knife	½" cementboard
Framing square	3" deck screws
Notched trowel	Fiberglass mesh tape
Tile cutter	Thinset mortar
Carpeted 2 × 4 mallet	Grout with latex additive
Grout float	Silicone caulk
Sponge	Grout sealer
Foam brush	L-brackets
Caulk gun	6d finish nails
1 × 2 hardwood	Drywall screws
2 × 4 lumber	Glue
Ceramic tile	

This island adds storage, countertop space, and seating to a kitchen, revealing the truly astonishing transformation this simple yet functional piece can achieve.

How to Build a Tiled Bi-Level Island

Build a 2 × 4 base for the island cabinet by cutting the 2 × 4s to length and joining them in a square frame that lays flat (wide sides down) on the floor. Use metal L-brackets to reinforce the joints. If you don't wish to move the island, fasten the frame to the floor in position with construction adhesive and/or deck screws.

Cut the bottom panels the same dimensions as the base frame from ¾" birch plywood. Attach it to the frame with finish nails. Then, cut the side panels to size and shape and fasten them to the edges with 6d finish nails and adhesive. Slip ¾" shims (scrap plywood works well) beneath the side panels before fastening them.

Cut the 2 × 4 cross supports to length and install them between the side panels at every corner, including the corners created by the L-shape cutout. Use 3" deck screws driven through the side panels and into the ends of the cross supports.

Prime and paint the cabinet interior and exterior.

(continued)

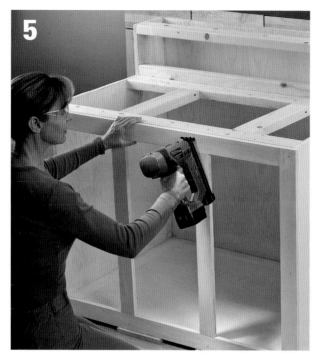

Build a face frame from 1 × 2 hardwood to fit the cabinet front. Attach it to the cabinet with 6d finish nails and hang the cabinet doors (we installed three 13"-wide overlay doors).

Cut strips of ¾" exterior plywood to make the subbases for the countertops and a backer for the backsplash. The lower counter subbase should overhang by 2" on the front and sides. The upper should overhang 2" on the sides and be centered on the cabinet front to back. Attach the backer and subbases with drywall screws driven down into the 2 × 4 cross supports.

Cut 2" wide strips of plywood for buildup strips and attach to the undersides of the subbases with glue and screws.

Attach the tile backerboard to the counter subbases, the backsplash, and tape seams; cover screw heads with compound (see page 114).

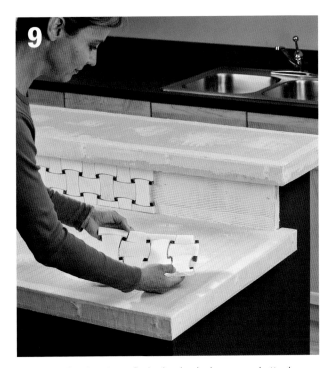

Cut mosaic sheets to fit the backsplash area and attach them with thinset adhesive (see Tile Backsplash, page 124).

Cut the edge tiles and fasten them around the perimeter of the subbase with thinset adhesive. The tiles should be flush or slightly below the bottoms of the buildup strips and project past the top surfaces so they will be level with the field tiles. If you are not using edge tiles with a bullnose top, install the tiles so they are level with the subbase surface and overhang them with the field tiles.

Install the field tiles for the countertops last (see How to Build a Tile Countertop, pages 113 to 119).

Choose a suitable grout color and apply it to the tile with a grout float. Buff off excess once it has dried. Seal the grout with grout sealer.

Concrete Countertop Island

Once used exclusively for outdoor building projects, concrete has expanded its range to become a premier material for indoor construction as well. Still utilized mostly to cast countertops and vanity tops, concrete is continually finding new applications inside the home, including fireplace hearths, floors, and even furnishings. Along with remarkable strength and extreme durability, concrete has charm and appeal unlike any other building material.

A concrete countertop may be cast in place or formed offsite and installed like a natural stone countertop. For a number of reasons, casting offsite makes more sense for most of us. In addition to keeping the mess and dust out of your living spaces, working in a garage or even outdoors lets you cast the countertops with the finished surface face-down in the form. This way, if you do a careful job building the form, you can keep the grinding and polishing to a bare minimum. In some cases, you may even be able to simply remove the countertop from the form, flip it over, and install it essentially as is.

Thorough planning and careful form construction are the keys to a successful concrete countertop project. One of the first issues to tackle is weight: concrete weighs about 140 pounds per cubic foot

(roughly 25 pounds per square foot for a 2" thick countertop). Most floors should be able to support a heavy countertop, but be sure to inspect floor joists and framing, especially in older homes, to determine if any reinforcement is needed. If you are unsure,

Tools & Materials ▸

Tape measure	Variable speed angle grinder
Table or circular saw	with grinding pads
Jigsaw	No. 3 rebar
Drill and right angle	3½" deck screws
drill guide	Poultry netting
Level	(or welded wire)
Carpenter's square	Concrete sealer
Rebar bender	Concrete mix
Reciprocating saw with	Coloring agent
metal cutting blade	Paste wax
Clamps	Fiber reinforcement (nylon)
Belt sander	Acrylic fortifier
Pad sander	Latex bonding agent
Concrete mixer	Silicone caulk
5-gal. buckets	¾" melamine

Concrete countertops have many pluses and few minuses. They are durable, heat resistant, and relatively inexpensive. But most of all, they are highly attractive and a great fit with contemporary styles.

consult a building professional, your local building inspector's office or a structural engineer.

The weight of the concrete is also a factor when it comes to cabinetry. Typical base cabinets should be reinforced at the back and across the top with ½" or ¾" plywood. Reinforcing cabinetry may increase the overall dimensions, which can cause problems with modular units or in areas with limited space.

After you design your project and determine the actual dimensions, you'll need to estimate the amount of concrete you'll need. Concrete is measured by volume in cubic feet; multiply the length by the wide and then by the thickness of the finished countertop for volume in cubic inches, then divide the sum by 1728 for cubic feet. For example, a countertop that will be 48-in.-long × 24-in.-wide × 3½-in.-thick will require 2⅓-cu.-ft. of mixed concrete (48 × 24 × 3.5 / 1728 = 2⅓). The best way to achieve consistent results when mixing concrete is to use premixed materials. One 60-lb. bag of premixed high-strength concrete equals ½-cu.-ft. of mixed concrete. A number of online concrete outlets also offer a virtual rainbow of dry-mix color pigments that are formulated with a water reducer admixture. Water reducers limit the amounts of water the concrete mix uses to help produce a stronger mix and a smoother finished produce.

As you mix the concrete materials, blend all dry ingredients thoroughly in a motorized mixer for five minutes prior to adding liquid ingredients. Do not mix the concrete until the form is completely built, with any sink or faucet knockouts and the reinforcement in place. For best results, mix the concrete in a single batch with a power mixer. Because the mixing container on power mixtures should never be more than half full (one-third full on some models), you'll need a relatively large mixer for all but the smallest countertops. For the island countertop projects shown here, a tow-behind nine cubic foot mixer was rented (yet another good reason for casting your countertop offsite). Once your casting is done, let the concrete cure for at least a week before you strip off the forms.

The basic supplies needed to build your countertop form and cast the countertop include: (A) Melamine-coated particleboard for constructing the form; (B) poultry netting or welded wire for reinforcement; (C) concrete sealer (product shown is adequate, but for better protection look for a sealer that has both penetrating and film-forming properties); (D) high/early bagged concrete mix rated for 5,000 p.s.i.; (E) coloring agent (liquid or powder); (F) grinding pads (shown are 5" diamond pads ranging from 50 grit to 1,500 grit for grinding and polishing); (G) paste wax; (H) buffing bonnet for polisher; (I) fiber reinforcement (nylon); (J) acrylic fortifier, latex bonding agent (or water reducing admixture if you can locate it); (K) black or colored silicone caulk; (L) faucet set if installing sink; (M) sink (self rimming shown); (N) No. 3 rebar (⅜").

How to Cast a Concrete Countertop

Cut ¾" melamine-coated particleboard into 2¼"-wide strips to make the form sides. Cut the sides to length (33½ and 41½", as shown here) and drill two countersunk pilot holes ⅜" in from the ends of the front and back form sides. Assemble the strips into a frame by driving a 2" coarse wallboard screws at each pilot hole and into the mating ends of the end form strips.

Mount a power drill in a right-angle drill guide (or use a drill press) and drill ¼"-dia. pilot holes for 3" deck screws at 6" intervals all the way through the tops of the form sides. Countersink the holes so the screw heads are recessed slightly from the surface.

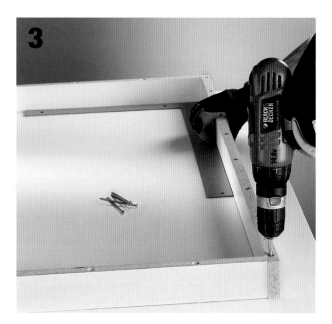

Center the form frame on the base, which should have the melamine side facing up. Test the corners with a carpenter's square to make sure they're square. Drive one 3½" deck screw per form side, near the middle. The screw heads should be slightly below the top edges of the forms. Check for square again, and continue driving the 3½" screws at 6" intervals through the pilot holes. Check for square frequently—the stress easily can pull the frame out of joint.

Make the sink knockout (if you're installing a sink). The sink we used requires a 14⅜" square cutout with corners that are rounded at a ½" radius. Cut three pieces of ¾"-thick MDF to 14⅜" square using a table saw if possible. With a compass, mark 1½"-radius curves at each corner for trimming. Make the trim cuts with a jigsaw (only if you stack and cut all three at once). Cut just outside the trim line and sand up to it with a sander for a smooth curve.

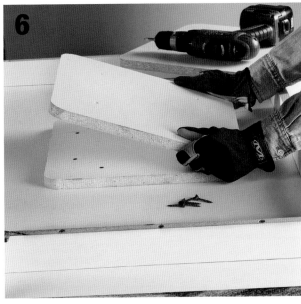

Use the rounded knockout blank as a template for marking and cutting the other two blanks to match. Clamp the three blanks together and sand the edges smooth and even. A belt sander on a stationary sanding station or an oscillating spindle sander works great for this. If you are strong and steady-handed, you can freehand the corners with a portable belt sander. Don't over-sand—this will cause the sink knockout to be too small.

Install the sink knockout. Because gluing the faces together can add height to the knockout (and cause the concrete finishing tools to bang into it when they ride on the form tops), attach each blank directly to the layer below it using countersunk screws. Keep the edges aligned perfectly, especially if you're planning to install an undermount sink.

Faucet Knockouts ▶

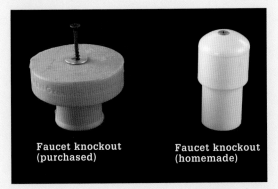

Faucet knockout (purchased)

Faucet knockout (homemade)

Option: If your sink faucet will not be mounted on the sink deck, you'll need to add knockouts for the faucet hole or holes, according to the requirements of the faucet manufacturer. You can order knockouts from a concrete countertop supplies distributor or create them with PVC plumbing pipe that has an outside diameter equal to the required faucet hole size. To anchor the PVC knockout, cover one end with a cap made for that size tubing. Drill a guide hole through the center of the cap so you can secure it with a screw. Position the knockout next to a form side and compare heights. If the knockout is taller, trim the uncapped tubing.

Seal any exposed edges with fast-drying polyurethane varnish, and then caulk the form once the varnish is dry. Run a very thin bead of colored silicone caulk (the coloring allows you to see where the caulk has been laid on the white melamine) in all the seams and then smooth carefully with a fingertip. In addition to keeping the wet concrete from seeping into gaps in the form, the caulk will create a slight roundover on the edges of the concrete. The smoother the caulk, the less grinding you'll have to do later. If you will be installing an undermount sink, also caulk around the sink knockout.

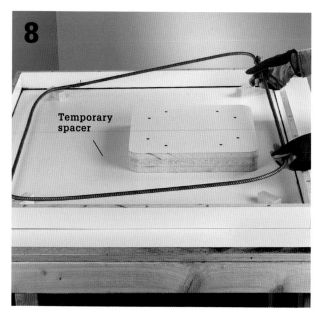

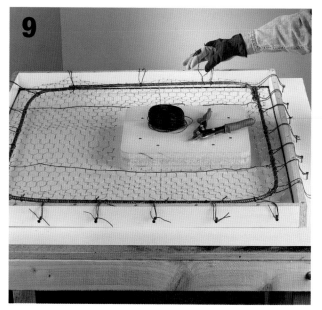

Add reinforcement to the form. For thicker castings, bend #3 (⅜") rebar to fit around the perimeter of the form using a rebar bender. The rebar needs to be at least 1" away from all edges (including knockouts) and 1" away from the top surface. Metal reinforcement can telegraph through concrete if it is too close to the visible surfaces. Tie the ends of the rebar with wire and set it in the form on temporary 1" spacers.

Hang the rebar loop with wires to suspend it, keeping it at least ½" away from the concrete surface. Drive a few screws into the outside faces of the form sides near the top and use wire ties to hang the rebar. Once all of the ties are in place, remove the temporary spacers. For extra insurance, add another reinforcing material, such as wire poultry netting, over the rebar and tie the two together.

Tip ▸

To keep the form from moving during the all-important pouring, finishing, and curing stages, attach or clamp the scrap plywood work top to the actual top. Check for level and insert shims between the work top and the bench top if needed. When possible, drive screws up through the bench top and into the work top to hold it steady. Otherwise, use clamps and check them regularly to make sure they're tight. If you're concerned about mess, put a sheet of 3-mil plastic on the floor.

Add all of the dry ingredients into a concrete mixer that's large enough to do the whole pour. The dry ingredients include high/early concrete mix rated to 5,000 p.s.i. and synthetic fiber reinforcement. If you are using dry pigment, also add this now. Run the mixer for several minutes to thoroughly blend the dry ingredients.

Blend the wet ingredients (water plus any liquid concrete colorant and a water reducer or acrylic fortifier) in a bucket and, with the mixer running, add them slowly to the dry ingredients. Add more water as necessary until the concrete is thoroughly hydrated, but still stiff.

Fill the countertop form, making sure to pack the concrete into the corners and press it through the reinforcement. Overfill the form slightly.

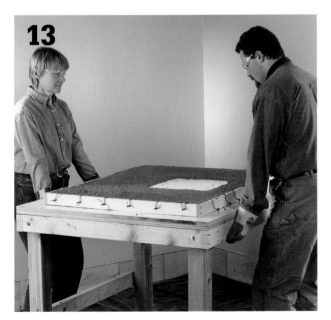

Vibrate the form vigorously as you work to settle the concrete into all the voids. You can rent a concrete vibrator for this purpose, or simply strike the form repeatedly with a rubber mallet. If you have a helper and a sturdy floor and worktable, lift up and down on the ends of the table, bouncing it on the floor to cause vibrations (this is a very effective method if you can manage it safely). Make sure the table remains level when you're through.

Strike off the excess concrete from the form using a 2 × 4 drawn along the top of the form in a sawing motion. If voids are created, pack them with fresh concrete and restrike. Do not overwork the concrete.

(continued)

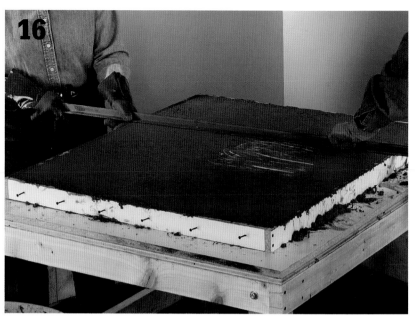

Once you are certain you won't need to vibrate the form any further, snip the wire ties holding the rebar loop and embed the cut ends attached to the rebar below the concrete surface.

Smooth the surface of the concrete with a metal screeding tool, such as a length of angle iron or square metal tubing. Work slowly with a sawing motion, allowing the bleed water to fill in behind the screed. Since this surface will be the underside of the countertop, no further tooling is required. Cover with sheet plastic and allow the concrete to dry and cure undisturbed for a full week.

Remove the plastic covering and then unscrew and remove the forms. Do not pry against the fresh concrete. In most cases, you'll need to cut apart the sink knockout to prevent damaging the countertop when removing it. Drill a starter hole and then carefully cut up to the edge of the knockout. Cut the knockout into chunks until you can remove it all (inset). The edges of the concrete will be fragile, so be very careful.

With a helper or two (or three), flip the countertop so the finished surface is exposed. Be extremely careful. The best technique is to roll the countertop onto an edge, position a couple of 2 × 4 sleepers beneath it (insulation board works very well), and then gently lower it onto the sleepers.

Option: To expose the aggregate and create a very polished surface that resembles natural stone, grind the surface. Use a series of increasingly fine diamond-wheel grinding pads (50-grit, then 100, 200, and 400) mounted on a shock-protected 5" angle grinder (variable speed). This is messy work and can go on for hours to get the desired result. Rinse the surface regularly with clean water and make sure it stays wet during grinding. For a gleaming surface, mount still finer pads (up to 1,500 grit) on the grinder and wet-polish.

Clean and seal the concrete with several coats of quality silicone-based concrete sealer (one with penetrating and film-forming agents). For extra protection and a renewable finish, apply a coat of paste wax after the last coat of sealer dries.

Undermount or self-rimming, it is easier to install the sink before the countertop is mounted on the cabinet. Attach the sink according to the manufacturer's directions. Self-rimming sinks likely will require some modifications to the mounting hardware (or at least you'll need to buy some extra-long screws) to accommodate the thickness of the countertop.

Make sure the island cabinet is adequately reinforced and that as much plumbing as possible has been installed, then apply a thick bead of panel adhesive or silicone adhesive to the tops of the cabinets and stretchers. With at least one helper, lower the countertop onto the base and position it where you wish. Let the adhesive dry overnight before completing the sink hookup.

Island Vent Hood

An island vent hood installation is a bit complicated because the unit must be supported from above, and because of the extra ductwork. Before installation, read the manufacturer's instructions carefully for recommended heights for cooktop and hood installation.

Most island vents weigh over 100 pounds, so you will need assistance during parts of the installation. Install the vent hood prior to installing the cooktop, if possible, to prevent damage to the cooktop. If not possible, protect the cooktop and countertop with a heavy moving pad. This installation is vented directly through the roof through attic space above the kitchen. You can also install the ductwork between ceiling joists and out to a side wall, or you can build a soffit around the ductwork. All vent hoods have a maximum permissible length for duct runs. The installation instructions will contain a chart giving equivalent lengths for each type of duct fitting. For example, a 90° elbow is the equivalent of 15 feet of round straight duct. A round roof cap is the equivalent of 26 feet of round straight duct.

Shopping Tips ▸

Professional-style cooktops require heavy-duty vent hoods. Check your cooktop manual for venting requirements.

Tools & Materials ▸

Measuring tape	Roof vent
Plumb bob	2 × 4 lumber
Ladder	3" #10 wood screws
Wallboard saw	Sheetmetal screws
Drill	NM cable
Reciprocating saw	Wire connectors
Screwdriver	Tape
Wire stripper	Metallic duct tape
6" round duct	Duct straps

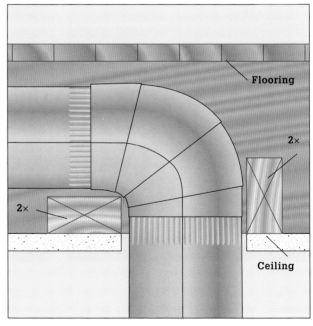

Variation: If you must install ductwork in the ceiling joists, turn one 2 × 4 brace flat to allow the duct to fit between the 2 × 4 and the flooring above.

How to Install an Island Vent Hood

Check manufacturer's directions for the distance from the front of the vent to the duct centerline and the necessary vent hood alignment over the cooktop. Use a plumb bob to find the position of the duct centerline over the cooktop. Mark the location of the duct centerline on the ceiling by poking a 12" length of hanger wire through the ceiling. In the attic, pull back the insulation surrounding the wire and the adjoining joists. Center a section of 6" duct over the wire hole and trace around it to mark the cutout for the duct. Using a wallboard saw or a rotary saw, cut out the hole.

Cut two lengths of 2 × 4 to fit between the joists. Check the manufacturer's instructions for the correct distance between the braces. Place the braces flush against the ceiling top. Drill pilot holes and install with a minimum of two 3" #10 wood screws driven through the joist and into the brace. The cross bracing and the ceiling surface must be level for proper installation of the vent hood. Insert the 6" round duct through the ceiling so it extends down 3 or 4 inches. This must be a female or external connection. Attach lengths of duct until you reach the roof deck.

Draw an outline of the duct on the roof deck. Drill a pilot hole, then saw through the sheathing and roofing material with a reciprocating saw to make the cutout for the vent tailpiece.

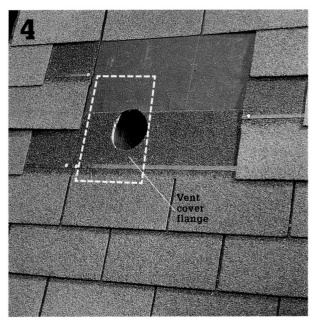

Vent cover flange

Remove a section of shingles from around the cutout, leaving the roofing paper intact. Remove enough shingles to create an exposed area that is at least the size of the vent cover flange.

(continued)

If the hole for the vent does not abut a rafter, attach a 2 × 4 brace between the roof rafters. Attach a hose clamp to the brace or rafter about 1" below the roof sheathing (top). Insert the vent tailpiece into the cutout and through the hose clamp, then tighten the clamp screw (bottom).

Apply roofing cement to the bottom of the vent cover flange, then slide the vent cover over the tailpiece. Nail the vent cover flange into place with self-sealing roofing nails, then patch in shingles around the cover.

Complete installation of the ductwork by securing each joint with self-tapping sheetmetal screws. Wrap each joint with metallic duct tape. Support the duct as it passes through the ceiling with duct straps.

Secure the upper support frame to the ceiling joists or the cross bracing with the screws provided. The screws must be driven into the center of the joists or cross braces. Check to make sure the frame is level in all directions. Insert the lower support frame and secure loosely. Adjust the lower support frame to the desired height above the countertop and tighten the screws. Make sure the support frame is level and plumb.

In the attic, run a branch circuit from a nearby junction box. (This may be a job for an electrician.) Route the cable through the ceiling hole. Pull the cable to reach the junction box, approximately 6" below the frame support. Tape the cable to the frame support.

10

Measure from the bottom of the duct flange in the ceiling to the bottom of the support frame. Add 1" for insertion into the ceiling duct and subtract 1¾" for the hood insertion. (This will vary; check the manufacturer's dimensions.) Cut 6" round duct to this length. Install the duct and attach with sheetmetal screws and metallic duct tape.

11

Slide the top decorative duct cover over the support frame to the ceiling and attach it to the support frame using the supplied decorative screws. Slide the bottom decorative duct cover over the support frame and the top duct cover. Secure with the provided stop screw to hold it in place while the hood is installed.

12

With a helper, lift the hood up to the support frame. Align the hood mounting studs with the support frame holes and guide the hood duct connector into the house duct. Install the nuts and lock washers to the mounting studs and tighten. Check that the hood is level in all directions. Make sure the duct is positioned over the hood connector. Seal the joint with metallic duct tape, not screws.

13

Strip 8" of cable. Thread the cable through a cable clamp and through a knockout into the junction box. Connect the white supply wire to the white vent wire with a wire connector. Connect the black supply wire to the black vent wire. Connect the green or bare supply wire to the green or yellow vent wire. Push the wires into the junction box and replace the cover without pinching the wires. Remove the stop screw and slide down the decorative cover.

Fixtures & Appliances

Appliances for kitchens include refrigerators, ranges, and dishwashers; fixtures include sinks, faucets, garbage disposers, and icemakers. In many ways, these items define our kitchens. Essentially, they do most of the work—along with the cook, of course. The conventional thinking on purchasing appliances and fixtures is that you should buy the best quality you can afford. Although some appliance sellers may offer free installation, you can often save a significant amount of money (and thereby upgrade your purchase) by doing the installation yourself.

In general, installing appliances and fixtures in your kitchen is a manageable job. An exception may be made however, when it comes to hooking up a gas range. Only professionals and very experienced do-it-yourselfers should attempt to make gas connections.

In This Chapter

- Appliance & Fixture Selection
- Ranges, Ovens & Cooktops
- Refrigerator Icemaker
- Dishwasher
- Food Disposer
- Range Hood/Vent Fan
- Drop-in Sink
- Undermount Sink
- Apron Sink
- Kitchen Faucets
- Kitchen Drains & Traps
- Hot Water Dispenser
- Pot Filler
- Carbon Water Filter
- Reverse-Osmosis Filtration System

Appliance & Fixture Selection

Selecting the right appliances and fixtures for your kitchen update or remodeling project requires a balancing act, with cost, energy efficiency, performance, and style thrown into the mix. It's fun to look through magazines and covet the cutting-edge kitchens featured, but be prepared for sticker shock when you are ready to make your selections. Focus on the features you really need and want, and look for appliances and fixtures that offer those options. For instance, a stainless steel kitchen may be appealing—but if your main goal is easy cleanup, you will be disappointed to discover that most stainless steel finishes prominently display fingerprints and water marks. As you read this section, consider which options you cannot live without, as well as those you just don't need. This will help you narrow your choices when you begin looking at the costs of various options.

Ranges, Cooktops & Ovens

A range, or stove, combines an oven and a cooktop in one unit. Ranges often cost less than two separate units, and they consume less space. Choosing separate units, however, gives you flexibility in placement and may allow you access to features not available in a range. Plus, you can choose appliances with different fuel sources: many cooks prefer gas cooktops and electric ovens. Cooktops can be placed in practically any enclosed cabinet with countertop. Ovens can be placed in islands, under counters, and at varying heights on walls.

The gas cooktop has the reputation of being difficult to clean, although sealed burners make this less of an issue. All gas cooktops have grates to hold the pots above the flames; make sure you can move these easily for cleaning. With electronic ignition, gas cooktops and ovens do not have pilot lights, so the risks of extinguished pilot lights are no longer an issue.

Gas ovens are often not as well insulated as self-cleaning electric ovens, so they may heat your kitchen space more. If you broil often, make sure the broiler is located in the main oven compartment and not in a separate, lower compartment. This eliminates bending and allows for greater broiling capacity.

Electric cooktops come in a variety of burner configurations. The traditional is the electric coil with drip plate. Solid disks are made of cast iron sealed to the cooktop. Halogen burners are underneath a glass cooktop and are heated by vacuum-sealed halogen lamps. Induction burners are also under a glass cooktop and have an electromagnetic coil that conducts electrical energy directly to the pot, requiring ferrous cookware (stainless steel, aluminum, and ceramic cookware will not work). The flat ceramic tops are smooth, but may require special cleaners.

A gas range is the preferred choice for most serious cooks because the heat is very controllable and achieves cooking temperatures immediately.

Electric ovens are conventional, convection, or multi-mode. A conventional oven is the standard oven with a heating element at the bottom for baking and an element at the top for broiling. A true convection oven has no elements in the oven cavity. Instead, the baking element and a fan are located outside the cavity. The fan circulates the heated air to produce an absolutely balanced heat—you can bake as many trays of cookies as you have oven racks. A more expensive option is the multimode oven, which uses conventional, convection, and microwave cooking.

Refrigerators

Buying a new refrigerator can be expensive, but running an older, inefficient refrigerator can account for as much as 20 percent of your household electrical costs. New energy and pollution standards created over the past twenty years have encouraged manufacturers to make refrigerators much more efficient. Refrigerators come in a number of styles and configurations. Slide-in refrigerators are the traditional style, usually 28" to 34" deep, though some may be 24" deep. Built-in refrigerators are wider than slide-ins, but only 24" deep so they are flush with base cabinets. Built-ins need space above for venting. Refrigerator and freezer configurations include top freezer, bottom freezer, and side-by-side. The top freezer is more efficient and easier to access, but the bottom freezer puts more of the refrigerator at a usable height. Side-by-side configurations are popular because both are easily accessed, and in-door ice servers are only available in this style. The major drawback of the side-by-side is the diminished width of the refrigerator side. A platter of hors d'oeuvres, a cookie sheet or a large roasting pan often won't fit in this narrow compartment.

New freezer and refrigerator options include commercial-grade refrigerators, individual drawers that look like cabinet drawers and can be located anywhere, dual-temperature wine coolers, and freestanding vertical freezer and refrigerator components that can be installed separately.

Dishwashers

Dishwashers, like refrigerators, have become more efficient and quieter. A dishwasher that doesn't require hand rinsing before loading will also save water—enough so that using a dishwasher actually conserves water. The key issues to consider when buying a dishwasher are the operating costs, noise reduction, cleaning power, and features. Operating costs can be determined by looking at the yellow Energy Guide tag. Noise reduction measures are often directly related to price. Look for sound-absorbent insulation around the tub (stainless steel tubs are regarded as the best), behind the door, over the top, and behind the access panel and toe kick. Because you won't usually be able to hear a dishwasher run through its cycles in a showroom, refer to consumer ratings magazines for sound-level comparisons. Avoid inexpensive dishwashers that do not have internal heating elements and rely on ambient heat in the water for cleaning.

A high-end stainless steel refrigerator/freezer can be an impressive centerpiece in a fancy kitchen, but a more modest, energy-efficient model is a better investment for most homeowners.

Washing dishes in an efficient dishwashing appliance consumes considerably less water and energy than washing and rinsing by hand.

Vent Fans

Vent fans and range hoods protect your kitchen surfaces and your health by exhausting the heat, steam, grease, and odors produced by cooking. Local codes may apply to venting systems, so check with a building inspector or HVAC contractor. To truly be effective, vent fans must vent to the outdoors, rather than filtering and recirculating the air. Vent fans are rated for airflow in cubic feet per minute (cfm) and by noise level measured in sones. Look for a high-flow rating with a low noise rating. Large cooktops, specialty grills, and wok burners require heavy-duty ventilation systems. Vent hoods over islands need to be more powerful because of the open, rather than enclosed, setting. Down-draft and pop-up vents pull the air down to exhaust, so they also need to be more powerful. Each vent will have specific limitations concerning size and length of ductwork; make sure your planned vent outlet is within these limits.

A vent fan can be a highly visible element of the room or it can be installed in a wall cabinet above the range where it is virtually invisible.

Food Disposal

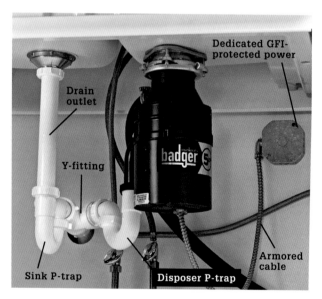

The main consideration when looking at food disposers is horsepower. Models come with ⅜- to 1-horsepower motors. A ¾ or 1 HP model is almost always worth the extra cost when it comes to operation and durability. The larger, more expensive models are quieter, carry longer warranties, and have more features. Most models are continuous feed, which means that a switch (usually on the wall, but occasionally sink or counter mounted) is flipped, the motor runs and items can be fed through the rubber gasket continuously. People with septic systems should be aware that a disposer adds to the overall load on the septic tank. Even though disposer units say they are safe for septic tanks and some even come with enzyme sprays to help promote the bacterial action, they still add to the amount of sludge in the tank.

A quality food disposer stays out of sight and out of mind. The more powerful the motor, the less likely it will bog down or clog.

Kitchen Sinks

Kitchen sinks are available in numerous stock configurations, sizes, and materials. The first choice to consider is the material. Stainless steel, cast iron, enameled steel, solid surface, fireclay, acrylic, and resin are all widely available sink materials, each with its own advantages and disadvantages. Custom sinks may be crafted from more unusual materials, such as copper, brass, soapstone, concrete, or granite.

Stainless steel sinks are easy to clean, long-lasting, and available in every possible bowl configuration (top mounts, undermounts, and apron fronts) and in every price range. Stainless steel may show water spots and the sinks can be noisy if they are not properly undercoated with sound-deadening material.

Cast-iron sinks have a fired-on porcelain finish. These sinks are durable, attractive, and are available in a wide range of designs and colors including top mount, undermount, and apron front. The only drawback of this type of sink is its hardness—you may break a few more glasses than with a stainless, solid-surface, or resin sink. The porcelain finishes can wear and chip over time.

Enameled steel is the inexpensive cousin to cast iron. The metal is thinner, the enamel is less durable than porcelain, and the designs available may be limited. However, if you can find a steel sink with a porcelain finish and polyester-resin backing, you will have a sink that costs and weighs less than cast iron and absorbs shock better.

Solid-surface sinks are available in a number of styles, but a limited range of colors. They are most frequently found in undermount styles rather than drop-ins. This is because the majority of solid surface sinks are integrated with a solid-surface counter, where they will be attached under the countertop in a seamless installation. Solid-surface sinks are

Replacing an old sink is a quick and easy way to make a significant improvement to your kitchen.

shock-absorbent, stain-resistant, and repairable. If you should happen to stain, gouge, or scorch the material, a seamless, invisible repair through sanding or patching can be made.

Fireclay is a vitreous-china product with a strong, smooth finish and a very hard, non-marking surface. These sinks are heavy and can be expensive. They are available in a number of apron-front designs. Acrylic and fiberglass sinks are inexpensive, shock-absorbing, and easy to clean but might not have good longevity. Resin sinks are composites of resin, pigment, quartz, or other minerals. This material does not chip, scratch, stain, crack or mark.

Universal Sink Design ▸

Sink depths of 8", 9", or 10" are becoming popular, but very tall or short users will find it difficult to reach the sink bottom comfortably. Raise or lower your sink countertop to enable the primary user to stand at the sink and easily reach the bottom without bending. Single-handle faucets are much easier to use, allowing for continuous temperature adjustment and easy on and off. Incorporating an anti-scald device makes the faucet safer for children.

Shopping Tips ▸

When purchasing a sink, also plan on buying a new strainer body or disposer sleeve, sink clips, and a fresh drain trap kit.

Look for a sink with a basin divider that is lower than the sink rim—this reduces splashing.

Drain holes located near the back of the basin create more usable space in the sink base cabinet.

Make sure your new sink has enough predrilled holes in the back deck and that they will work with your faucet configuration (or, choose your sink first and buy fittings to match).

Faucets

You'll find many options when choosing a new kitchen faucet. The best place to start the process is with your sink. In the past, most faucets were mounted directly to the sink deck, which had three or four predrilled holes to accommodate the faucets, spout, sprayer, and perhaps a liquid soap dispenser or an air gap for the dishwasher. Modern kitchen faucets don't always conform to this setup; many of them are designed to be installed in a single hole in the sink deck or in the countertop. If you plan to keep your old sink, look for a faucet that won't leave empty holes in the deck. Generally, it's best to replace like for like, but unfilled stainless sink holes can be filled with snap-in plugs or a soap dispenser.

The two most basic kitchen faucet categories are single-handle and two-handle. Single-handled models are popular because you can adjust the water temperature easily with just one hand. Another difference is in the faucet body. Some faucets have the taps and the spout mounted onto a faucet body, so the spacing between the tailpieces is preset. Others, called widespread faucets, have independent taps and spouts that can be configured any way you please, as long as the tubes connecting the taps to the spouts reach. This type is best if you are installing the faucet in the countertop (a common way to go about it with new countertops such as solid-surface, quartz, or granite). In the past, kitchen faucets almost always had a remote pull-out sprayer. The sprayer was attached to the faucet body with a hose directly below the mixing valve. While this type of sprayer is still fairly common, many faucets today have integral pull-out spouts. These spouts are very convenient and less prone to failure than the old-style sprayers.

A single-handled, high-arc faucet with traditional remote sprayer. The mounting plate is decorative and optional.

Single-handled faucets may require four holes, as does this model with its side sprayer and matching soap/lotion dispenser.

Two-handled faucets are less common, but remain popular choices for traditional kitchens. The gooseneck spout also has a certain elegance, but avoid this type if you have a shallow sink that's less than 8" deep.

A single-handled faucet with pull-out spray head requires only one hole in your sink deck or countertop—a real benefit if your sink is not predrilled or if it is an undermount model.

Energy Star & Energy Guide Labels ▶

If you're in the market for a new appliance, it's time to start paying attention to those yellow-and-black ENERGYGUIDE labels you see pasted to the front of many new products. The labels, required by the Federal Trade Commission, help consumers quickly compare models for their energy efficiency. The box in the middle of each label provides the "energy use" of all models in a given class, with an arrow showing where that particular model falls within the range. The label also gives you an estimated annual operating cost for the appliance.

Energy Star is the Department of Energy's wide-reaching program that awards Energy Star status to the most efficient products in a given class. The program applies to major appliances, windows, doors, HVAC systems, and other household items. In general, Energy Star products exceed the federal government's energy-efficiency standards and perform within the top 25 percent of their categories.

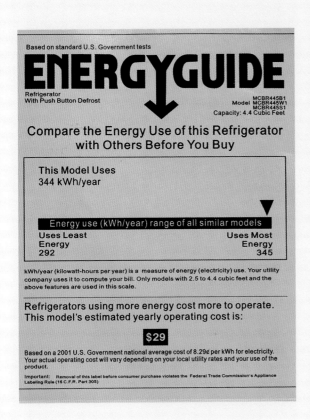

Additional Resources ▶

- U.S. Department of Energy (DOE): www.energy.gov
- Energy Star: www.energystar.gov
- Consumer Reports, for unbiased analysis of appliance performance and other shopping considerations, online at www.consumerreports.org
- American Council for Energy-Efficient Economy: www.aceee.org
- Your local utility provider
- Your state's energy authority; some states offer rebates on high-efficiency appliances
- Association of Home Appliance Manufacturers: www.aham.org
- The Green Guide: www.thegreenguide.com

Ranges, Ovens & Cooktops

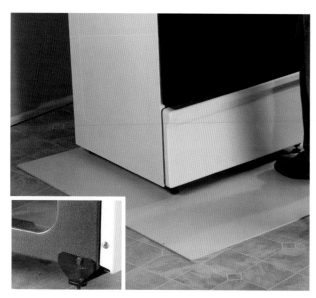

For the most part, installing a new range is simply a matter of positioning it, leveling it, and making sure it is hooked up to a receptacle and gas connection. If you are comfortable working with gas and plumbing, hooking up a gas range or cooktop is not difficult. But in many municipalities only a licensed installer can make gas hook-ups. Ask your local building department if you are unsure (your appliance retailer is also a good source for information).

When moving a range for painting or cleaning, removing it for replacement, or installing a new range, make sure you protect the flooring. Use an appliance dolly to lift a new range from the side only—not the front or the back. If the range will not fit through doors, remove the oven door handle. An electric range or cooktop must have its own dedicated 240-volt circuit. Gas ranges and cooktops also need a grounded 3-hole electrical outlet to power the electronic ignition, clock, and timers.

Protect your flooring when moving a range, whether it is an old one on the way out or a brand-new one being installed. Typically, ranges have adjustable feet that can gouge floor coverings. A piece of cardboard, tagboard, or a carpet scrap can be slipped under the appliance.

Installing Electric Ranges

Receptacles for electric ranges should look like this. They are 50-amp, combination 125/250 volt fittings with a three-slot configuration that will only work with electric range appliance cords. They provide 125-volt power to run lights, clocks, and timers and 250-volt service to the heating elements.

A dedicated circuit with a double pole 50-amp breaker supplies power to the high-voltage receptacle for your electric range. Most codes require 6-gauge copper service entrance round (SER) cable for the circuit. If your circuit does not meet these standards, contact a qualified electrician to upgrade the circuit. *Note: Always shut off power at the main service panel before removing a service panel cover.*

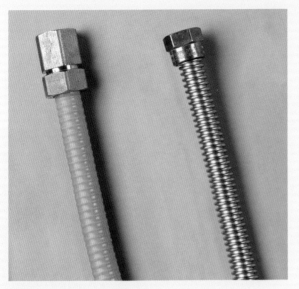

Flexible appliance connectors are required for hooking a gas inlet port up to a gas supply valve. Flexible connectors are usually made of stainless steel, and some areas require that the steel be protected with a PVC coating. These are sold in a variety of lengths. Buy the shortest connector that will reach from the supply valve to the inlet port.

Shut off gas at the nearest in-line shutoff or stopcock valve, as well as the supply valve you will be hooking up to. When closed, a stopcock valve is perpendicular to the gas pipe as seen here.

Use two wrenches to securely attach the appliance connector tube to the gas supply valve. One wrench should be used to hold the tube securely and the other to tighten the male tube coupling onto the female supply valve. Be sure to wrap a layer of gas-rated (yellow) Teflon tape around the supply valve threads before attaching the coupling. Do not overtighten the coupling.

Attach the other end of the flexible appliance connector tube to the gas inlet port in your range or cooktop. Also use yellow Teflon tape to lubricate the threads at this union. Turn on the gas supply and immediately test all connections with leak detector solution. If the connections pass, slide the appliance into position, taking care not to cause stress on or kinks in the connector tube.

Refrigerator Icemaker

There's nothing really tricky about installing a refrigerator unless your new model has a built-in icemaker. If your old refrigerator was equipped with an icemaker, you should already have a water supply line running to the refrigerator area. If there is no supply line, contact a plumber to install one for you if you do not know how. Most icemakers either come preinstalled or are purchased as an accessory when you buy your new refrigerator. But if you have an older refrigerator with no icemaker and you'd like it to have one, all is not lost. Inspect the back of the unit, behind the freezer compartment. If your refrigerator has the required plumbing to support an icemaker, you will see a port that is covered with backing. In that case, all you need to do is take the make and model information to an appliance parts dealer, and they can sell you an aftermarket icemaker. Plan to spend $100 to $200.

Tools & Materials ▶

Screwdrivers
Nut drivers
Needle-nose pliers
Duct or masking tape
Electric drill and assorted bits
Channel-type pliers
Open-end or
  adjustable wrench

Icemaker kit
Saddle valve or T-fitting
  (for supply tube)
Putty knife
Tape

A built-in icemaker is easy to install as a retrofit appliance in most modern refrigerators. If you want to have an endless supply of ice for home use, you may wonder how you ever got along without one.

How Icemakers Work ▶

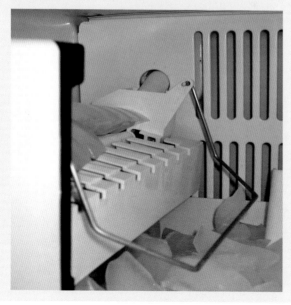

An icemaker receives its supply of water for making cubes through a ¼" copper supply line that runs from the icemaker to a water pipe. The supply line runs through a valve in the refrigerator and is controlled by a solenoid that monitors the water supply and sends the water into the icemaker itself, where it is turned into ice cubes. The cubes drop down into a bin, and as the ice level rises, they also raise a bail wire that's connected to a shutoff. When the bin is full, the bail wire will be high enough to trigger a mechanism that shuts off the water supply.

Aftermarket automatic icemakers are simple to install as long as your refrigerator is icemaker-ready. Buy the correct model for your appliance and do careful installation work—icemaker water supply lines are very common sources for leaks.

How to Install a Refrigerator Icemaker

1

Remove all the contents from the refrigerator and freezer compartments and store them in ice chests or in a neighbor's refrigerator. Unplug the unit and pull it out from the wall. Then open the freezer door and remove the icemaker cover plate at the back of the compartment.

On the back of the refrigerator, remove the backing or unscrew the icemaker access panel that covers the icemaker port.

3

Water port

Wiring harness port

Locate and clear the ports. One opening is for the water line. The other is for a wiring harness. Usually, these holes are filled with insulation plugs that keep the cold air inside the freezer from leaking out into the room. Remove these plugs with needle-nose pliers.

4

Install the water tube assembly (part of the icemaker kit) in its access hole on the back of the refrigerator. This assembly features a plastic elbow attached to the plastic tube that reaches into the freezer compartment.

5

Hook up the harness. Icemaker kits usually come with a wiring harness that joins the icemaker motor to the power supply wires. Push this harness through the access hole and into the freezer compartment. Seal the hole with the plastic grommet supplied with the harness.

(continued)

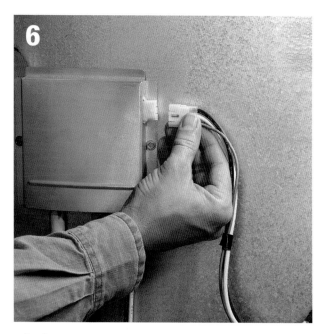

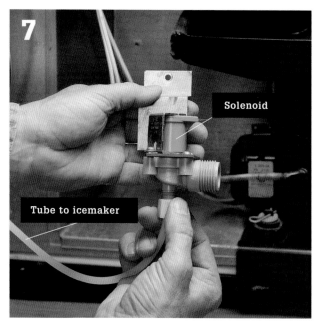

Join the end of the icemaker wiring harness to the power connector that was preinstalled on the back of the refrigerator. This connection should be flat against the back. If it isn't, tape it down with duct tape or masking tape.

Attach the water tube at the top of the refrigerator to the solenoid that is mounted at the bottom with a plastic water line. Run the tube down the back of the refrigerator and attach it to the solenoid valve with a compression fitting. This job is easier to do before you attach the solenoid assembly to the refrigerator cabinet.

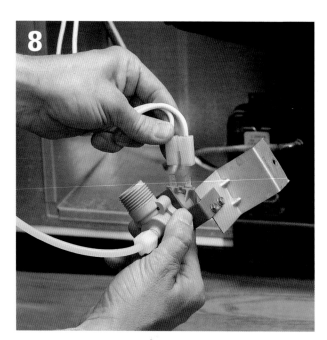

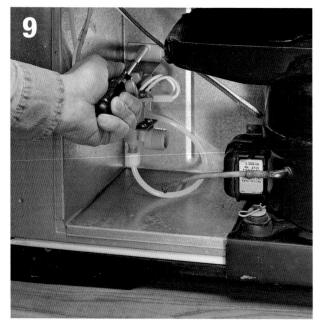

Identify the two snap connectors on the wiring harness. One goes to the preinstalled wires on the refrigerator and the other is attached to the solenoid. Just push this second connector onto the brass tabs, usually at the top of the solenoid.

Attach the solenoid to a mounting bracket that should be installed on the cabinet wall at the bottom of the refrigerator. Mounting holes may be predrilled in the cabinet for this purpose. But if not, drill holes to match the bracket and the size of the screws. Then attach the bracket and make sure to attach the solenoid ground wire to one of these screws.

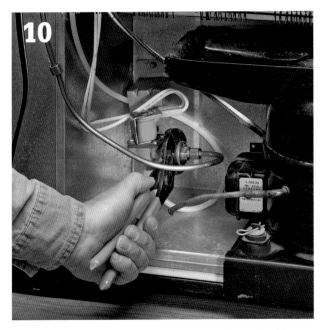

Install the water-inlet copper tube once the solenoid is mounted. Attach it by tightening the nut on one end with channel-type pliers. The other end of the tube is held to the refrigerator cabinet with a simple clamp. Make sure the end of this tubing is pointing straight up.

Join the water-inlet tube to the water supply tubing (from the house plumbing system) with a brass compression coupling. Tighten the compression nuts with an open-end or adjustable wrench.

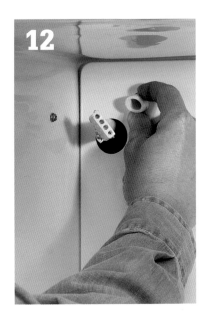

Make sure the water tube and the wiring harness (from the back of the refrigerator) are free inside the freezer compartment. If they are caught on the cabinet, loosen them until they are easily accessible.

Connect the wire harness to the plug on the icemaker unit. Also connect the water supply tube to the back of the icemaker with a spring clip or hose clamp.

Install the icemaker. Remove any small rubber caps that may be installed in the mounting screw holes with a narrow putty knife. Lift the unit and screw it to the freezer wall. The mounting bracket holes are usually slotted to permit leveling the unit. Plug in the refrigerator and test the icemaker.

Dishwasher

A dishwasher that's past its prime may be inefficient in more ways than one. If it's an old model, it probably wasn't designed to be very efficient to begin with. But more significantly, if it no longer cleans effectively, you're probably spending a lot of time and hot water prerinsing the dishes. This alone can consume more energy and water than a complete wash cycle on a newer machine. So even if your old dishwasher still runs, replacing it with an efficient new model can be a good green upgrade.

In terms of sizing and utility hookups, dishwashers are generally quite standard. If your old machine is a built-in and your countertops and cabinets are standard sizes, most full-sized dishwashers will fit right in. Of course, you should always measure the dimensions of the old unit before shopping for a new one to avoid an unpleasant surprise at installation time. Also be sure to review the manufacturer's instructions before starting any work.

Tools & Materials ▸

Screwdrivers	Cable connector
Adjustable wrench	Teflon tape
2-ft. level	Hose clamps
⅝" automotive heater hose	Wire connectors
Automotive heater hose	Carpet scrap
4" of ½" copper tubing	Bowl

Replacing an old, inefficient dishwasher is a straightforward project that usually takes just a few hours. The energy savings begin with the first load of dishes and continue with every load thereafter.

Efficient Loading ▸

To get the best circulation of water for effective wash action, follow these tips when loading dishes:

- Make sure dishes are loaded so water can reach all of the soiled surfaces.
- Be sure that larger items are not blocking smaller items from the wash action.
- Place all items in both racks so that they are separated and face the center of the dishwasher. This will help to ensure that water reaches all soiled surfaces.
- Place glasses with the open end facing downward to allow proper washing action.
- Do not place glasses over the tines, but between them. This will allow the glasses to lean toward the spray arm and will improve washing. It also promotes drying by reducing the amount of water remaining on the top of the glass after the wash cycle is complete.
- Do not allow flatware to "nest." This prevents proper water distribution between the surfaces.
- Load flatware, except knives, with some handles up and some down to prevent nesting. For safety, knives should always be loaded handles up.

How to Replace a Dishwasher

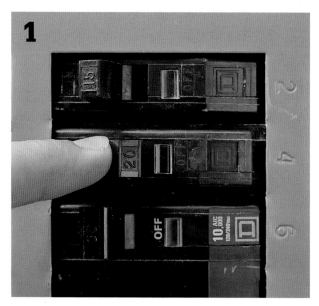

Shut off the electrical power to the dishwasher circuit at the service panel. Also, turn off the water supply at the shutoff valve, usually located directly under the floor.

Disconnect the old plumbing connections. First unscrew the front access panel. Once the access panel is removed, disconnect the water supply line from the L-fitting on the bottom of the unit. This is usually a brass compression fitting, so just turning the compression nut counterclockwise with an adjustable wrench should do the trick. Use a bowl to catch any water that might leak out when the nut is removed.

Disconnect the old wiring connections. The dishwasher has an integral electrical box at the front of the unit where the power cable is attached to the dishwasher's fixture wires. Take off the box cover and remove the wire connectors that join the wires together.

Disconnect the discharge hose, which is usually connected to the dishwasher port on the side of the garbage disposer. To remove it, loosen the screw on the hose clamp and pull it off. You may need to push this hose back through a hole in the cabinet wall and into the dishwasher compartment so it won't get caught when you pull the dishwasher out.

5

Detach the unit from the surrounding cabinets. Remove the screws that hold the brackets to the underside of the countertop. Then put a piece of cardboard or old carpet under the front legs to protect the floor from getting scratched, and pull the dishwasher out.

6

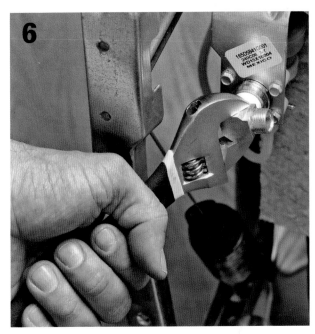

Prepare the new dishwasher. Tip it on its back and attach the new L-fitting into the threaded port on the solenoid. Apply some Teflon tape or pipe sealant to the fitting threads before tightening it in place to prevent possible leaks.

7

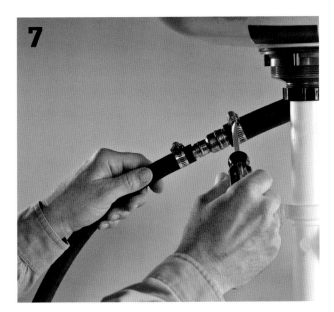

Attach a length of new automotive heater hose, usually ⅝" diameter, to the end of the dishwasher's discharge hose nipple with a hose clamp. The new hose you are adding should be long enough to reach from the discharge nipple to the port on the side of the kitchen sink garbage disposer.

8

Prepare for the wiring connections. Like the old dishwasher, the new one will have an integral electrical box for making the wiring connections. To gain access to the box, remove the box cover. Then install a cable connector on the back of the box and bring the power cable from the service panel through this connector. Power should be shut off at the main service panel at all times.

(continued)

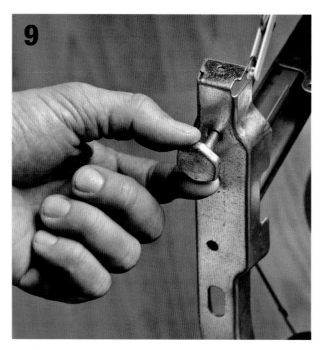

9

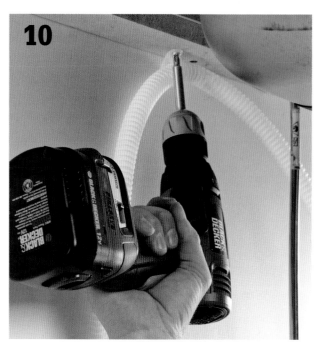

10

Install a leveling leg at each of the four corners while the new dishwasher is still on its back. Just turn the legs into the threaded holes designed for them. Leave about ½" of each leg projecting from the bottom of the unit. These will have to be adjusted later to level the appliance. Tip the appliance up onto the feet and slide it into the opening. Check for level in both directions and adjust the feet as required.

Once the dishwasher is level, attach the brackets to the underside of the countertop to keep the appliance from moving. Then pull the discharge hose into the sink cabinet and install it so there's a loop that is attached with a bracket to the underside of the countertop. This loop prevents waste water from flowing from the disposer back into the dishwasher.

Lengthening a Discharge Hose ▶

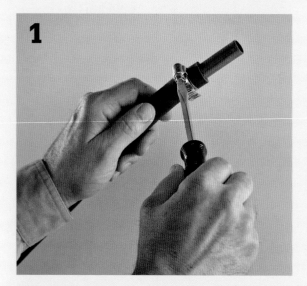

1

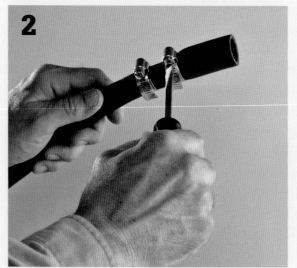

2

If the discharge hose has to be modified to fit onto the disposer port, first insert a 4"-long piece of ½" copper tubing into the hose and hold it in place with a hose clamp. This provides a nipple for the rubber adapter that fits onto the disposer.

Clamp the rubber disposer adapter to the end of the copper tubing nipple. Then tighten the hose clamp securely.

11

Discharge tube from dishwasher

Drain

Push the adapter over the disposer's discharge nipple and tighten it in place with a hose clamp. If you don't have a disposer, this discharge hose can be clamped directly to a modified sink tailpiece that's installed below a standard sink strainer.

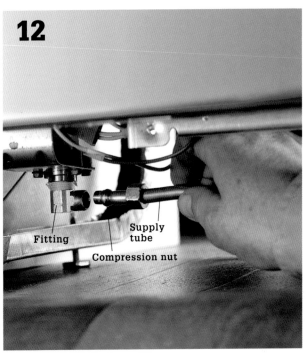

12

Fitting

Supply tube

Compression nut

Adjust the L-fitting on the dishwasher's water inlet valve until it points directly toward the water supply tubing. Lubricate the threads slightly with a drop of dishwashing liquid and tighten the tubing's compression nut onto the fitting. Use an adjustable wrench and turn the nut clockwise.

13

Complete the electrical connections by tightening the connector's clamp on the cable and then joining the power wires to the fixture wires with wire connectors. Attach the ground wire (or wires) to the grounding screw on the box, and replace the cover.

14

Install the access panel, usually by hooking it on a couple of prongs just below the dishwasher's door. Install the screws (if any) that hold it in place, and turn on the water and power supplies. Replace the toe-kick panel at the bottom of the dishwasher.

Variation: Installing a Raised Dishwasher

Raising the dishwasher 6 to 9" makes it much easier to load and unload. You'll eliminate a lot of stooping, which is especially important for people with sore backs. A raised dishwasher is also much easier for wheelchair users to operate.

These directions are for raising an existing dishwasher 8¼"—the height of a 2 × 8 and a sheet of ½" plywood. These directions cover the new extra space above the toe kick with a piece of matching cabinetry. Because the platform will cover the previous access holes, you will need to cut new access holes in the side cabinets. A raised dishwasher ideally should have 12" of countertop available on one side as a "landing" area for dish unloading.

If your dishwasher currently abuts the sink, you will need to move it, since the sink needs to have clearance of 12" on one side and 21" on the other. Because dishwashers are meant to be built in, the directions include the creation of side panels to house the portion of the dishwasher that extends above the countertop.

Tools & Materials ▸

Circular saw
Drill
Framing square
Jigsaw
2 × 8 lumber
1 × 3 lumber

½" plywood
Screws (2", 1 ¼", & ¾")
½" × 2" angle irons
½" × 4" mending plates
Masking tape
Edge banding

Part	Name	Measurements	Material	No.
A	Platform sides	24"*	2 × 8	2
B	Platform cross braces	21"*	2 × 8	2
C	Platform top	24" × 24"	½" plywood	1
D	Floor panel	24" × 8¼"*	½" plywood	
E	Cleat	21"	1 × 3	1

*approximate measurement, cut to fit.

How to Make a Raised Platform for a Dishwasher

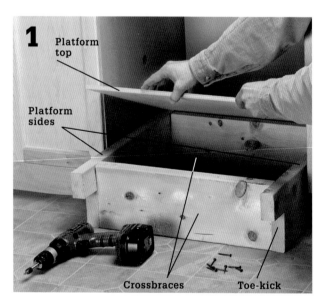

1
Platform top
Platform sides
Crossbraces
Toe-kick

Remove the dishwasher completely. Cut a 4 × 4" notch in each platform side piece. (Make sure this matches your existing toe-kick space. Most toe-kick cutouts are 4 × 4" and covered with molding.) Place the cross brace to align with the back of the toe-kick cutout. Place the other cross brace at the back. Drill pilot holes and attach with 2" screws. Cut the ½" plywood to fit the platform and attach with 1¼" screws. Place the platform into the dishwasher opening.

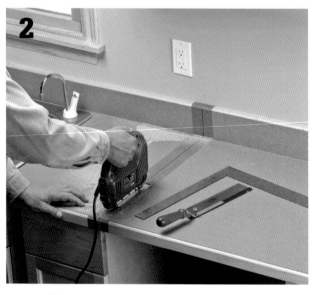

2

Put masking tape on top of the counter and use a framing square to mark cutting lines flush with the cabinet edges on each side of the opening. Use a jigsaw to cut the countertop. To cut the backsplash, use a jamb saw or a reciprocating saw. The masking tape prevents the laminate from chipping.

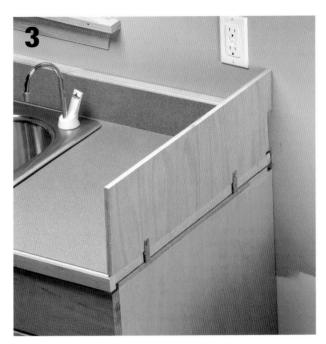

Cut the plywood side panels to size. For frameless cabinets, cut the length to match the front edge of the cabinet sides. Use a compass to scribe the backsplash cutouts for the side panels and cut using a jigsaw. Apply edge banding to the exposed edge and install with the mending plates.

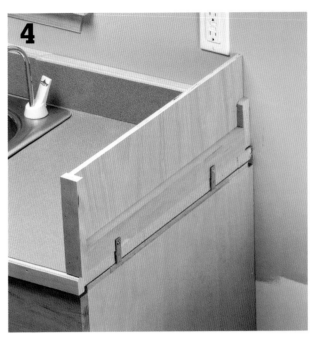

For framed cabinets, cut the length to match the cabinet front edge minus the face frame. Use a compass to scribe the backsplash cutouts for the side panels, cut using a jigsaw. Install a matching face frame filler strip. Use scrap lumber and mending plates to set the panels back from the edge.

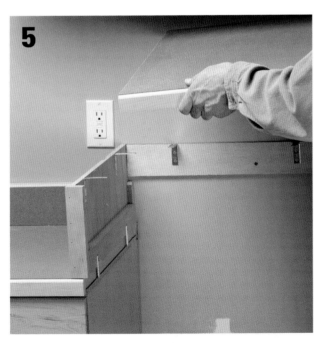

Cut the new countertop to size and apply the edge trim to match. Attach a 1 × 3 cleat to the wall using 2" screws. Install the countertop using two angle irons per side and ¾" screws.

Make the necessary connections and slide the dishwasher into the new space. Make the final connections (see page 169). Reattach the access panel cover (if present), but leave off the toe-kick plate. Purchase or make a floor panel to match your cabinets and install it across the front of the platform and the dishwasher toe-kick space. Install the toe-kick molding to match.

Food Disposer

Food disposers are standard equipment in modern homes, and most of us have come to depend on them to macerate our plate leavings and crumbs so they can exit the house along with waste water from the sink drain. If your existing disposer needs replacing, you'll find that the job is relatively simple, especially if you select a replacement appliance that is the same model as the old one. In that case, you can probably reuse the existing mounting assembly, drain sleeve, and drain plumbing.

Most food disposers are classified as "continuous feed" because they can only operate when an ON/OFF switch on the wall is being actively held down. Let go of the switch, and the disposer stops. Each appliance has a power rating between one-third and one HP (horsepower). More powerful models bog down less under load and the motors last longer because they don't have to work as hard. They are also costlier.

Disposers are hardwired to a switch mounted in an electrical box in the wall above the countertop. If your kitchen is not equipped for this, consult a wiring guide or hire an electrician. The actual electrical hookup of the appliance is quite simple (you only have to join two wires) but hire an electrician if you are not comfortable with the job.

Tools & Materials ▸

Screwdriver	Putty knife
Channel-type pliers	Mineral spirits
Spud wrench (optional)	Plumber's putty
Hammer	Wire caps
Hacksaw or tubing cutter	Hose clamps
Kitchen drain supplies	Threaded Y-fitting
Drain auger	Electrical tape

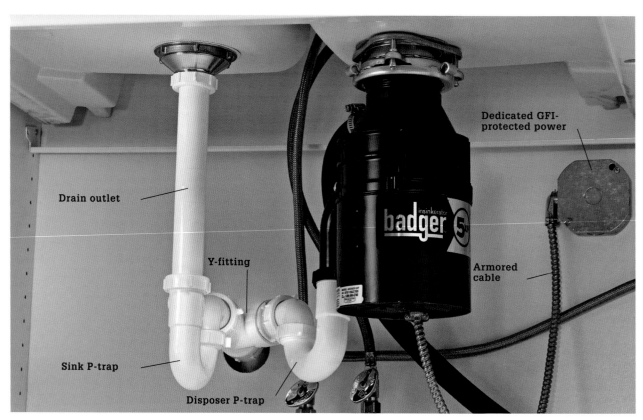

A properly functioning food disposer that's used correctly can actually help reduce clogs by ensuring that large bits of organic matter don't get into the drain system by accident. Many plumbers suggest using separate P-traps for the disposer and the drain outlet tube as shown here.

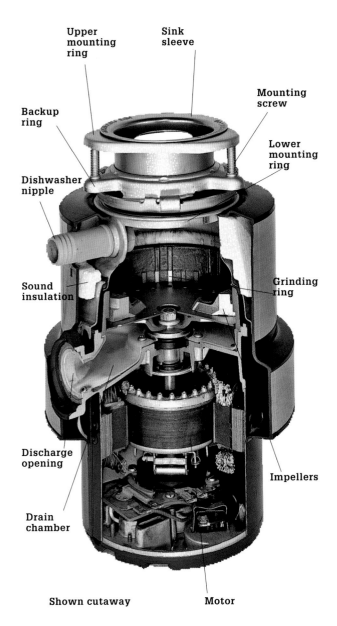

Upper mounting ring

Sink sleeve

Mounting screw

Backup ring

Lower mounting ring

Dishwasher nipple

Sound insulation

Grinding ring

Discharge opening

Drain chamber

Impellers

Shown cutaway

Motor

A food disposer grinds food waste so it can be flushed away through the sink drain system. A quality disposer has a ½–horsepower, self-reversing motor that will not jam. Other features to look for include foam sound insulation, a grinding ring, and overload protection that allows the motor to be reset if it overheats. Better food disposers have a 5-year manufacturer's warranty.

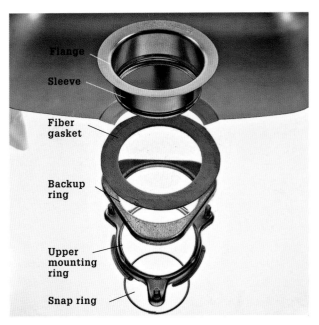

Flange

Sleeve

Fiber gasket

Backup ring

Upper mounting ring

Snap ring

The disposer is attached directly to the sink sleeve, which comes with the disposer and replaces the standard sink strainer. A snap ring fits into a groove around the sleeve of the strainer body to prevent the upper mounting ring and backup ring from sliding down while the upper mounting ring is tightened against the backup ring with mounting screws. A fiber gasket seals the connection from beneath the sink.

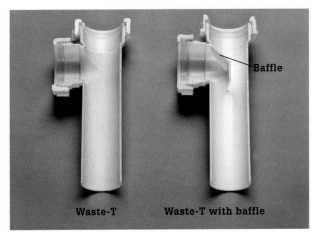

Baffle

Waste-T   **Waste-T with baffle**

Kitchen and drain tees are required to have a baffle if the tee is connected to a dishwasher or disposer. The baffle is intended to prevent discharge from finding its way up the drain and into the sink. However, the baffle also reduces the drain flow capacity by half, which can cause the dishwasher or disposer to back up. You cannot, by most codes, simply replace the tee with another that has no baffle. The safest way to get around the problem is to run separate drains and traps to a Y-fitting at the trap arm (as shown on previous page).

How to Install a Food Disposer

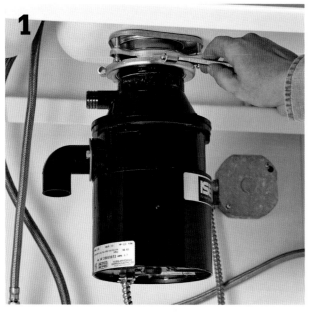

1

Remove the old disposer if you have one. You'll need to disconnect the drainpipes and traps first. If your old disposer has a special wrench for the mounting lugs, use it to loosen the lugs. Otherwise, use a screwdriver. If you do not have a helper, place a solid object directly beneath the disposer to support it before you begin removal. *Important:* Shut off the electrical power at the main service panel before you begin removal. Disconnect the wire leads, cap them, and stuff them into the electrical box.

Tip ▶

Alternate: If you are installing a disposer in a sink that did not previously have one, remove the old sink strainer and drain tailpiece. Scrape up any old plumber's putty and clean the sink thoroughly around the drain opening with mineral spirits.

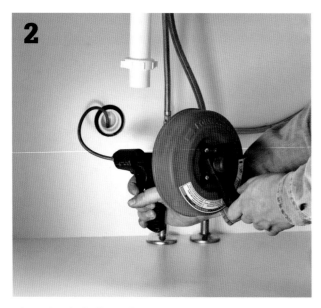

2

Clear the drain lines all the way to the branch drain before you begin the new installation. Remove the trap and the trap arm first.

3

Upper mounting ring

Lower mounting ring

Snap ring

Disassemble the mounting assembly and then separate the upper and lower mounting rings and the backup ring. Also remove the snap ring from the sink sleeve. See photo, page 173.

4

Press the flange of the sink sleeve for your new disposer into a thin coil of plumber's putty that you have laid around the perimeter of the drain opening. The sleeve should be well-seated in the coil.

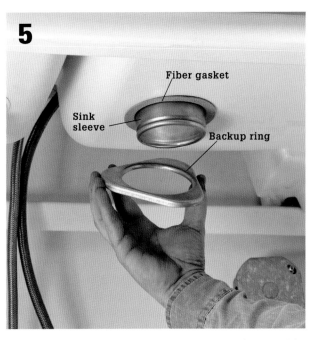

5

Slip the fiber gasket and then the backup ring onto the sink sleeve, working from inside the sink base cabinet. Make sure the backup ring is oriented the same way it was before you disassembled the mounting assembly.

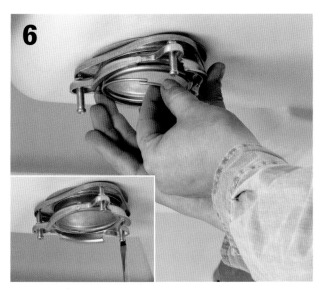

6

Insert the upper mounting ring onto the sleeve with the slotted ends of the screws facing away from the backup ring so you can access them. Then, holding all three parts at the top of the sleeve, slide the snap ring onto the sleeve until it snaps into the groove. Tighten the three mounting screws on the upper mounting ring until the tips press firmly against the backup ring (inset photo). It is the tension created by these screws that keeps the disposer steady and minimizes vibrating.

7

Make electrical connections before you mount the disposer unit on the mounting assembly. Shut off the power at the service panel if you have turned it back on. Remove the access plate from the disposer. Attach the white and black feeder wires from the electrical box to the white and black wires (respectively) inside the disposer. Twist a small wire cap onto each connection and wrap it with electrical tape for good measure. Also attach the green ground wire from the box to the grounding terminal on your disposer.

(continued)

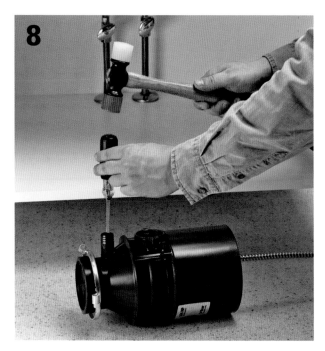

Knock out the plug in the disposer port if you will be connecting your dishwasher to the disposer. If you have no dishwasher, leave the plug in. Insert a large flathead screwdriver into the port opening and rap it with a mallet. Retrieve the knock plug from inside the disposer canister.

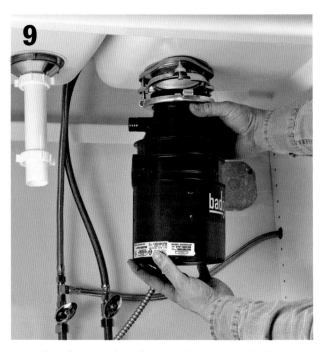

Hang the disposer from the mounting ring attached to the sink sleeve. To hang it, simply lift it up and position the unit so the three mounting ears are underneath the three mounting screws and then spin the unit so all three ears fit into the mounting assembly. Wait until after the plumbing hookups have been made to lock the unit in place.

Attach the discharge tube to the disposer according to the manufacturer's instructions. It is important to get a very good seal here, or the disposer will leak. Go ahead and spin the disposer if it helps you access the discharge port.

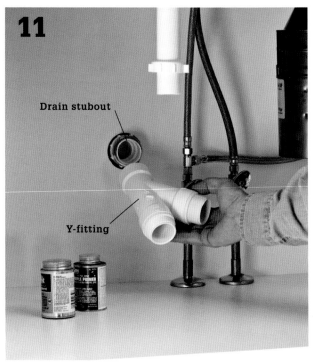

Attach a Y-fitting at the drain stubout. The Y-fitting should be sized to accept a drain line from the disposer and another from the sink. Adjust the sink drain plumbing as needed to get from the sink P-trap to one opening of the Y.

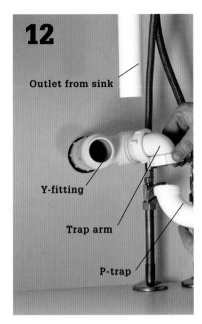

12

Outlet from sink

Y-fitting

Trap arm

P-trap

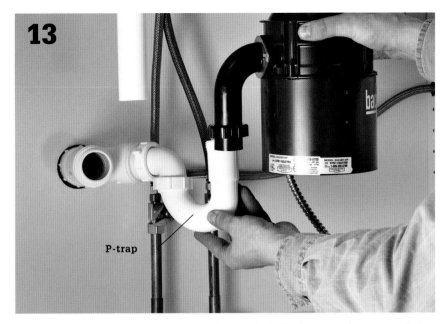

13

P-trap

Install a trap arm for the disposer in the open port of the Y-fitting at the wall stubout. Then, attach a P-trap or a combination of a tube extension and a P-trap so the low end of the trap will align with the bottom of the disposer discharge tube.

Spin the disposer so the end of the discharge tube is lined up over the open end of the P-trap, and confirm that they will fit together correctly. If the discharge tube extends down too far, mark a line on it at the top of the P-trap and cut through the line with a hacksaw. If the tube is too short, attach an extension with a slip joint. You may need to further shorten the discharge tube first to create enough room for the slip joint on the extension. Slide a slip nut and beveled compression washer onto the discharge tube and attach the tube to the P-trap.

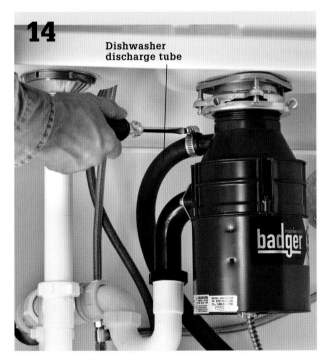

14

Dishwasher discharge tube

15

Connect the dishwasher discharge tube to the inlet port located at the top of the disposer unit. This may require a dishwasher hookup kit (see page 168).

Lock the disposer into position on the mounting ring assembly once you have tested it to make sure it is functioning correctly and without leaks. Lock it by turning one of the mounting lugs with a screwdriver until it makes contact with the locking notch.

Range Hood/Vent Fan

Range hoods are vent fans that are mounted directly over a slide-in range or a cooktop. Some are meant to be seen while others are designed to be hidden in a cabinet or soffit.

Effective ventilation is important for ridding your kitchen of cooking odors, excess moisture (think: mold), smoke, and exhaust fumes from gas burners. If you don't already have a good vent system in place, you should consider installing one to improve your indoor air quality. Recirculating vent fans—those without a duct running outside—also should be replaced, since all they really do is pretend to filter the air before blowing it right back into the kitchen.

The two main types of mechanical ventilation are overhead hoods and downdraft (or cooktop) fans. Overhead systems include the basic under-cabinet types and the higher-end suspended styles with exposed ducting extending from the ceiling. Overheads are more effective and require less suction than downdraft vents, primarily because they work with nature rather than against it: Hot air rises, so all that steam, grease, and fragrant cooking air is easy to capture inside a hood for transfer to the outdoors. Downdraft fans have to work much harder

in reversing the natural flow of air and vapor. Also, many downdraft systems tend to draw heat away from burners (especially gas burners), so your pans don't heat as evenly when the fan is on.

Sizing is important with hood systems. The hood should be at least as wide as, but preferably up to 6" wider than, the cooktop and at least 20" deep. The power, or capacity, of the fan is another critical factor. Expert recommendations vary. Some say a standard hood fan should move 40 cfm (cubic feet per minute) for every 12" of cooktop width; for example, a 30"-wide cooktop gets a 100 cfm fan, which is the minimum required under many building codes. The National Kitchen & Bath Association recommends 150 cfm as a minimum for hood fans.

The manufacturer of your range or cooktop may have its own recommendations. Undersizing a fan results in inadequate ventilation, but oversizing it could potentially lead to a dangerous backdrafting into the home.

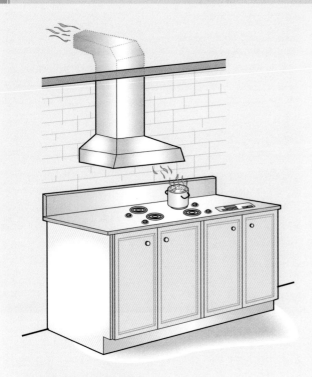

Overhead vent hoods are the best all-around performers.

Downdraft systems have no hood to capture rising exhaust and must pull the hot air down in order to evacuate it.

Windows are a low-tech option. They can introduce cross breezes but are less effective than fan systems at eliminating cooking exhaust.

How to Install a Range Hood

Install the vent duct in the wall first, then cut a hole in the back of the range hood cabinet and mount the cabinet over the duct. Cut a vent hole in the bottom of the cabinet to match the opening on the top of the hood.

Make sure the circuit power is turned off at the service panel, then join the power cable wires to the lead wires inside the range hood. Use wire connectors for this job.

Get someone to help lift the range hood into place and hold it there while you attach it. Drive two screws through both sides and into the adjacent cabinets. If the hood is slightly small for the opening, slip a shim between the hood and the walls, trying to keep the gaps even.

Run ductwork from the cabinet to the exhaust exit point. Use two 45° adjustable elbows to join the duct in the wall to the top of the range hood. Use sheet metal screws and duct tape to hold all parts together and keep them from moving.

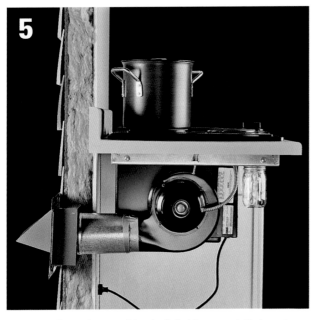

Downdraft cooktop: With a built-in blower unit that vents through the back or bottom of a base cabinet. A downdraft cooktop is a good choice for a kitchen island or peninsula.

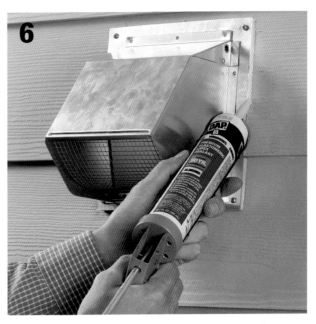

Wall vent: If the duct comes out through the sidewall of the house, install a vertical duct cap. Make sure to seal around the perimeter of the cap with exterior caulk.

Ceiling vent: If the duct goes through an overhang soffit, you'll need a transition fitting to connect the round duct to a short piece of rectangular duct. Once these parts are installed, add a protective grille to keep animals and insects from getting into the duct.

Roof vent: For ducts that pass through the roof, cut an access hole through the roofing and sheathing, then install a weatherproof cap on top of the duct and under the roofing shingles. Make a waterproof seal by caulking the cap with plastic roof cement.

Drop-in Sink

Most drop-in, self-rimming kitchen sinks are easy to install. Drop-in sinks for do-it-yourself installation are made from cast iron coated with enamel, stainless steel, enameled steel, acrylic, fiberglass, or resin composites. Because cast-iron sinks are heavy, their weight holds them in place, and they require no mounting hardware.

Stainless steel and enameled-steel sinks weigh less than cast-iron, and most require mounting brackets on the underside of the countertop. Some acrylic and resin sinks rely on silicone caulk to hold them in place. If you are replacing a sink, but not the countertop, make sure the new sink is the same size or larger than the old sink. All old silicone caulk residue must be removed with acetone or denatured alcohol, or the new caulk will not stick.

Tools & Materials ▸

Caulk gun	Plumber's putty or silicone caulk
Spud wrench	Mounting clips
Screwdriver	Jigsaw
Sink	Pen or pencil
Sink frame	Wrench

Shopping Tips ▸

- When purchasing a sink, you also need to buy strainer bodies and baskets, sink clips, and a drain trap kit.
- Look for basin dividers that are lower than the sink rim—this reduces splashing.
- Drain holes in the back or to the side make for more usable space under the sink.
- When choosing a sink, make sure the predrilled openings will fit your faucet.

Drop-in sinks, also known as self-rimming sinks, have a wide sink flange that extends beyond the edges of the sink cutout. They have a wide back flange to which the faucet is mounted directly.

How to Install a Self-rimming Sink

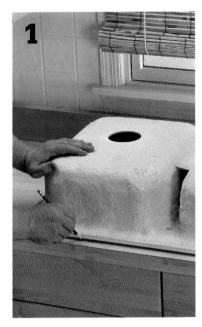

Invert the sink and trace around the edges as a reference for making the sink cutout cutting lines, which should be parallel to the outlines, but about 1" inside of them to create a 1" ledge. If the sink comes with a template for the cutout, use it.

Drill a starter hole and cut out the sink opening with a jigsaw. Cut right up to the line. Because the sink flange fits over the edges of the cutout, the opening doesn't need to be perfect, but, as always, you should try to do a nice, neat job.

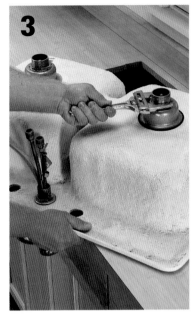

Attach as much of the plumbing as makes sense to install prior to setting the sink into the opening. Having access to the underside of the flange is a great help when it comes to attaching the faucet body, sprayer, and strainer, in particular.

Apply a bead of silicone caulk around the edges of the sink opening. The sink flange most likely is not flat, so apply the caulk in the area that will make contact with the flange.

Place the sink in the opening. Try to get the sink centered right away so you don't need to move it around and disturb the caulk, which can break the seal. If you are installing a heavy cast-iron sink, it's best to leave the strainers off so you can grab onto the sink at the drain openings.

For sinks with mounting clips, tighten the clips from below using a screwdriver or wrench (depending on the type of clip your sink has). There should be at least three clips on every side. Don't overtighten the clips—this can cause the sink flange to flatten or become warped.

Undermount Sink

Undermounted sinks have become quite popular in contemporary kitchens for reasons that are both practical and aesthetic. On the aesthetic side, they look updated and sleek. Practically, they are easier to clean than rimmed sinks because you eliminate that area around the rim seal where stuff always collects.

Most sink manufacturers make sinks that are designed for undermounting, and if you don't mind paying the $100 to $200 premium, a true undermount sink is the best choice. But if your decision-making is driven more by your frugal side, you can undermount a self-rimming (drop-in) stainless steel sink with little difficulty using readily available undermount clips. (Self-rimmers also come in a much wider range of styles). *Note: You can undermount any sink you wish, including heavy cast-iron models, if you support the sink from below instead of hanging it from clips.* Not all countertops are suitable for undermounting a sink. The countertop material needs to be contiguous in nature. That is, the edges that are created when you cut through it need to be of the same material as the surface. Solid-surface, granite, butcher block, and concrete are good candidates for undermounting. Post-form and any laminated or tiled countertops are not. (Some new products that claim to seal countertop substrate edges around a sink opening are emerging, but are not yet proven or readily available). If you are not able to locate solid-surface seam adhesive or undermount clips, you can use the same installation method for undermounting that is shown in the apron sink mounting project on pages 190 to 195 instead.

Tools & Materials ▸

2HP or larger plunge router	Belt sander
½" template following router bit	Solid-surface scraps
Roundover bit	Solid-surface seam adhesive with applicator gun
MDF or particleboard for template	Denatured alcohol
Jigsaw	Undermount clips
Drill and bits	Silicone caulk
Abrasive pads	Pipe clamps
Laminate trimmer	Pad sander

Before

After

Undermounted sinks have a sleek appearance and make cleanup easy, but they are only a good idea in countertops that have a solid construction, such as solid-surfacing, stone, quartz, or butcher block. Laminate and tile countertops are not compatible with undermount sinks.

Amateurs & Solid-surface ▸

Solid-surface countertop material is generally installed only by certified installers. But a simple job like mounting a non-solid-surface undermount sink can be done by a skilled amateur if you have access to adhesive and an applicator gun (without these, you can still mount a sink using the apron sink method shown on pages 192 to 195).

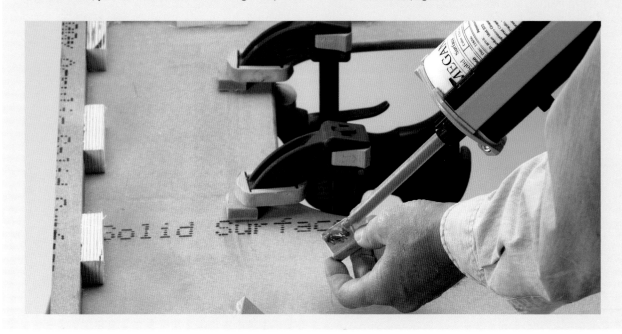

How to Make a Sink Cutout Template

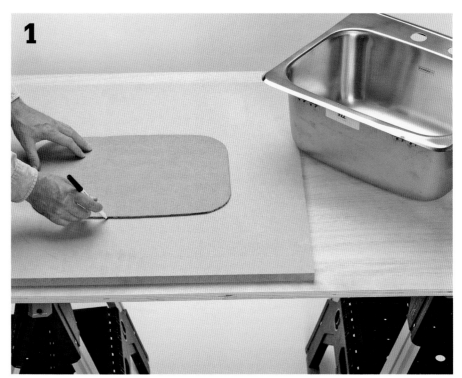

1

If you are undermounting a self-rimming sink, do not use the sink template provided by the manufacturer. Instead, make your own custom router template to use with a router and pattern-following bit. The template should be sized and shaped so the cutout you make with your pattern-following bit is the same shape and about ⅛" larger than the basin opening in each direction. You can plot the cutout directly onto a piece of MDF, or make a preliminary paper or cardboard template and trace it onto the MDF.

(continued)

2

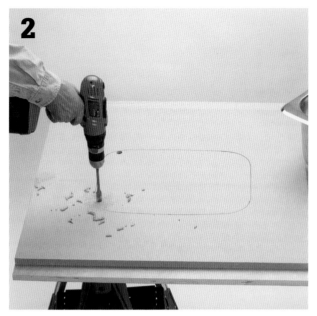

Drill a few starter holes just inside the template outline to create access for your jigsaw blade. If the cutout has sharp radii at the corners, look for a bit or hole-cutter of the same radius and carefully drill out the corners.

3

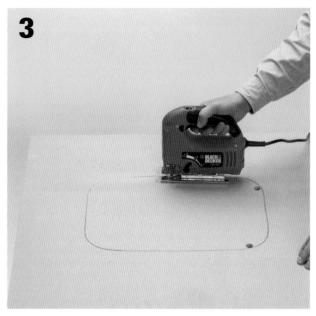

Connect the starter holes by cutting just inside the cutout line with a jigsaw. You can use a straightedge cutting guide for straight runs if you have little confidence in your ability to cut straight.

4

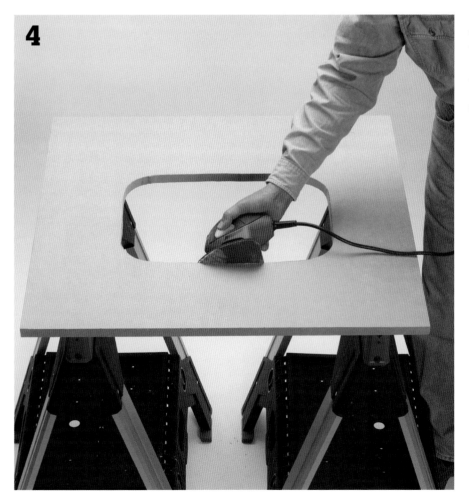

Use a belt sander or pad sander to smooth out the cutting lines and to remove material until the cutout hits the lines precisely. A drum sander attachment mounted in a power drill is useful for smoothing out rounded corners.

How to Undermount a Sink

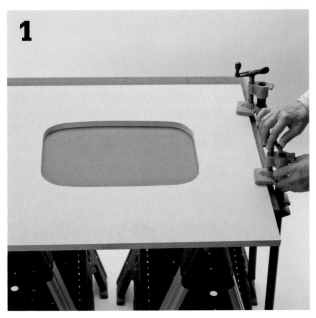

Remove the countertop from the cabinet and transport it to a work area with good light and ventilation. Set the countertop section on sawhorses and then clamp the router template (see previous page) securely so the opening is centered exactly over the planned cutout area. Make sure the router bit won't be cutting into your work area.

Use a two-fluted, ⅛" pattern-following bit (preferably carbide tipped) with a ½" shank into a plunge router with a minimum motor size of 2HP. Retract the bit and position the router so the bit is an inch or so away from the edge of the template. Turn the router on and let it develop to full velocity. Then, plunge the router bit into the countertop material until the bit breaks all the way through.

Pull the router bit toward the template edge until the bit sleeve contacts the edge, then slowly cut through the countertop, following the template. Pace is important here: Cutting too fast will cause chatter, cutting too slowly will cause burning or melting. Cut three continuous sides of the opening, hugging the template edge.

(continued)

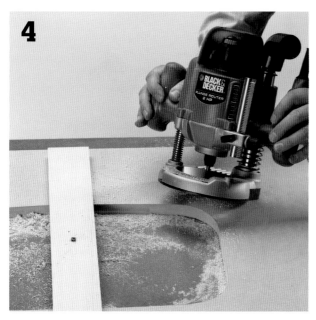

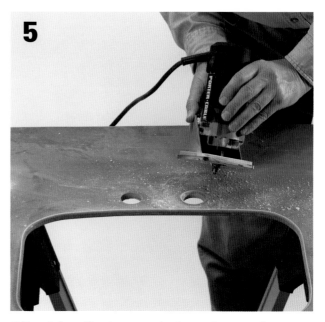

After routing three sides of the opening, stop routing and screw a support board to the waste piece. The ends of the support board should extend onto the template. Position the support so it is near the center, but not in the way for completing the fourth side of the cut. Finish the cut. The support board will prevent the waste from breaking off as the cut nears completion.

If the sink outline has any chatter or the cutout is not perfectly smooth, make another pass with a straight bit before you remove the template. Remove the template and make a 1/8" roundover cut on both the top and bottom of the sink cutout. If you know exactly where your faucet hole or holes need to be, cut them with a hole saw and round over their tops and bottoms as well.

Mount the sink on the countertop before you reinstall it on the cabinet. Cut several 1 × 1" mounting blocks from the solid-surface waste cutout. You'll also need to purchase some seam adhesive to glue the mounting blocks to the underside of the countertop. After they're cut, break all the block edges with a stationary sander or by clamping a belt sander belt-side up and using it as a stationary sander (breaking the edges reduces the chance that the blocks will crack).

7

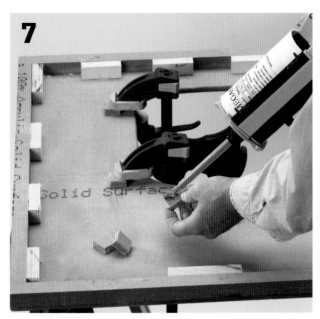

Clean the blocks and the underside of the solid-surface around the cutouts with denatured alcohol. Apply solid-surface seam adhesive to the blocks and bond them to the underside of the countertop, set back ¾" from the cutout. Install three blocks along the long sides of the cutout and two on the front-to-back sides. Clamp the blocks while the adhesive sets up.

8

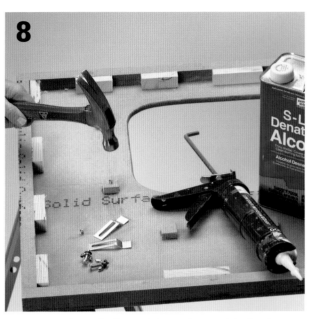

Drill pilot holes, ¼" **-dia × ¾" deep,** for the sink clips into each mounting block. The holes should be in the centers of the mounting blocks. Tap the brass inserts for the mounting clips into the holes in the mounting blocks.

9

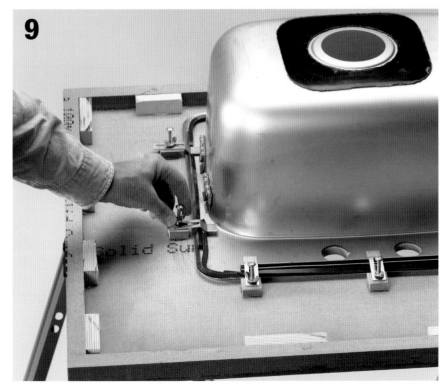

Clean the sink rim and the underside of the countertop with denatured alcohol. When the alcohol has dried, apply a bead of 100% silicone adhesive caulk to the sink rim. Carefully center the sink over the opening and press it in place. Hand-tighten the wing nuts onto the mounting nuts to secure the clips that hold the sink bowl. Replace the countertop and hook up the faucet and drain. For information on installing a kitchen faucet see pages 196 to 199.

Apron Sink

Despite their vintage look, apron sinks are relative newcomers in modern kitchen design. Also known as farmer's sinks or farmhouse sinks, they are notable for having an exposed front apron that usually projects past the cabinets. Although they can be double-bowl fixtures, most apron sinks are single bowl, and most are made from fireclay (a durable enameled porcelain). Other materials sometimes used for apron sinks include enameled cast iron, copper, stainless steel, and composite. The model seen here, made by Kohler (see Resources, page 282), is a fireclay sink.

Apron sinks typically are not suspended from above as other undermount sinks are: they're just too heavy. Instead, you either attach wood ledgers to the cabinet sides to support a board that bears the sink from below, or you build a support platform that rests on the floor. Either way, the sink is not actually connected to the countertop except with caulk at the seams. As kitchen sinks go, apron sinks are definitely on the high-end side, with most models costing over $1,000. But they create a focal point that makes them rather unique. Plus, they have a warm, comforting appearance that people who own them find appealing.

Tools & Materials ▸

Countertop material	Wood finish
Shims	Brush
Carpenter's square	Framing lumber
Straightedge	Sheet stock
Jigsaw	Caulk gun
Belt sander	Silicone adhesive
Pad sander	Strainer
Spindle sander	Drain tailpiece
Router or laminate trimmer	¾" plywood or MDF
Drill/driver	

Apron sinks, also called farmer's sinks or farmhouse sinks, can be nestled into a tiled countertop (called a tile-in) or pressed up against the underside of a solid countertop. Either way, they can be gorgeous.

Because they are usually mounted underneath the countertop, apron sinks tend to be fairly shallow (otherwise, most people would strain their backs doing dishes in them). Make sure you know the exact dimensions of your sink before ordering countertops or planning your sink installation.

Sink support for apron sinks comes from below. A typical strategy is to build a U-shaped ledger that's mounted to the walls of neighboring cabinets or supported with a post structure from below. If you're attaching the ledgers to cabinet walls, it may be necessary to reinforce them.

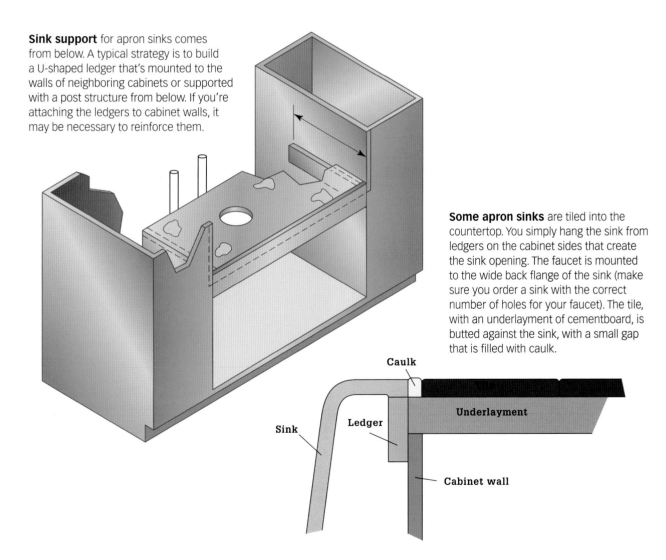

Some apron sinks are tiled into the countertop. You simply hang the sink from ledgers on the cabinet sides that create the sink opening. The faucet is mounted to the wide back flange of the sink (make sure you order a sink with the correct number of holes for your faucet). The tile, with an underlayment of cementboard, is butted against the sink, with a small gap that is filled with caulk.

Caulk

Underlayment

Sink

Ledger

Cabinet wall

How to Install an Apron Sink in a Butcher Block Countertop

If you are undermounting the sink, outline the sink opening in your countertop material. Plan the opening to create an equal reveal of approximatel ½" on all three sides (which basically means making the opening 1" smaller than the overall sink dimensions). For the 22 × 25" sink seen here, the opening cut into the butcher block is 24" wide and 21" deep (½" reveal in the back plus ½" projection of the sink in front).

Mount a downstroke blade in a jigsaw (see pages 98 to 101 and be sure to read the material on working with butcher block if that is your countertop surface). Cut out the waste to form the sink opening, cutting just inside the cutting lines. Support the waste wood from below so it does not break out prematurely.

Sand up to the cutting lines with a belt sander after the waste is removed. The goal is to create a smooth, even edge.

Sand into the corners of the cutout with a detail sander or, if you own one, a spindle sander (you can mount a small-diameter sanding drum in an electric drill, but be sure to practice first on some scrap wood).

Flip the countertop and sand the cutout along the bottom edges of the opening to prevent any splintering.

Round over the top edges of the cutout with a piloted roundover bit mounted in a small router or a laminate trimmer.

Apply several coats of urethane varnish to the exposed wood around the opening. This wood will have a high level of water exposure, so take care to get a good, even coat. Where possible, match the finish of the countertop (if any).

Measure and draw layout lines for a wood support frame to be attached to the adjoining cabinet walls. Attach the frame members (2 × 4) to the cabinet sides first and then face-screw through the front frame member and into the ends of side members.

(continued)

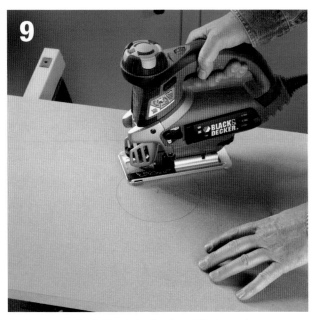

Cut a support platform to size from ¾" plywood or MDF, then layout and cut a drain clearance hole (if your drain will include a garbage disposer, make the hole large enough to accommodate the disposer easily). Also cut holes for the water supply lines if they come up through the floor and there is not enough room between the platform and the wall for the lines to fit.

Remove the countertop section containing the sink cutout, if feasible (if you can't remove the countertop, see sidebar next page). Then, screw the platform to the frame.

Set the sink on the platform and confirm that it is level with the cabinet tops by setting a straightedge so it spans the sink opening. If necessary, shim under the sink to bring it to level (if the sink is too high you'll need to reposition the frame members).

Apply silicone adhesive to the sink rim and then carefully replace the countertop section before the silicone adhesive sets up. Reattach the countertop.

Hook up the drain plumbing and install the faucet. If you are drilling through the countertop material to install a faucet, make sure your installation hole or holes align with the preformed holes in the back flange of the sink.

Option for Unremovable Countertops ▸

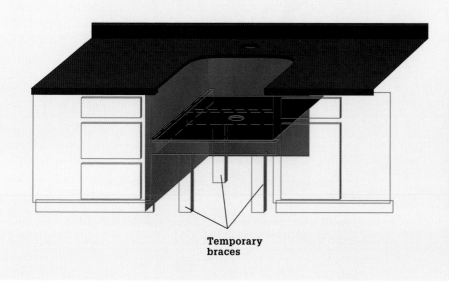

Temporary braces

If you are not able to remove the countertop, you'll need to raise the sink up against the underside of the countertop once you've caulked the rim. Create a 3-piece 2 × 4 frame and platform (as seen in Step 8) but do not attach it to the cabinets. Instead, support the platform with braces. With help, set the sink on the platform and raise it from below after the silicone adhesive has been applied to the sink rim. When the sink rim is tight against the countertop, attach the frame members to the cabinet sides with screws.

Kitchen Faucets

Most new kitchen faucets feature single-handle control levers and washerless designs that rarely require maintenance. Additional features include brushed metallic finishes, detachable spray nozzles, or even push-button controls.

Connect the faucet to hot and cold water lines with easy-to-install flexible supply tubes made from vinyl or braided steel. If your faucet has a separate sprayer, install the sprayer first. Pull the sprayer hose through the sink opening and attach it to the faucet body before installing the faucet.

Where local codes allow, use plastic tubes for drain hookups. A wide selection of extensions and angle fittings lets you easily plumb any sink configuration. Manufacturers offer kits that contain all the fittings needed for attaching a food disposer or dishwasher to the sink drain system.

Tools & Materials ▸

Adjustable wrench	Scouring pad
Basin wrench or channel-type pliers	Scouring cleaner
	Plumber's putty
Hacksaw	Flexible vinyl or braided steel supply tubes
Faucet	
Putty knife	Drain components
Screwdriver	Penetrating oil
Silicone caulk	

Modern kitchen faucets tend to be single-handle models, often with useful features such as a pull-out head that functions as a sprayer. This Price Pfister™ model comes with an optional mounting plate that conceals sink holes when mounted on a predrilled sink flange.

How to Install a Kitchen Sink Faucet

Shut off the hot and cold water at the faucet stop valves. Assemble the parts of the deck plate that cover the outer mounting holes in your sink deck (unless you are installing a two-handle faucet or mounting the faucet directly to the countertop, as in an undermount sink situation). Add a ring of plumber's putty in the groove on the underside of the base plate.

Set the base plate onto the sink flange so it is correctly aligned with the predrilled holes in the flange. From below, tighten the wing nuts that secure the deck plate to the sink deck.

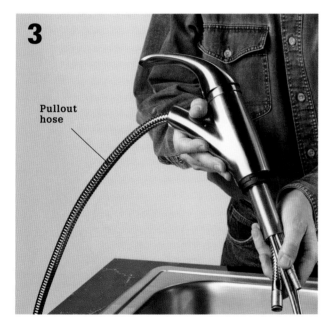

Pullout hose

Retract the pullout hose by drawing it out through the faucet body until the fitting at the end of the hose is flush with the bottom of the threaded faucet shank. Insert the shank and the supply tubes down through the top of the deck plate.

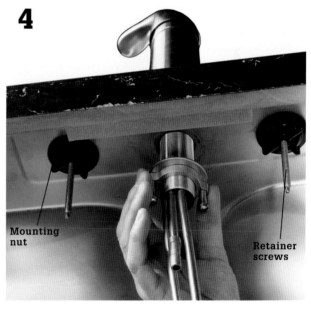

Mounting nut

Retainer screws

Slip the mounting nut and washer over the free ends of the supply tubes and pullout hose, then thread the nut onto the threaded faucet shank. Hand tighten. Tighten the retainer screws with a screwdriver to secure the faucet.

(continued)

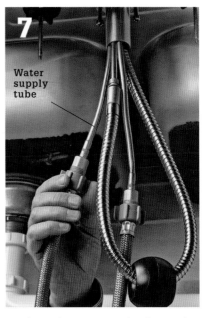

Slide the hose weight onto the pullout hose (the weight helps keep the hose from tangling, and it makes it easier to retract).

Connect the end of the pullout tube to the outlet port on the faucet body using a quick connector fitting.

Hook up the water supply tubes to the faucet inlets. Make sure the lines are long enough to reach the supply risers without stretching or kinking.

Water supply tube

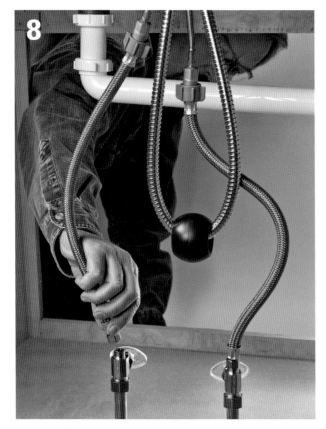

Connect the supply lines to the supply risers at the stop valves. Make sure to get the hot lines and cold lines attached correctly.

Attach the spray head to the end of the pullout hose and turn the fitting to secure the connection. Turn on the water supply and test. Tip: Remove the aerator in the tip of the spray head and run hot and cold water to flush out any debris.

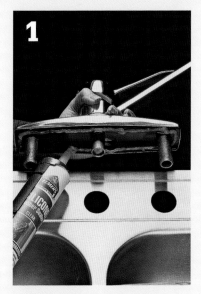

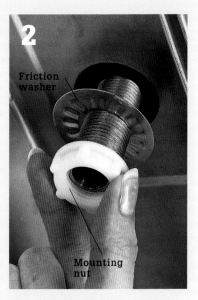

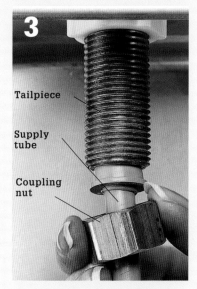

Apply a thick bead of silicone caulk to the underside of the faucet base and then insert the tailpieces of the faucet through the appropriate holes in the sink deck. Press down lightly on the faucet to set it in the caulk.

Slip a friction washer onto each tailpiece and then hand tighten a mounting nut. Tighten the mounting nut with channel-type pliers or a basin wrench. Wipe up any silicone squeeze-out on the sink deck with a wet rag before it sets up.

Connect the supply tubes to the faucet tailpieces. (Make sure the tubes you buy are long enough to reach the stop valves and that the coupling nuts will fit the tubes and tailpieces).

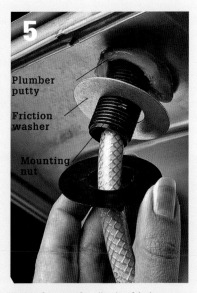

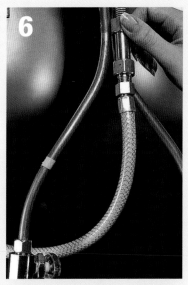

Apply a ¼" bead of plumber's putty or silicone caulk to the underside of the sprayer base. With the base threaded onto the sprayer hose, insert the tailpiece of the sprayer through the opening in the sink deck.

From beneath, slip the friction washer over the sprayer tailpiece and then screw the mounting nut onto the tailpiece. Tighten with channel-type pliers or a basin wrench. Wipe off any excess putty or caulk on the sink deck from around the base.

Screw the sprayer hose onto the hose nipple on the bottom of the faucet. Hand tighten and then give the nut one-quarter turn with channel-type pliers or a basin wrench. Turn on the water supply at the shutoff, remove the aerator, and flush debris from the faucet.

Kitchen Drains & Traps

Kitchen sink drains don't last forever, but on the plus side, they're very easy and inexpensive to replace. The most common models today are made of PVC plastic pipe and fittings held together with slip fittings. In addition to making the installation fairly forgiving, the slip fitting makes the drain easy to disassemble if you get a clog. The project shown here is a bit unusual by today's standards, because it does not include either a dishwasher drain or a garbage disposer. But you will see how to add each of these drain systems to your kitchen sink in the following chapters.

You can buy the parts for the kitchen drain individually (you can usually get better quality materials this way) or in a kit (see photo, next page). Because most kitchen sinks have two bowls, the kits include parts for plumbing both drains into a shared trap, often with a baffle in the T-fitting where the outlet line joins with the tailpiece from the other bowl. If you are installing a disposer, consider installing individual traps to eliminate the baffle, which reduces the flow capacity by half.

Tools & Materials ▸

Flat screwdriver
Spud wrench
Trap arm
Mineral spirits
Cloth
Strainer kit

Plumber's putty
Teflon tape
Washers
Waste-T fitting
S- or P-trap

Kitchen sink drains include a strainer basket (A), tailpiece (B), continuous waste T (C), P- or S-trap (D), outlet drain lines (E), trap arm (F), and wall stubout (G).

Drain Kits ▸

Kits for installing a new sink drain include all the pipes, slip fittings, and washers you'll need to get from the sink tailpieces (most kits are equipped for a double bowl kitchen sink) to the trap arm that enters the wall or floor.

For wall trap arms, you'll need a kit with a P-trap. For floor drains, you'll need an S-trap. Both drains normally are plumbed to share a trap. Chromed brass or PVC with slip fittings let you adjust the drain more easily and pull it apart and then reassemble if there is a clog. Kitchen sink drains and traps should be 1½" O.D. pipe—the 1¼" pipe is for lavatories and doesn't have enough capacity for a kitchen sink.

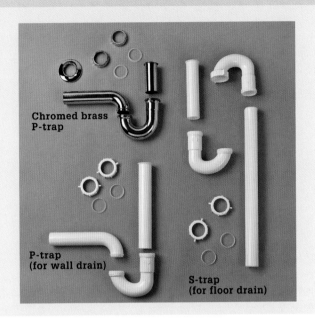

Chromed brass P-trap

P-trap (for wall drain)

S-trap (for floor drain)

Tips for Choosing Drains ▸

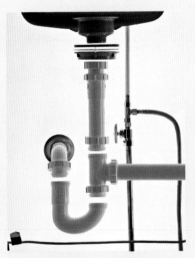

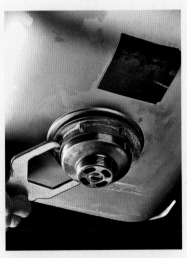

Wall thickness varies in sink drain pipes. The thinner plastic material is cheaper, but it is more difficult to obtain a good seal than with the thicker, more expensive tubing. The thin product is best reserved for lavatory drains, which are far less demanding.

Slip joints are formed by tightening a male-threaded slip nut over a female-threaded fitting, trapping and compressing a beveled nylon washer to seal the joint.

Use a spud wrench to tighten the strainer body against the underside of the sink bowl. Normally, the strainer flange has a layer of plumber's putty just above the sink drain and a pair of washers (one rubber, one fibrous) to seal below.

How to Hook Up a Kitchen Sink Drain

If you are replacing the sink strainer body, remove the old one and clean the top and bottom of the sink deck around the drain opening with mineral spirits. Attach the drain tailpiece to the threaded outlet of the strainer body, inserting a non-beveled washer between the parts if your strainer kits include them. Lubricate the threads or apply Teflon tape so you can get a good, snug fit.

Apply plumber's putty around the perimeter of the drain opening and seat the strainer assembly into it. Add the washers below as directed and tighten the strainer locknut with a spud wrench (see photo, previous page) or by striking the mounting nubs at the top of the body with a flat screwdriver.

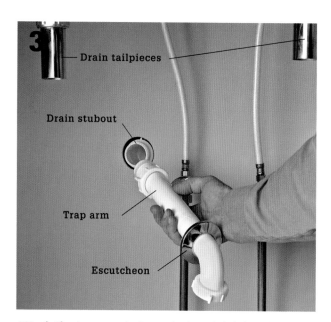

Drain tailpieces

Drain stubout

Trap arm

Escutcheon

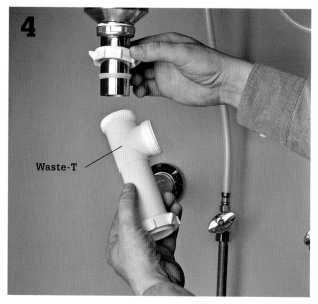

Waste-T

Attach the trap arm to the male-threaded drain stubout in the wall, using a slip nut and a beveled compression washer. The outlet for the trap arm should point downward. *Note: The trap arm must be higher on the wall than any of the horizontal lines in the set-up, including lines to dishwasher, disposer, or the outlet line to the second sink bowl.*

Attach a waste-T-fitting to the drain tailpiece, orienting the opening in the fitting side so it will accept the outlet drain line from the other sink bowl. If the Waste-T is higher than the top of the trap arm, remove it and trim the drain tailpiece.

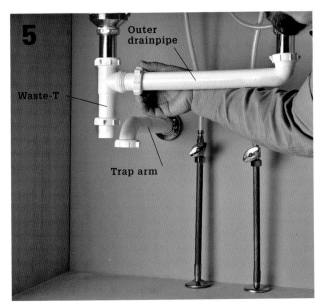

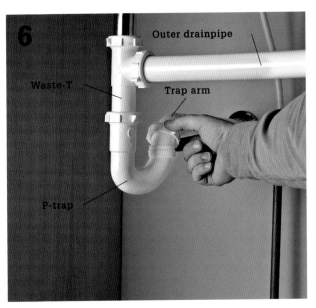

Joint the short end of the outlet drainpipe to the tailpiece for the other sink bowl and then attach the end of the long run to the opening in the waste-T. The outlet tube should extend into the T ½" or so—make sure it does not extend in far enough to block water flow from above.

Attach the long leg of a P-trap to the waste-T and attach the shorter leg to the downward-facing opening of the trap arm. Adjust as necessary and test all joints to make sure they are still tight, and then test the system.

Variation: Drain in Floor ▶

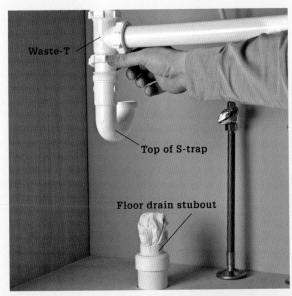

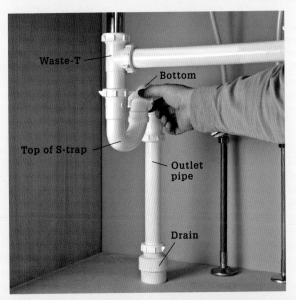

If your drain stubout comes up out of the floor instead of the wall, you'll need an S-trap to tie into it instead of a P-trap. Attach one-half of the S-trap to the threaded bottom of the waste-T.

Attach the other half of the S-trap to the stubout with a slip fitting. This should result in the new fitting facing downward. Join the halves of the S-trap together with a slip nut, trimming the unthreaded end if necessary.

Hot Water Dispenser

It's still easy to find a refrigerator without a cold water dispenser in its door, but you have to walk past a lot of product before you see one. This says something about people liking convenience. In many ways, a hot water dispenser is even more convenient than a cold water dispenser. There are boxes and boxes of beverages and food that need only a trickle of hot water to achieve their destiny: coffee, tea, hot chocolate, instant soup, hot cereals, and just plain old hot water and lemon to name a few. And there's no faster way to get this hot water than with a hot water dispenser. These units are designed to fit in the spare hole on many kitchen sink decks. But, if the sink doesn't have this hole, you can replace the spray hose with the dispenser. Or, if you want to keep the hose, just drill an extra hole in your sink or countertop to accommodate the dispenser faucet.

Note: Installing this appliance requires both plumbing and wiring work. If you are unsure of your skills in these areas, hire a professional. (Be sure to check your local codes before starting.)

Tools & Materials ▸

Power drill with ¾"-dia. bit
Utility knife
Wire stripper
Screwdrivers
Adjustable wrench
14/2 NM electrical cable
Flexible cable conduit
Duplex electrical box
Conduit box connector

Switched receptacle
Measuring tape
Wire connectors
Brass plug
Hot water dispenser kit
Cable connectors
15-amp circuit breaker
Tubing cutter

Switch Receptacle ▸

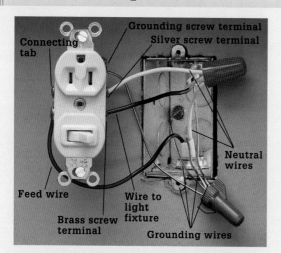

Three wires are connected to the switch/receptacle. One hot wire is the feed wire that brings power into the box. It is connected to the side of the switch that has a connecting tab. The other hot wire carries power out. It is connected to the brass screw terminal on the side that does not have a connecting tab. The white, neutral wire is pigtailed to the silver screw terminal. The grounding wires must be pigtailed to the switch/receptacle green grounding screw and to the grounded metal box.

On-demand hot water is not only convenient, it can help to conserve both energy and water.

How to Install a Hot Water Dispenser

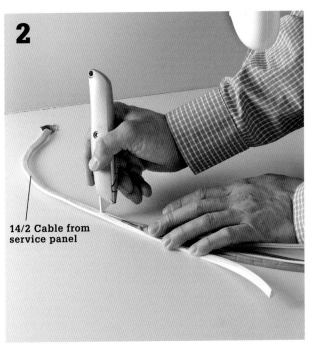

Drill an access hole for a new power cable (in flexible conduit) in the bottom of the sink compartment cabinet. Use a drill and a ¾"-dia. bit. Go into the basement and drill a hole up through the flooring that will align with the first hole or make other arrangements to run circuit wire.

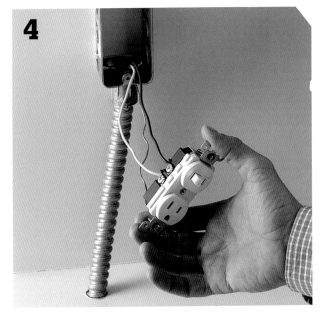

14/2 Cable from service panel

Fish a 14/2 or 12/2 cable from the electric service panel up through the hole in the floor. Strip the sheathing from the cable with a utility knife. Also strip the insulation from the wires with a wire stripper. Do not nick the wire insulation.

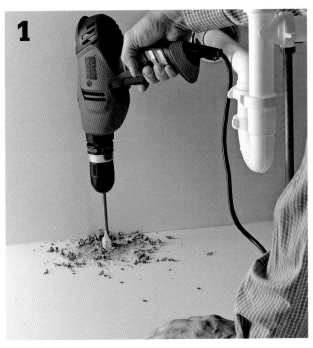

Slide a piece of flexible conduit over the wires, so the wires are protected from the point where they leave the cabinet floor to where they enter the electrical box. Attach the conduit to the box with a box connector so at least 8" of wire reaches into the box.

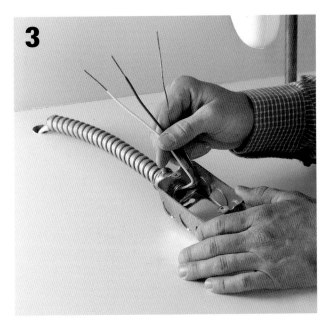

Install a switched receptacle. Mount a duplex metal box on the cabinet wall. Connect the black power wire to the brass screw on the switch. Attach the white neutral wire to the silver screw on the receptacle. Attach the ground wire to the receptacle ground terminal.

(continued)

Tie into the water supply. Water for the dispenser comes from the cold water supply line under the kitchen sink. Mount a tee on this pipe, below its shutoff valve, by alternately tightening the tee bolts on both sides with a wrench.

Determine the best place for the dispenser heater, usually on the back cabinet wall, so its pigtail plug will reach the switched receptacle. Screw its mounting bracket to the wall and hang the heater on this bracket.

To replace a spray hose with the dispenser faucet, remove the nut that holds the sprayer to the sink. Then remove the end of the hose from its port on the bottom of the faucet using an adjustable wrench. This will free the hose so it can be pulled out from above the sink. Plug the spray hose part on the faucet.

Squeeze the supply tubes of the dispenser faucet together so they can fit into the hole, and drop it in place. The unit is held securely by a washer and locking screw that is tightened from below the sink.

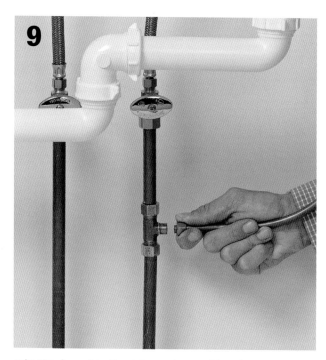

Join the faucet to the sink supply tee with a piece of flexible tubing. Measure this piece, make the cut with a tubing cutter, and install compression nuts and ferrules on both ends. Slide one end of the tubing into the valve and tighten the nut with a wrench.

Attach the two copper water tubes to the heater with compression fittings. Tighten them with a wrench. On the model seen here, the heater unit has three tubes. One supplies cold water to the heater, one supplies hot water to the faucet, and a third clear plastic hose acts as a vent and is attached to an expansion tank within the heater.

Slide the end of the plastic vent tube onto the nipple on top of the tank and attach it according to the manufacturer's instructions. On some models a spring clip is used for this job; other models require a hose clamp.

Install the heater power supply cable in the service panel. Begin by turning off the main power breaker. Then, remove the outside door panel and remove one of the knockout plates from the top or side of the box. Install a cable clamp inside this hole, push the cable through the clamp, and tighten the clamp to secure the cable.

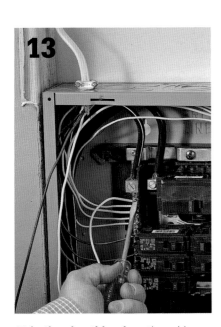

Strip the sheathing from the cable inside the panel and remove the insulation from the ends on the black and white cable wires. Loosen a lug screw on the neutral bus bar and push the white wire under the lug. Attach the ground wire to the grounding bus bar. Tighten both these screws securely.

Loosen the lug screw on a standard 15-amp breaker and put the end of the black (hot) cable wire under this lug. Tighten the lug with a screwdriver. Then install the breaker in the hot bus bar by pushing it into place.

Once a new breaker is installed, the service panel cover has to be modified to fit over it. Break out the protective plate that covers the breaker position with pliers. Screw the cover to the panel, and turn on the main breaker. Turn on the water supply to the dispenser and plug it into the receptacle. Turn on the receptacle switch, wait fifteen minutes, and check that the system is working properly.

Pot Filler

Kitchen design trends are moving ever closer to replicating commercial kitchens in the home. One example of this trend is the pot filler. A long-neck faucet that mounts on the wall behind the cooktop, a pot filler allows you to dispense water directly into large pots on the cooktop. This saves lugging pots of water from the sink to the stove.

Although horizontally mounted models are available, most pot fillers are attached to the wall. Almost all are designed for cold water only. Some have two valves, one at the wall and another at the end of the spout. Other models can be turned on with a foot pedal for safe, hands-free use. A pot filler will require code-approved supply pipe ½" in most cases) connected with a permanent union at another supply line or the main. The best time to run a new supply is during a remodel. But retrofitting a new supply line and mounting a pot filler is not too difficult as a standalone project. Using PEX supply pipe will make running the new supply line in finished walls easier.

A pot filler is a cold-water tap that you install above your cooktop so you can add water to large stock pots without having to carry a full pot of water around the kitchen.

Tools & Materials ▶

Hack saw
PEX tools
PEX pipe

Pot filler
Protector plates
PEX fittings

Reciprocating saw
Wallboard tools
Pipe joint compound

Wallboard
patching materials

Plan the route for the new supply line. In most cases, you will enter the stud cavity of the wall and run a new line directly upward, past the backsplash height of the countertop (A). If the countertop backsplash is removable, avoid wallboard patching by installing the tubing behind the backsplash (B). You may also be able to run the supply line underneath the kitchen if there is an unfinished basement (C).

How to Install a Pot Filler

Shut off the water supply and locate the cold-water supply riser at the kitchen sink. Cut into the riser and install a T-fitting, or replace the existing shutoff valve on the riser with a multiple-outlet shutoff valve, with an outlet for the ½" supply pipe for the pot filler.

Plan the route for the new supply line beginning at the T-fitting and working toward the cooktop area. Determine the height of the new line and then snap chalklines from the sink to the cooktop. With the electrical power shut off, remove wall coverings 2" above and below the chalkline and at the location for the pot filler outlet. Make sure the location is high enough to clear your tallest stock pot.

Drill ¾" holes in the framing for the supply tubes. Install protector plates if the holes are within 1¼" of the stud edge. Run ½" PEX from the supply riser through the holes to the pot filler location (inset).

Attach the new PEX supply line to the T-fitting at the supply riser, installing an accessible shutoff valve on the new line.

At the cooktop, install the faucet union as specified by the manufacturer. Add blocking as needed. The pot filler installed here attaches to a drop-ear L-fitting mounted to the blocking. Apply pipe joint compound to the faucet inlet and thread it onto the L-fitting.

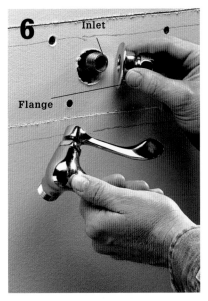

Cut and install the wallboard patch. Fit the flange over the inlet. Apply pipe joint compound to the threads of the faucet body. Assemble and adjust the faucet according to the manufacturer's instructions. Test the faucet before refinishing the wallboard.

Carbon Water Filter

Carbon-activated water filters are the most popular systems for home drinking water because they are inexpensive, easy to install, and they effectively improve the taste and odor of most municipal tap water. Most systems remove common contaminants, such as chlorine, lead, cysts, and particulates. Filters are readily available from home centers, hardware stores, and online through many manufacturers.

There are three main types of carbon filters: faucet-mounted, countertop, and under-counter. Faucet-mounted install directly to the kitchen faucet and have a simple diverter switch to provide filtered water directly from the tap. These are the easiest to use of the three systems, and they take up no counter or cabinet space. Countertop models also feed from the faucet spout but have a separate filter unit that sits on your countertop. Diverted water flows through the filter and out through a spout on the filter unit. Under-counter filters install under the sink and connect directly to the cold water supply piping.

A separate, countertop-mounted spout delivers the filtered water. When shopping for a filter system, compare ratings for contaminant reduction as well as flow rate and filter service life. Under-counter units typically offer the greatest service life per filter cartridge, followed by countertop models. Faucet-mounted filters typically offer considerably shorter service life before requiring a new cartridge. When comparing prices, be sure to calculate the long-term costs for cartridge replacement.

Tools & Materials ›

Adjustable wrench
Channel-type pliers
Drill and bits
Tubing cutter or utility knife

Screwdrivers
Teflon tape
Plumber's putty
Filter system

Faucet-mounted filters are the easiest to install. Remove the faucet aerator, then thread the filter unit onto the spout and hand-tighten. Slowly turn on the cold water tap, then check for leaking. If necessary, carefully tighten the collar using pliers. Flush the filter before use as recommended.

Countertop water filters also are easy to install. First, remove the faucet aerator. Then, thread the filter's diverter valve onto the spout using the appropriate adapter and gaskets. Place the filter unit and supply tubing in a convenient location. Test the system and check for leaks, carefully tightening the diverter with pliers if necessary. Flush the filter as recommended.

How to Install an Under-Counter Filter System

1

Shut off the cold water supply to the kitchen faucet at the fixture shutoff valve or the main house valve; drain the faucet. Remove the supply tubing from the faucet stud using a wrench. Wrap the stud with Teflon tape, then thread the filter's water supply fitting onto the stud and tighten carefully. Apply the tape and connect the supply tubing to the fitting.

2

Secure the mounting bracket to the filter unit, then mount the unit at a convenient location under the sink, following the manufacturer's directions. Be sure to leave plenty of room for removing the filter housing for filter replacement.

3

Remove the sprayer from the sink, if necessary, or cut a new hole through the countertop, following the countertop manufacturer's recommendations (some materials require a professional fabricator). Assemble the filter spout as directed, and then mount the spout into the sink hole, using plumber's putty as a sealant.

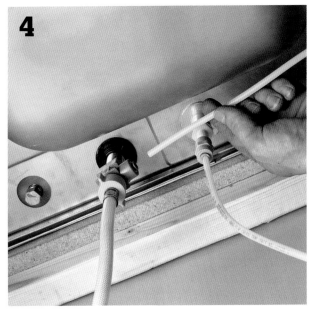

4

Cut lengths of tubing to run between the water supply, filter unit, and spout, making sure the cuts are square and the tubing ends are free of scratches, kinks, and rough spots. Connect the tubing at the push-in (or other) fittings. Test and flush the system as directed.

Reverse-Osmosis Filtration System

Not all water is created equal. Some water tastes better than other water. Some water looks better than other water. And some has more impurities, too. Because no one wants to drink bad water, the bottled water business has exploded over the past twenty years. Home filtration systems have also grown by leaps and bounds, in part because there are so many different types of filters available.

For example, sediment filters will remove rust, sand, and suspended minerals, like iron. A carbon filter can remove residual chlorine odors, some pesticides, and even radon gas. Distillation filters can remove bacteria and organic compounds, while a traditional water softener can neutralize hard water. Many of the most toxic impurities, heavy metals like mercury, lead, cadmium, and arsenic, are best removed with a reverse-osmosis (RO) system like the one shown here.

These filters are designed to treat cooking and drinking water. The system holds the treated water in a storage tank and delivers it to a sink-mounted faucet on demand. RO units feature multiple filter cartridges: in this case a pre-filter unit, followed by the RO membrane, followed by a carbon post-filter.

Tools & Materials ▸

Plastic gloves
Screwdrivers
Electric drill
Adjustable wrench

Teflon tape
Saddle valve
Rubber drain saddle

Reverse-osmosis filters can be highly effective for removing specific contaminants from drinking water. Because the filtration process wastes a lot of fresh water, it's a good idea to have your water professionally tested before investing in an RO system.

Point-of-use Filters ▸

Point-of-use water filtration systems typically are installed in the sink base cabinet, with a separate faucet from the main kitchen faucet. The setup shown here has an extra filter to supply a nearby refrigerator icemaker.

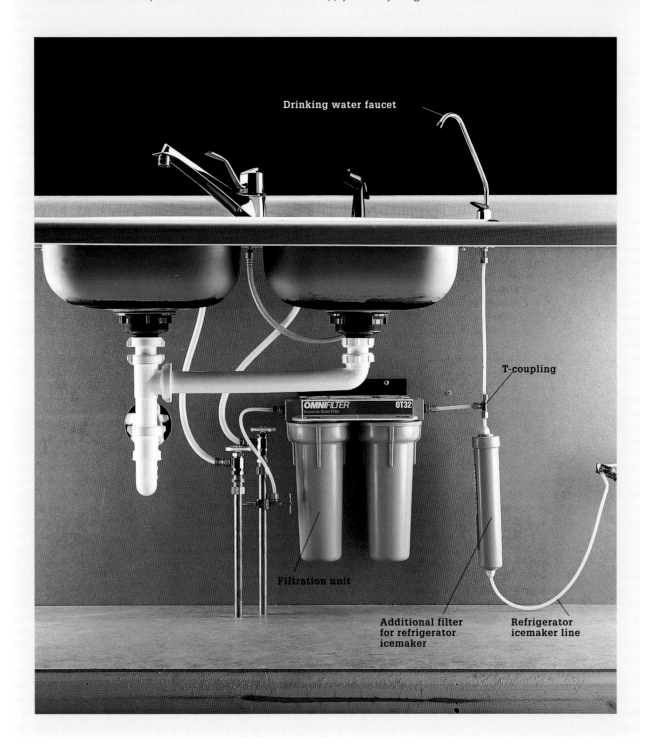

Drinking water faucet

T-coupling

Filtration unit

Additional filter
for refrigerator
icemaker

Refrigerator
icemaker line

How to Install a Reverse-osmosis Water Filter

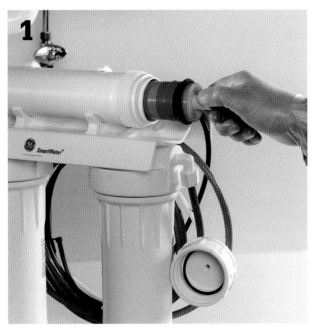

Remove the cartridge from the bag and install it in the filter unit (be sure to wear plastic gloves). The RO membrane filter is shipped in a separate bag that is filled with antibacterial fluid. Make sure to touch only the ends of the cartridge when you handle it or you can damage the membrane.

Establish the best location for the filter inside your kitchen sink cabinet, following manufacturer's instructions. Then drive mounting screws in the cabinet wall to support the unit.

Assemble the filtration system and then hang it on the cabinet wall. The best system layout may be to locate the filter on one wall and the storage tank on the opposite wall.

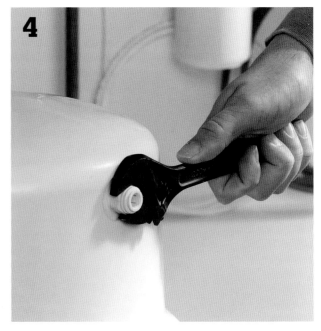

Wrap the threads of the valve a couple of times with Teflon tape and screw it into the tank. Finger-tighten it, then turn it one more turn with an adjustable wrench.

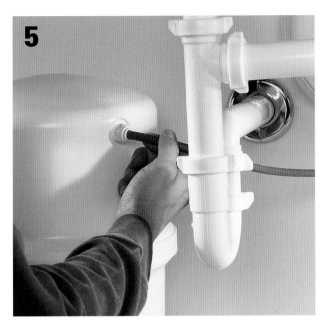

Connect the filter to the tank with plastic tubing. In most units, the joint between the two is made with a compression fitting. On this filter, the fitting is a push-type collar. Simply insert the hose into the collar until it will not go any farther.

Use a push-type compression fitting on the end of the tubing to connect the water storage tank and the faucet. To install it, push the end of the fitting over the bottom of the faucet shank until the fitting bottoms out.

Attach a plastic space (if provided) and jamb nut to the shank of the faucet. After the nut is finger tight, snug it securely with an adjustable wrench. This unit came with a C-shaped collar and jamb nut, but a round collar would need to have hoses threaded through it prior to mounting the faucet.

Remove the cover from an unused sink hole or remove the spray hose or bore a mounting hole in the sink or into the countertop. Once you have prepared a suitable hole for the faucet stem, insert it from above.

(continued)

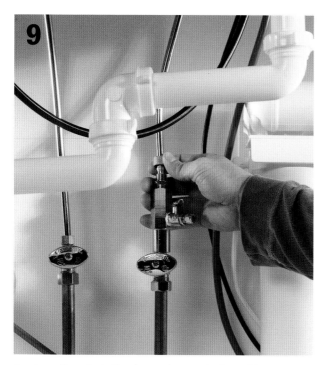

Replace the shutoff valve at the supply riser with a new valve containing an additional outlet for tubing. The water supply to the filter comes from the cold-water supply line that services the kitchen sink faucet.

Attach the filter supply tube to the port on the shutoff valve with a compression fitting. Push the end of the tubing onto the valve, then push the ferrule against the valve and thread the compression nut into place. Finger-tighten it, then turn it one more full turn with a wrench.

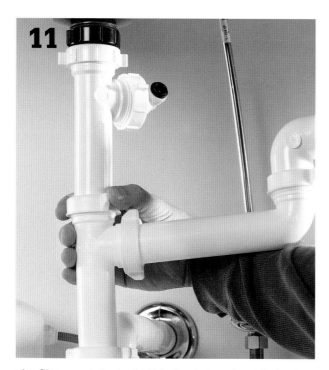

The filter must also be tied into the drain system. The best way to do this is to replace the drain tailpiece with a new fitting that contains an auxiliary port.

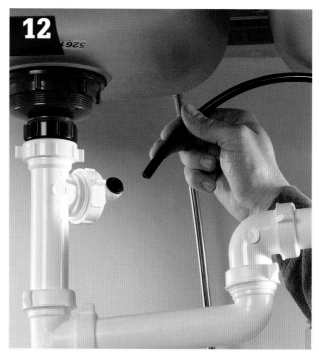

Attach the tubing from the drain to the auxiliary port on the tailpiece. Finish up by turning on the water and checking the system for leaks. Be sure to filter and drain at least two tanks of water to clean any contaminants from the system before drinking the water.

Installing a Whole-House Water Filtration System ▸

A whole-house water filtration system is installed along the supply pipe carrying water to the house, located after the water meter, but before any other appliances in the pipeline. A whole-house system reduces the same elements as an under-sink system and can also help reduce the iron flowing into the water softener, prolonging its life.

Always follow the manufacturer's directions for your particular unit. If your electrical system is grounded through the water pipes, make sure to install ground clamps on both sides of the filtration unit with a connecting jumper wire. Globe valves should be installed within 6" of the intake and the outtake sides of the filter.

Filters must be replaced every few months, depending on the manufacturer. The filtration unit cover unscrews for filter access.

Shut off the main water supply and turn on the faucets to the drainpipes. Position the unit after the water meter, but before any other appliances in the supply pipe. Measure and mark the pipe to accommodate the filtration unit. Cut the pipe at the marks with a pipe cutter. Join the water meter side of the pipe with the intake side of the unit and house the supply side of the pipe with the outtake side of the unit. Tighten with a wrench.

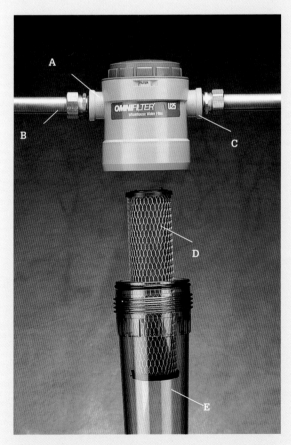

A whole-house water filtration system: (A) intake side, (B) supply pipe from the water meter pipe, (C) outtake side to the house supply pipe, (D) filter, and (E) filtration unit cover.

Install a filter and screw the filtration unit cover to the bottom of the filtration unit. Attach a jumper wire to the pipes on the other side of the unit, using pipe clamps. Open the main water supply lines to restore the water supply. Allow faucets to run for a few minutes, as you check to make sure that the system is working properly.

Flooring

Your kitchen floor is more than just a surface—it also helps to create the room's style by adding color, texture, and personality. You can use flooring to complement your countertops and cabinets or create a point of contrast. Using different types of flooring can help define task and traffic areas, giving a large kitchen floor a bit more style. Flooring choices can help the kitchen flow into other rooms or create more visible boundaries.

Almost any material can and has been used as kitchen flooring, and with new processes of factory lamination, many inexpensive and easy-to-install options are available. The only floor covering that is truly not suited to kitchen use is carpeting. Non-slip area rugs, however, are a good way to add color, texture, and help break up a large expanse of one material. Different flooring options have different merits, especially in the kitchen. It pays to think carefully about what you want, because the cost and labor involved in flooring projects mean you won't soon want to change it.

In This Chapter

- Flooring Selection
- Sheet Vinyl
- Resilient Tile
- Laminate Flooring

Flooring Selection

The floor is the largest surface in a kitchen and therefore has great potential for setting the kitchen's tone. Options for kitchen flooring have expanded immensely in the past few years. Many of these options are perfect for do-it-yourselfers looking to give their kitchen a stylish facelift. Or perhaps your kitchen has a resilient sheet floor that is in good shape but has a dated pattern or colors. A new floating floor can be installed over existing resilient flooring in a weekend—or even just a matter of hours in a smaller kitchen.

Not all types of flooring are suitable for kitchens. Carpeting is perhaps the worst choice, since it traps odors and moisture and presents cleaning nightmares. Solid wood floors are a better choice than carpeting, but they are fairly susceptible to damage from sources you are likely to encounter in the kitchen, including dropped pans or knives and spilled liquids or steam. Ceramic tile floors are popular in kitchens, but suffer from a few notable drawbacks. The grout lines tend to present cleaning problems, the hardness of the surface can lead to fatigue if you are standing and cooking for long periods. The hardness also is completely unforgiving if you drop a piece of glassware, and the tile itself is likely to fracture if you drop a heavy pot or pan.

If you are willing to overlook some environmental considerations, vinyl flooring products are well suited for kitchens. Sheet vinyl is impervious, easy to clean, and available in a greatly expanded assortment of styles and colors, many of which mimic other flooring types. It is also very comfortable underfoot. Resilient vinyl tile has similar good points. Newer laminate floors are good choices as well. Boasting the look of wood (and, increasingly, other flooring types), laminate flooring products have a very hard wear layer that holds up well to abuse but without the hardness of concrete. Following a more in-depth examination of kitchen flooring options, you'll find three how-to sequences that show you exactly how our preferred kitchen floor coverings (vinyl, vinyl tile, and laminate) are installed.

Kitchen floors should be water and moisture resistant and very easy to clean. If given a choice, some homeowners prefer a floor that conceals spills. This cork floor, when treated with a durable water resistant finish, has the added advantages of an on-trend appearance and a soft feel underfoot.

Sheet Vinyl

Sheet vinyl creates a versatile, flexible surface. Sheets come in 6 ft. and 12 ft. wide rolls, with either a felt or a polyvinyl chloride (PVC) backing, depending on the type of installation. Installation is easy. Sheet vinyl with felt backing is glued to the floor using the full-spread method, meaning the entire project area is covered with adhesive. More rigid PVC-backed sheet vinyl needs to be glued only along the edges (called the perimeter-bond method). And newer, extra-thick "no-glue" vinyl will lie flat and hold its position with little or no glue and no fasteners.

Sheet vinyl is priced per square yard and is considered one of the most inexpensive floor coverings. Most building centers carry a limited selection, but if you shop at a flooring store you'll find virtually unlimited colors and patterns, many of which do a very good job of emulating other floor types, such as parquet and ceramic tile or even natural stone. Largely because the manufacturing process for vinyl produces toxins and pollutants, resilient sheet flooring and tile are not high on the list of green floor covering products. Their relatively light weight, however, means they can be transported with some efficiency.

Resilient sheet vinyl has long been a kitchen standard. It is available in hundreds of colors and patterns at flooring distributors and design centers.

Resilient Tile

Resilient floor tile is made of vinyl. Some types have a homogenous structure and are rigid (these resemble linoleum when laid) and others are of multilayered construction with a photographic pattern layer covered by a clear wear layer. Tiles typically come in 12" squares and are available with or without self-adhesive backing. The self-adhesive versions are usually thin, lower in quality, and tend to become unstuck fairly easily.

Resilient tiles are easy to install, but because tile floors have a lot of seams, they're less suitable for high-moisture areas than sheet vinyl. They also require a very smooth layer of underlayment. The rigid, homogeneous vinyl tile normally does not have a hard wear layer, so it is susceptible to scratching and should be treated regularly with floor wax or other protective coatings. Multilayer vinyl tile is designed as a no-wax floor covering product.

Resilient vinyl tiles are laid in much the same way as ceramic tiles, but they create a surface that is more comfortable.

Laminate Flooring

Strip flooring made from laminated materials has taken over a big portion of the residential floor coverings market, especially among DIYers. Laminate flooring offers many of the visual benefits of hardwood, with better quality products doing a convincing job of replicating the warmth and even the texture of real wood. Although some laminate flooring is designed to be set into mastic, the majority of the products sold today are floating floors, often with profiled tongue-and-grooved edges that click together to form a mechanical joint. When assembled, the planks form a solid mass that "floats" on a layer of cushioned underlayment. This makes laminate very easy to install, and its growing popularity has done away with earlier limitations on colors and patterns.

Hardwood Floors

Hardwood strip flooring is a very traditional floor covering with many benefits. It is durable, beautiful, comfortable to walk and work on, and it can be resurfaced and refinished several times over its useful life. It is also somewhat susceptible to water damage and to dents, gouges, and other forms of damage that can happen easily in kitchens. It is a relatively expensive floor covering. While planks are the most common type of solid wood flooring, parquet tiles created by assembling narrow wood strips into tiles are readily available. Oak and maple are the most common hardwood flooring species available. Fir and pine flooring is not hard to find, but it is too soft for the rigors of a kitchen environment. Typically, wood flooring has tongue-and-grooved edges and is installed by direct nailing to a plywood subfloor. An underlayment of rosin paper is recommended. It can also be glued down.

Laminate flooring comes in narrow panels or strips that have click-together tongue-and-grooved edges and ends.

Solid hardwood flooring is perfectly acceptable for most kitchen installations. Its natural wood tones can never be perfectly duplicated by other flooring types.

Bamboo

As a popular wood alternative that's far too nice to be considered "the next best thing to wood," bamboo is steadily making its way into the mainstream flooring market. Because it can be harvested every three to five years (and without killing the plant, as an added bonus), bamboo is classified as a "rapidly renewable resource." Hardwood trees, by contrast, can take twenty-five years or more to reach maturity prior to harvesting.

Bamboo flooring is available in solid-strip and engineered versions. The latter has a similar construction to engineered wood flooring and can be installed with floating or glue-down methods. Solid bamboo products install much like traditional hardwood—they're typically nailed or glued to the subfloor—and are sold prefinished or can be sanded and finished on-site just like hardwood.

When shopping for bamboo flooring, compare products and varieties for their sustainability in kitchens. Vertical-grain (edge grain) bamboo typically stands up better to moisture than horizontal grain (flat grain), while carbonized bamboo (which has been steamed to produce darker coloring) may be somewhat softer than natural-color products. It's also important to buy from a reputable, experienced manufacturer to ensure high performance standards and (hopefully) ethical and sustainable practices in harvesting and producing the materials.

Cork

Cork is a natural material that boasts a cook-friendly "give" underfoot and an uncommon advantage over other kitchen floors: it's quiet. Due to its porous structure, cork has remarkable sound-deadening properties, which can be a welcome feature in a room full of hard, sound-reflecting surfaces. As a raw material, cork is the dead bark stripped from dead oak trees (harvesting doesn't damage the tree), but most cork flooring is made with material recycled from cork stopper manufacturing.

Cork flooring materials come in glue-down tiles and glue-down or snap-together planks and may include a wood, layered cork, or PVC backing.

A kitchen floor made of grass. Bamboo (a woody grass) is a popular and widely available alternative to hardwood flooring.

Cork lends a rich, natural character to kitchen floors and helps to keep noise levels down.

Sheet Vinyl

Preparing a perfect underlayment is the most important phase of resilient sheet vinyl installation. Cutting the material to fit the contours of the room is a close second. The best way to ensure accurate cuts is to make a cutting template. Some manufacturers offer template kits, or you can make one by following the instructions on page 225. Be sure to use the recommended adhesive for the sheet vinyl you are installing. Many manufacturers require that you use their glue for installation. Use extreme care when handling the sheet vinyl, especially felt-backed products, to avoid creasing and tearing.

Tools & Materials ▸

Linoleum knife	Heat gun
Framing square	1⁄16" V-notched trowel
Compass	Straightedge
Scissors	Vinyl flooring
Non-permanent	Masking tape
felt-tipped pen	Heavy butcher or brown
Utility knife	wrapping paper
Straightedge	Duct tape
1⁄4" V-notched trowel	Flooring adhesive
J-roller	3⁄8" staples
Stapler	Metal threshold bars
Flooring roller	Nails
Chalkline	

How to Make a Cutting Template

Place sheets of heavy butcher paper or brown wrapping paper along the walls, leaving a ⅛" gap. Cut triangular holes in the paper with a utility knife. Fasten the template to the floor by placing masking tape over the holes.

Follow the outline of the room, working with one sheet of paper at a time. Overlap the edges of adjoining sheets by about 2" and tape the sheets together.

To fit the template around pipes, tape sheets of paper on either side. Measure the distance from the wall to the center of the pipe, then subtract ⅛".

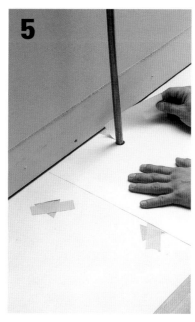

Transfer the measurement to a separate piece of paper. Use a compass to draw the pipe diameter on the paper, then cut out the hole with scissors or a utility knife. Cut a slit from the edge of the paper to the hole.

Fit the hole cutout around the pipe. Tape the hole template to the adjoining sheets.

When completed, roll or loosely fold the paper template for carrying.

How to Install Perimeter-bond Sheet Vinyl

Unroll the flooring on any large, flat, clean surface. To prevent wrinkles, sheet vinyl comes from the manufacturer rolled with the pattern-side out. Unroll the sheet and turn it pattern-side up for marking.

For two-piece installations, overlap the edges of the sheets by at least 2". Plan to have the seams fall along the pattern lines or simulated grout joints. Align the sheets so the pattern matches, then tape the sheets together with duct tape.

Make a paper template (see page 225) and position it. Trace the outline of the template onto the flooring using a non-permanent felt-tipped pen.

Remove the template. Cut the sheet vinyl with a sharp linoleum knife or a utility knife with a new blade. Use a straightedge as a guide for making longer cuts.

Cut holes for pipes and other permanent obstructions. Cut a slit from each hole to the nearest edge of the flooring. Whenever possible, make slits along pattern lines.

Roll up the flooring loosely and transfer it to the installation area. Do not fold the flooring. Unroll and position the sheet vinyl carefully. Slide the edges beneath undercut door casings.

Cut the seams for two-piece installations using a straightedge as a guide. Hold the straightedge tightly against the flooring, and cut along the pattern lines through both pieces of vinyl flooring.

Remove both pieces of scrap flooring. The pattern should now run continuously across the adjoining sheets of flooring.

Fold back the edges of both sheets. Apply a 3" band of multipurpose flooring adhesive to the underlayment or old flooring, using a ¼" V-notched trowel or wallboard knife.

Lay the seam edges one at a time onto the adhesive. Make sure the seam is tight, pressing the gaps together with your fingers, if needed. Roll the seam edges with a J-roller or wallpaper seam roller.

Apply flooring adhesive underneath flooring cuts at pipes or posts and around the entire perimeter of the room. Roll the flooring with the roller to ensure good contact with the adhesive.

If you're applying flooring over a wood underlayment, fasten the outer edges of the sheet with ⅜" staples driven every 3". Make sure the staples will be covered by the base molding.

Variation: No-glue Sheet Vinyl

The latest in the sheet-vinyl world is a "loose-lay" (no-glue) product. It has a fiberglass backing, which makes it cushier than standard felt-backed vinyl. The fiberglass backing also makes this sheet product thicker and more dimensionally stable. Consequently, it only needs to be glued at seams or under heavy appliances. Also, rather than using glue, you use acrylic double-sided adhesive tape.

No-glue sheet vinyl is installed in much the same way as other resilient sheet goods. Cutting the material to size is the most difficult part of the project. Fortunately, the major manufacturers have kits available to help you do it right.

This loose-lay sheet vinyl can be installed over many surfaces, including a single layer of sheet vinyl or vinyl tile, underlayment-grade plywood, concrete, or ceramic tile. Do not install over particleboard, cushioned vinyl flooring, carpet, strip wood, or plank flooring. Use embossing leveler to fill textured vinyl or ceramic grout lines, or use patching compound on plywood to create a flat, smooth surface.

Do not use carpet tape for this product, as it will cause discoloration. Use standard threshold transition moldings where the sheet vinyl meets other floor surfaces.

Supplies for installing no-glue sheet vinyl include a floor leveler and patching compound for preparing the floor, reinforced double-sided tape, and a seaming kit for larger installations.

Tip ▶

Thicker than standard sheet vinyl flooring, no-glue sheet vinyl is designed to remain flat and stay put without the use of glues or other adhesives.

Leave gaps. To allow for the normal movement and expansion of the floor and wall surfaces, the flooring must be cut ³⁄₁₆" to ¼" away from all vertical surfaces such as walls, cabinets, or pipes. Use a jamb saw to undercut door trim—this will allow for expansion. Make sure vinyl is not contacting the wall surface behind the door trim. Check the fit of the no-glue flooring and then carefully remove the flooring.

Place acrylic double-face tape in areas that will be under heavy appliances such as stoves and refrigerators. Make an X with three pieces of tape—one long piece and two short pieces—so that the tape does not overlap. Place acrylic double-face tape at doorways and under seam lines. Leave the paper covering in place and press the tape down so it adheres well to the subfloor.

Center the tape under the two sides at seam lines. Press one side of the vinyl into place first. Place the second vinyl sheet and press it into place. Use a seam sealer kit to seal the seams.

Drive nails into the wall surface—not through the vinyl flooring—when installing the baseboard or base shoe. Anchoring the flooring with perimeter nails may result in buckling of the vinyl surface when the floor expands or contracts. Also, do not press the molding down into the vinyl. Leave a small gap between the molding and the floor surface so the vinyl is not constricted.

Resilient Tile

As with any tile installation, resilient tile requires carefully positioned layout lines. Before committing to any layout, conduct a dry run to identify potential problems.

Keep in mind the difference between reference lines and layout lines. Reference lines mark the center of the room and divide it into quadrants. If the tiles don't lay out symmetrically along these lines, you'll need to adjust them slightly, creating layout lines. Once layout lines are established, installing the tile is a fairly quick process. Be sure to keep joints between the tiles tight and lay the tiles square.

Tiles with an obvious grain pattern can be laid so the grain of each tile is oriented identically throughout the installation. You can also use the quarter-turn method, in which each tile has its pattern grain running perpendicular to that of adjacent tiles. Whichever method you choose, be sure to be consistent throughout the project.

Tools & Materials ▸

Tape measure	Resilient tile
Chalkline	Flooring adhesive
Framing square	⅛" spacer blocks
Utility knife	Metal threshold bars
¹⁄₁₆" notched trowel	and screws
Ceramic tile cutter	

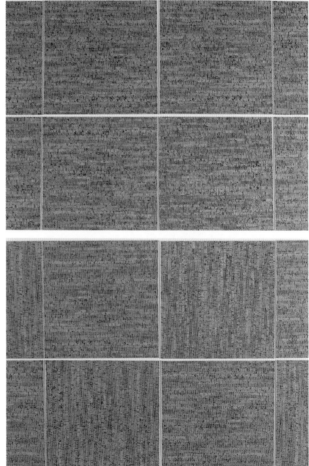

Check for noticeable directional features, like the grain of the vinyl particles. You can set the tiles in a running pattern so the directional feature runs in the same direction (top) or in a checkerboard pattern using the quarter-turn method (bottom).

How to Install Resilient Tile

Lay out perpendicular reference lines that divide the room into roughly equivalent quadrants.

Check the reference lines for squareness using the 3-4-5 triangle method. Measure along reference line X and make a mark 3 ft. from the centerpoint. Measure from the centerpoint along reference line Y and make a mark at 4 ft.

Create a new line that is parallel to reference line X and runs through a tile joint near line X if it's necessary to shift the layout. The new line, X1, is the line you'll use when installing the tile. Use a different colored chalk to distinguish between lines.

Dry-fit tiles along the new line, X1. If necessary, adjust the layout line as in steps 1 and 2.

(continued)

Apply adhesive around the intersection of the layout lines using a trowel with 1/16" V-shaped notches. Hold the trowel at a 45° angle and spread adhesive evenly over the surface.

Spread adhesive over most of the installation area, covering three quadrants. Allow the adhesive to set according to the manufacturer's instructions, then begin to install the tile at the intersection of the layout lines. You can kneel on installed tiles to lay additional tiles.

Complete the first three quadrants, and then spread adhesive over the remaining quadrant and finish setting the tile.

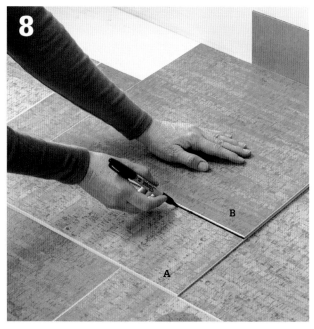

Cut tiles to fit along the walls. Place the tile to be cut (A) face up on top of the last full tile you installed. Position a 1/8"-thick spacer against the wall, then set a marker tile (B) on top of the tile to be cut. Trace along the edge of the marker tile to draw a cutting line.

To mark tiles for cutting around outside corners, make a cardboard template to match the space, keeping a ⅛" gap along the walls. After cutting the template, check to make sure it fits. Place the template on a tile and trace its outline.

9

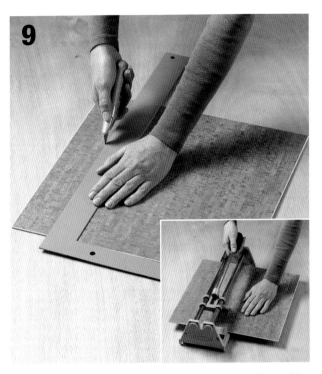

Cut the tile to fit using a utility knife and straightedge. Hold the straightedge securely against the cutting line to ensure a straight cut. *Option:* You can use a ceramic-tile cutter to make straight cuts in thick vinyl tiles (see inset).

10

Install the cut tiles next to the walls. If you're precutting all the tiles before installing them, measure the distance between the wall and install the tiles at various points in case the distance changes.

11

Continue installing the tile in the remaining quadrants until the room is completely covered. Check the entire floor. If you find loose areas, press down on the tiles to bond them to the underlayment. Install metal threshold bars at room borders where the new floor joins another floor covering.

Laminate Flooring

Laminate flooring comes in a floating system that is simple to install, even if you have no experience with other home-improvement projects. You may install a floating laminate floor right on top of plywood, concrete slab, sheet vinyl, or hardwood flooring. Just be sure to follow the manufacturer's instructions.

The flooring is available in planks or squares in a variety of different sizes, colors, and faux finishes— including wood and ceramic. The part you see is really a photographic print. Tongue-and-grooved edges lock the pieces together, and the entire floor floats on the underlayment. At the end of this project there are a few extra steps to take if your flooring manufacturer recommends using glue on the joints.

The rich wood tones of beautiful laminate planks may cause you to imagine hours of long, hard installation work, but this is a DIY project that you can do in a single weekend. Buy the manufactured planks at a home-improvement or flooring store and install laminate flooring with the step-by-step instructions offered in the following pages.

Tools & Materials ▸

Hammer	Drill with Forstner bit
Circular saw	Hole saw
Utility knife	Jigsaw
Underlayment	Painter's tape
½" wall spacers	Clamps
Tapping block	Rubber mallet
Scrap rigid foam insulation	Drawbar
Speed square	Thin cloth and ratchet
Scissors	Finish nails
Manufacturer glue	Strap clamps
Adhesive tape	Threshold and screws

Ripcut the planks from the back side to avoid splintering the top surface. For accurate straight cuts, mark the cut with a chalk line. If your pencil line is not straight, double-check your tracing—your wall may not be perfectly straight, in which case you should cut along your hand-drawn pencil line.

Place another piece of flooring next to the piece marked for cutting to provide a stable surface for the foot of the saw. Also, clamp a cutting guide to the planks at the correct distance from the cutting line to ensure a straight cut.

If you need to cut the planks to fit snugly against another plank or a wall with an obstacle such as a heat vent: Measure in to the appropriate cutline to fit the board flush with the adjacent board or wall (on the other side of the obstacle). Draw a line across the plank in this location. Then measure the obstacle and transfer those measurements to the plank. Drill a starter hole just large enough to fit your jigsaw blade into it. Cut the plank along the drawn lines, using a jigsaw. Set the board in place by locking the tongue-and-grooved joints with the preceding board.

How to Install a Floating Floor

Start in one corner and unroll the underlayment to the opposite wall. Cut the underlayment to fit using a utility knife or scissors. Overlap the second underlayment sheet according to the manufacturer's recommendations, and secure the pieces in place with adhesive tape.

Work from the left corner of the room to the right and set wall spacers and dry lay planks (tongue side facing the wall) against the wall. The spacers allow for expansion. If you are flooring a room more than 26 ft. long or wide, you need to buy appropriate-sized expansion joints. *Note: Some manufacturers suggest facing the groove side to the wall.*

Final uncut plank ends here

Set a new plank right side up, on top of the previously laid plank, flush with the spacer against the wall at the end run. Line up a speed square with the bottom plank edge and trace a line. That's the cutline for the final plank in the row.

Press painter's tape along the cutline on the top of the plank to prevent chipping when cutting. Score the line drawn in step 3 with a utility knife. Turn the plank over and extend the pencil line to the back side.

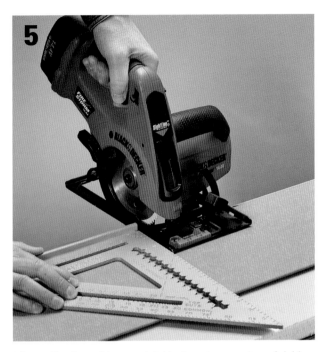

Clamp the board to a work table face down on top of rigid foam insulation or plywood. The foam reduces chipping. Clamp a speed square on top of the plank, as though you are going to draw another line parallel to the cutline—use this to eye your straight cut. Place the circular saw's blade on the waste side of the actual cutline.

To create a tight fit for the last plank in the first row, place a spacer against the wall and wedge one end of a drawbar between it and the last plank. Tap the other end of the drawbar with a rubber mallet or hammer. Protect the laminate surface with a thin cloth.

Continue to lay rows of flooring, making sure the joints are staggered. This prevents the entire floor from relying on just a few joints, which keep the planks from lifting. Staggering also stengthens the floor, because the joints are shorter and more evenly distributed.

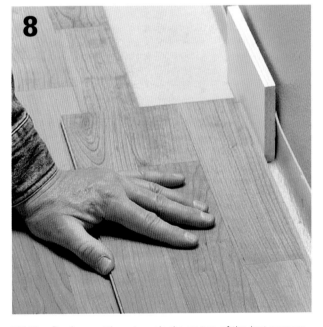

Fit the final row: Place two planks on top of the last course; slide the top plank up against the wall spacer. Use the top plank to draw a cutline lengthwise on the middle plank. Cut the middle plank to size using the same method as in step 3, just across the grain. The very last board must be cut lengthwise and widthwise to fit.

How to Work Around Obstacles

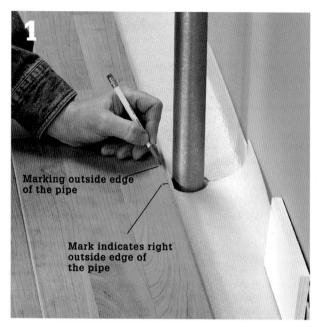

Position a plank end against the spacers on the wall next to the obstacle. Use a pencil to make two marks along the length of the plank, indicating the points where the obstacle begins and ends.

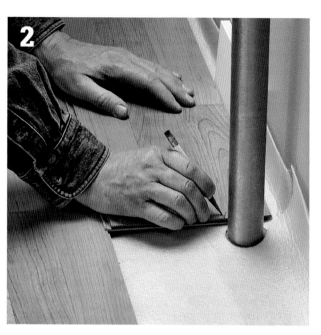

Snap the plank into the previous row, then position the plank end against the obstacle. Make two marks with a pencil, this time on the end of the plank to indicate where the obstacle falls along the width of the board.

Use a speed square to extend the four lines. The space at which they intersect is the part of the plank that needs to be removed to make room for the obstacle to go through it. Use a drill with a Forstner bit or a hole saw the same diameter as the space within the intersecting lines, and drill through the plank at the X. You'll be left with a hole; extend the cut to the edges with a jigsaw.

Install the plank by locking the tongue-and-groove joints with the preceding board. Fit the end piece in behind the pipe or obstacle. Apply manufacturer-recommended glue to the cut edges, and press the end piece tightly against the adjacent plank. Wipe away any excess glue with a damp cloth.

How to Install Laminate Flooring Using Adhesive

Dry-fit each row, then completely fill the groove of the plank with the glue supplied or recommended by the manufacturer.

Close the gaps between the end joints and the lengthwise joints using a rubber mallet and block to gently tap the edge or end of the last plank. Use a drawbar for the last planks butted up to a wall. Wipe away excess glue in the joints with a damp cloth before it dries.

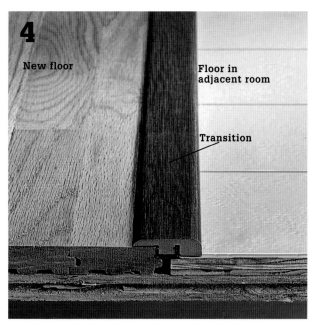

New floor

Floor in adjacent room

Transition

Use strap clamps to hold a few rows of planks together as adhesive dries (about an hour). Fit one end of the strap clamp over the plank nearest the wall and the other end (the one with the ratchet lever) over the last plank. Use the ratchet to tighten straps until the joints are snug.

Install transition thresholds at room borders where the new floor joins another floor covering. These thresholds are used to tie together dissimilar floor coverings, such as laminate floorings and wood or carpet. They may also be necessary to span a distance in height between flooring in one room and the next.

Lighting

Lighting does many jobs in the kitchen. It can set the mood, illuminate the task at hand, highlight a detail, or simply create beautiful patterns. Despite how important lighting is, a great many kitchens are poorly lit.

One common kitchen lighting problem is the centrally placed ceiling fixture with no other lighting sources. Unfortunately, this central fixture creates strong shadows at every workstation because the cook's body is always between the light source and the work area. Fortunately, this can be remedied in a number of creative and beautiful ways highlighted in this chapter.

Another kitchen lighting scheme, considered a step up from the single fixture, was the suspended ceiling with banks of fluorescent lights. The problem with fluorescent lighting is that it can make everything look green. In this chapter you will learn that light sources have different impacts on color. We'll cover lighting for tasks, accent and ambient lighting, and decorative lighting using photo examples of each. Also included are how-to directions for installing track and cable lighting, under-, in-, and above-cabinet lighting, recessed lights, and a ceiling fan with a light fixture.

In This Chapter

- Lighting Selection
- Ceiling Lights
- Canister Lights
- Undercabinet Lights

Lighting Selection

Kitchen lighting is a big deal—for homeowners everywhere and, of course, for the entire kitchen remodeling industry. When confronted with the endless variety of fixture options, designers and their clients can be tempted to go a little nuts, often ending up with a complex array of interesting yet marginally effective lights. By contrast, lighting a kitchen with a green focus can be quite straightforward. The main objective should be comfortable and effective illumination without unnecessary and inefficient fixtures cluttering the plan. Most people like bright kitchens, and with good reason: It's the home's primary gathering place and the stage for most of the household's everyday "work." A kitchen must be warm and inviting for all users at any hour. With that in mind, it's important to note that a green lighting plan is not about putting up with dim lighting or commercial-style ambience; it's about setting the right fixtures in the right places. It's also about maximizing natural daylight.

In a green kitchen, natural daylight, reflective surfaces, and judicious use of fixtures create a bright, dynamic environment with limited energy use.

Artificial Lighting

Kitchen lighting is often broken down into three main categories based on function. Ambient lighting provides the room with most of its general illumination. This is most often achieved with bright overhead fixtures that reflect light off of surrounding surfaces and set the overall light level in the room. The cumulative light from other fixtures also contributes to ambient lighting. Task lighting provides focused light in specific work areas, such as the cooktop, sink, and countertops. The third category, accent lighting, is used more sparingly and creatively to highlight special features or for decorative effect.

Ambient and task lighting together make up the core of a kitchen plan. With those types of lighting satisfied, accent fixtures can be added to provide layering and enhance the dynamics of light and shadow.

When it comes to overhead lighting, one or two well-placed fixtures will meet the demands of most kitchens. The most effective overhead fixtures are ceiling-mounted units that project light all around as well as onto the ceiling. Glass or acrylic globes offer the best illumination, while fixtures with opaque sides or shades limit brightness by focusing the light downward.

One of the most popular choices for overhead lighting is the recessed "can" fixture, which people like for its flush installation that doesn't break up the ceiling plane. However, because all of the light is directed downward, you need several fixtures to yield the same levels as one or two globe-type fixtures; thus, it is a less-green option. If you do opt for recessed cans, choose products rated "IC-AT," meaning the fixture housing can be covered with insulation and the cans are airtight to limit air infiltration.

The kitchen on the left has several recessed fixtures just for overhead lighting, while the greener kitchen on the right takes advantage of reflective surfaces and is brightly illuminated with only one overhead fixture.

When it comes to task lighting, nothing gets the job done more effectively or efficiently than under-cabinet fluorescent tube fixtures. These inexpensive units fit into the recess below most standard cabinets and can be plugged into a countertop receptacle or hard-wired with a wall-switch control (see pages 254 to 257). Their energy efficiency is unmatched by other fixture types, providing about 50 lumens per watt (or lpw—the true measure of lighting efficiency). A single bulb can burn for up to 20,000 hours before needing replacement.

Other popular types of under-cabinet lighting include halogen, xenon, and LED. Of the three, LED are the most energy-efficient but by far the most expensive. Halogen lights, which contain incandescent bulbs, are popular for their bright, even light, but they come with two significant drawbacks: They operate at only 20 lpw and they get very hot—hot enough to warm a stack of plates or even melt chocolate in the cabinet above the fixture. Xenon bulbs produce about 15 lpw and may require a separate transformer that you have to hide as part of the installation.

Ambient (and decorative) lighting may be less important from a practical view, but it can play a critical role in the overall quality of light in the kitchen. Eating areas, such as a bar or breakfast nook, often call for more atmospheric lighting. Dimmers let you set the light level to suit the mood of the specific meal or activity. Some compact fluorescent lamps (CFLs) and fixtures are available with dimming capability, so be sure to get the right products for the application.

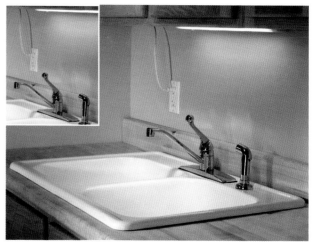

Fluorescent under-cabinet lights run cool (unlike incandescents) and provide the most light with the least amount of electricity. The simplest way to add under-cabinet lighting is with plug-in fixtures (inset), while hard-wired installations don't use up outlet space.

Positioning Task Lights ▸

Here's a good rule of thumb for effective task lighting: Let nothing come between the light and the task. Lights placed under cabinets, inside range hoods, and directly over sinks follow the rule; overhead lights and soffit-mounted fixtures don't. Always place task lights where your body or head won't cast a shadow over your work.

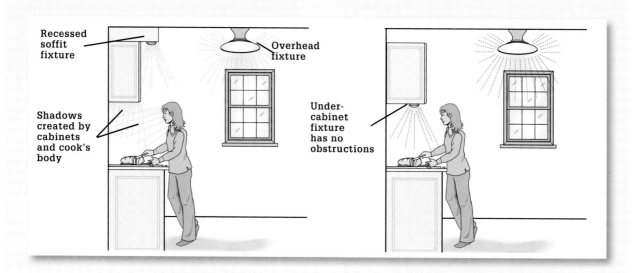

Natural Lighting

Nothing adds more life to a kitchen than a window. With a view to the outdoors, cooking and cleaning up feel less like work, and the room doesn't have the sense of isolation that can plague windowless kitchens. Operable windows on more than one wall can usher in generous cross-breezes to flush the kitchen with fresh air. And all that natural light reduces the need for artificial lighting during the day.

When adding windows to a kitchen, orientation is a critical consideration. Glare and heat gain, primarily from south- and west-facing windows, can hinder visibility and make the room uncomfortably hot with the afternoon sun. North-facing windows offer more even light throughout the day, while east-facing windows can bring in pleasant morning sun without the heat gain from midday and afternoon sun exposure. On southern windows, you can use exterior awnings to block the hot summer sun but let in light and warmth in the winter when the sun is at a lower angle. Of course, not every kitchen can accommodate windows or has the luxury of an exterior view. But good alternatives exist. Skylights work well in kitchens because they dramatically brighten the room even on cloudy days, and they psychologically expand the space. As with windows, skylights should face north or east whenever possible. If glare and heat gain are unavoidable, look into skylights with prismatic or translucent glazing, or provide means for shading the unit when needed. Where an attic above the kitchen makes a skylight impractical, a tubular skylight may be a viable alternative. Another way to bring natural light into a kitchen is to remove a wall or bank of cabinets to join the kitchen with an adjacent room that has windows. If the kitchen has a standard entry door, you can replace it with a glazed unit or add a transom or awning window above to increase daylighting.

Adding a well-placed window is always a good investment, particularly in kitchens.

Ceiling Lights

Ceiling fixtures don't have any moving parts and their wiring is very simple, so, other than changing bulbs, you're likely to get decades of trouble-free service from a fixture. This sounds like a good thing, but it also means that the fixture probably won't fail and give you an excuse to update a room's look with a new one. Fortunately, you don't need an excuse. Upgrading a fixture is easy and can make a dramatic impact on a room. You can substantially increase the light in a room by replacing a globe-style fixture by one with separate spotlights, or you can simply install a new fixture that matches the room's décor.

Tools & Materials ▸

Replacement light fixture
Wire stripper
Voltage sensor

Insulated screwdrivers
Combination tool
Wire connectors

Installing a new ceiling fixture can provide more light to a space, not to mention an aesthetic lift. It's one of the easiest upgrades you can do.

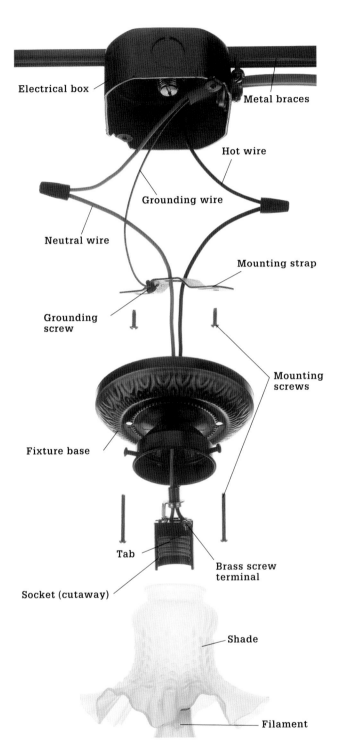

Electrical box

Metal braces

Hot wire

Grounding wire

Neutral wire

Mounting strap

Grounding screw

Mounting screws

Fixture base

Tab

Brass screw terminal

Socket (cutaway)

Shade

Filament

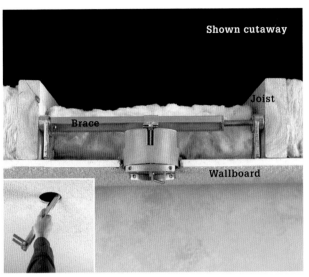

Shown cutaway

Joist

Brace

Wallboard

If the new fixture is much heavier than the original fixture, it will require additional bracing in the ceiling to support the electrical box and the fixture. The manufacturer's instructions should specify the size and type of box. If the ceiling is finished and there is no access from above, you can remove the old box and use an adjustable remodeling brace appropriate for your fixture (shown). The brace fits into a small hole in the ceiling (inset). Once the bracing is in place, install a new electrical box specified for the new fixture.

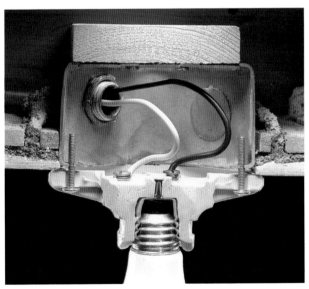

No matter what ceiling light fixtures look like on the outside, they all attach in basically the same way. An electrical box in the ceiling is fitted with a mounting strap, which holds the fixture in place. The bare wire from the ceiling typically connects to the mounting strap. The two wires coming from the fixture connect to the black and the white wires from the ceiling.

Inexpensive light fixtures have screw terminals mounted directly to the backside of the fixture plate. Often, as seen here, they have no grounding terminal. Some codes do not allow this type of fixture, but even if your hometown does approve them, it is a good idea to replace them with better quality, safer fixtures that are UL-approved.

How to Replace a Ceiling Light

1

Shut off the power to the ceiling light and remove the shade or diffuser. Loosen the mounting screws and carefully lower the fixture, supporting it as you work (do not let light fixtures hang by their electrical wires alone). Test with a voltage sensor to make sure no power is reaching the connections.

2

Remove the twist connectors from the fixture wires or unscrew the screw terminals and remove the white neutral wire and the black lead wire (inset).

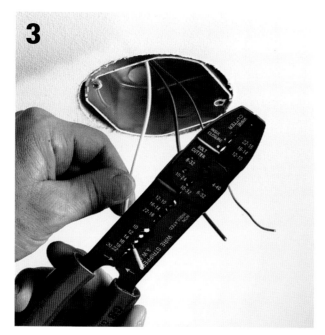

3

Check the ends of the wires coming from the ceiling electrical box before you install the new fixture. They should be clean and free of nicks or scorch marks. If they're dirty or worn, clip off the stripped portion with your combination tool. Then strip away about ¾" of insulation from the end of each wire.

4

Attach a mounting strap to the ceiling fixture box if there is not one already present. Your new light may come equipped with a strap, otherwise you can find one for purchase at any hardware store.

5

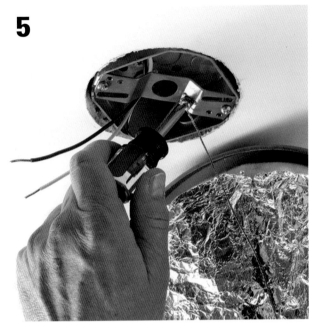

Lift the new fixture up to the ceiling (you may want a helper for this) and attach the bare copper ground wire from the power supply cable to the grounding screw or clip on the mounting strap. Also attach the ground wire from the fixture to the screw or clip.

6

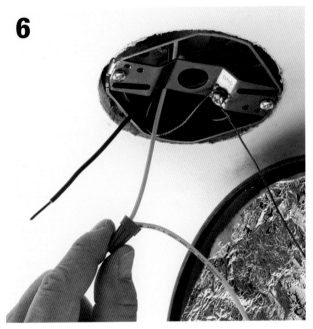

Support the fixture with a ladder or a helper and then join the white wire lead and the white fixture wire with a wire connector (often supplied with the fixture).

7

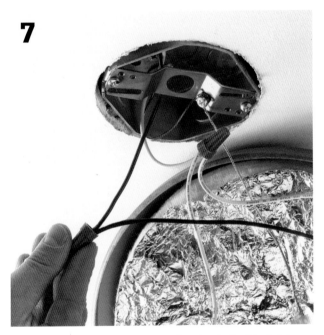

Connect the black power supply wire to the black fixture wire with a wire connector.

8

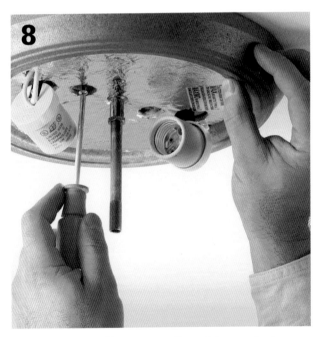

Position the new fixture mounting plate over the box so the mounting screw holes align. Drive the screws until the fixture is secure against the ceiling.

Canister Lights

Recessed lights are versatile fixtures suited for a variety of situations. Fixtures rated for outdoor use can also be installed in roof soffits and overhangs for accent and security lighting. Recessed fixtures can also be installed over showers or tubs. Be sure to use fixture cans and trims rated for bathroom use.

There are recessed lighting cans in all shapes and sizes for almost every type of ceiling or cabinet. Cans are sold for unfinished ceilings (new construction) or for finished ceilings (retrofit installation). Cans are also rated as insulation compatible or for uninsulated ceilings. Be sure to use the correct one for your ceiling to prevent creating a fire hazard.

Choose the proper type of recessed light fixture for your project. There are two types of fixtures: those rated for installation within insulation (left), and those which must be kept at least 3" from insulation (right). Self-contained thermal switches shut off power if the unit gets too hot for its rating. A recessed light fixture must be installed at least ½" from combustible materials.

Tools & Materials ▸

Recessed-lighting can for new construction or remodeling and trim	Circuit tester	Chalkline	Drywall saw
	Cable ripper	Pliers	NM cable
Tape measure	Combination tool	Fish tape	Wire staples

Recessed ceiling lights often are installed in series to provide exacting control over the amount and direction of light. Spacing the canisters in every other ceiling joist bay is a common practice.

Recessed ceiling light housings come in many sizes and styles for various purposes and budgets. Some are sold with trim kits (below) included. Some common types are: new construction recessed housing (sold in economical multipacks) (A); airtight recessed housings (for heated rooms below unheated ceilings) (B); shallow recessed housings (for rooms with 2 × 6" ceiling joists) (C); small aperture recessed housing (D); recessed slope ceiling housing (for vaulted ceilings) (E).

Trim kits for recessed ceiling lights may be sold separately. Common types include: recessed open trim with baffle (A, F); recessed eyeball trim (B); baffle trim (C); shower light trim (D); airtight recessed open trim (E).

How to Install Canister Lights

Mark the location for the light canister. If you are installing multiple lights, measure out from the wall at the start and end of the run, and connect them with a chalkline snapped parallel to the wall. If the ceiling is finished, see the next page.

Install the housing for the recessed fixture. Housings for new construction (or remodeling installations where the installation area is fully accessible from either above or below) have integral hanger bars that you attach to each joist in the joist bay.

Run electric cable from the switch to each canister location. Multiple lights are generally installed in series so there is no need to make pigtail connections in the individual boxes. Make sure to leave enough extra cable at each location to feed the wire into the housing and make the connection.

Run the feeder cables into the electrical boxes attached to the canister housings. You'll need to remove knockouts first and make sure to secure the cable with a wire staple within 8" of the entry point to the box.

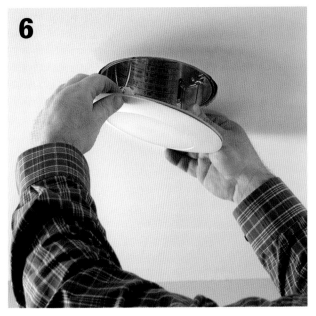

Connect the feeder wires to the fixture wires inside the junction box. Twist the hot lead together with the black fixture wire, as well as the black lead to other fixtures further downline. Also connect the neutral white wires. Join the ground wires and pigtail them to the grounding screw or clip in the box. Finish the ceiling, as desired.

Attach your trim kit of choice. Normally, these are hung with torsion spring clips from notches or hooks inside the canister. This should be done after the ceiling is installed and finished for new construction projects. With certain types of trim kits, such as eyeball trim, you'll need to install the light bulb before the trim kit.

How to Connect a Recessed Fixture Can in a Finished Ceiling

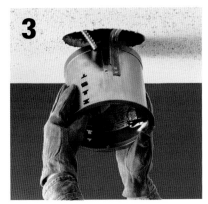

Make the hole for the can. Most fixtures will include a template for sizing the hole. Fish 14/2 cable from the switch location to the hole. Pull about 16" of cable out of the hole for making the connection.

Remove a knockout from the electrical box attached to the can. Thread the cable into the box; secure it with a cable clamp. Remove sheathing insulation. Connect the black fixture wire to the black circuit wire, the white fixture wire to the white circuit wire, and then connect the ground wire to the grounding screw or grounding wire attached to the box.

Retrofit cans secure themselves with spring-loaded clips into the hole. Install the can in the ceiling by depressing the mounting clips so the can will fit into the hole. Insert the can so that its edge is tight to the ceiling. Push the mounting clips back out so they grip the drywall and hold the fixture in place. Install the trim piece.

Undercabinet Lights

Hardwired undercabinet lights illuminate the kitchen countertop and sink areas that fall in the shadow of ceiling lights. Most of these light fixtures, which are often called strip lights, utilize fluorescent, halogen, or xenon bulbs that emit very low levels of heat and are therefore very efficient.

If you are doing a kitchen remodel with all-new cabinets, run the new light circuit wiring before the cabinets are installed. For a retrofit, you'll need to find an available power source to tie into. Options for this do not include the dedicated 20-amp small-appliance circuits that are required in kitchens. The best bet is to run new circuit wire from a close-by ceiling light switch box, but this will mean cutting into the walls to run cable. Another option is to locate a receptacle that's on the opposite side of a shared wall, preferably next to a location where a base cabinet is installed in the kitchen. By cutting an access hole in the cabinet back, you can tie into the receptacle box and run cable through the wall behind the cabinets, up to the upper cabinet location, and out the wall to supply the fixture that's mounted to the underside of the upper cabinet.

You can purchase undercabinet lights that are controlled by a wall switch, but most products have an integral on/off button so you can control lights individually.

Tools & Materials ▸

Circuit tester	Undercabinet lighting kit
Utility knife	Hanging straps
Wallboard saw	14/2 NM cable
Hammer	Wire connectors
Screwdriver	Switch box
Drill and hole saw	Switch
Jigsaw	Electrical junction box
Cable Clamp	Panel adhesive
Wire stripper	

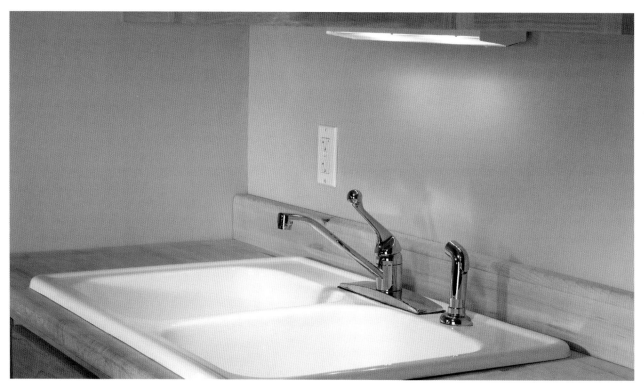

Undercabinet lights provide directed task lighting that brings sinks and countertop work surfaces out from the shadows. Hardwired lights may be controlled either by a wall switch or an onboard on/off switch located on the fixture. *Note: Do not supply power for lights from a small-appliance circuit.*

How to Install a Hardwired Undercabinet Light

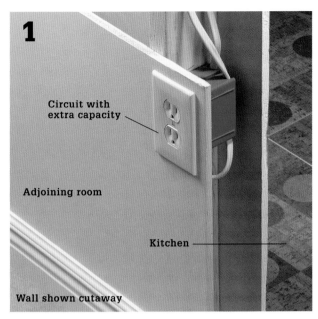

1

Circuit with
extra capacity

Adjoining room

Kitchen

Wall shown cutaway

Look in the adjoining room for a usable power source in the form of a receptacle that has a box located in the wall behind your base cabinets. Unlike the small-appliance circuit with outlets in your backsplash area, these typically are not dedicated circuits (which can't be expanded). Make sure that the receptacle's circuit has enough capacity to support another load. Shut the power to the receptacle off at the main service panel and test for power.

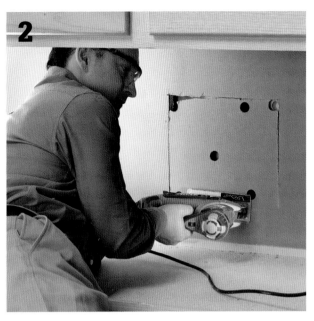

2

Cut a hole in the base cabinet back panel to get access to the wall behind it in roughly the area where you know the next-door receptacle to be. Use a keyhole saw or drywall saw and make very shallow cuts until you have positively identified the locations of the electrical box and cables. Then finish the cuts with a jigsaw.

3

Drill an access hole into the kitchen wall for the cable that will feed the undercabinet light. A ½" dia. hole should be about the right size if you are using 12-ga. or 14-ga. sheathed NM cable.

4

Cut a small access hole (4 × 4" or so) in the back panel of the base cabinet directly below the undercabinet light location.

(continued)

5

Feed the cable into the access hole at the light location until the end reaches the access hole below. Don't cut the cable yet. Reach into the access hole and feel around for the free cable end and then pull it out through the access hole once you've found it. Cut the cable, making sure to leave plenty of extra on both ends.

6

String the cable into a piece of flexible conduit that's long enough to reach between the two access holes in the base cabinets. Attach a connector to each end of the conduit to protect the cable sheathing from the sharp edges of the cut metal. Tip: *To make patching the cabinet back easier, drill a new access hole for the cable near the square access hole.*

7

Hang the conduit with hanger straps attached to the base cabinet frame or back panel, drilling holes in the side walls of the cabinet where necessary to thread the conduit through. On back panels, use small screws to hang the straps instead of brads or nails. Support the conduit near both the entrance and the exit holes (the conduit should extend past the back panels by a couple of inches).

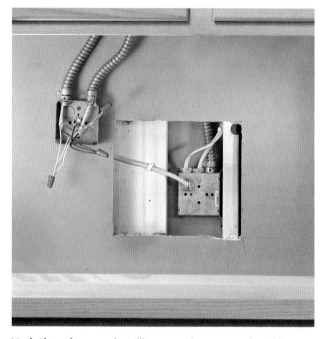

Variation: If you are installing more than one undercabinet light, run the cable down from each installation point as you did for the first light. Mount an electrical junction box to the cabinet back near the receptacle providing the power. Run the power cables from each light through flexible conduit and make connections inside the junction box. Be sure to attach the junction box cover once the connections are made.

8

Remove the receptacle from the box you are tying into and insert the new circuit cable into one of the knockouts using a cable clamp. Check a wire capacity chart to make sure the box is big enough for the new conductors. Replace it with a larger box if necessary. Reinstall the receptacle once the connections are made.

9

Install the undercabinet light. Some models have a removable diffuser that allows access to the fixture wires, and these should be screwed to the upper cabinet prior to making your wiring hookups. Other models need to be connected to the circuit wires before installation. Check your manufacturer's installations.

10

Connect wires inside the light fixture according to the light manufacturer's directions. Make sure the incoming cable is stapled just before it enters the light box and that a cable clamp is used at the knockout in the box to protect the cable. Restore the power and test the light.

11

Cut patches of hardboard and fit them over the access holes, overlapping the edges of the cutouts. Adhere them to the cabinet backs with panel adhesive.

Easy Updates

Sometimes all your kitchen requires to get a new lease on life is one or two quick projects. From a fresh coat of paint to a clever pantry conversion, the projects on the following pages could be classified as "high payback" on your investment of time and money.

An easy update may have a purely visual purpose, such as painting walls or cabinets. It may be more of an organizational improvement, such as a pantry conversion project. It may add a new dimension to your kitchen as a living space, as when building a built-in banquette. Or the main purpose could be improving the safety of your family by taking a few simple childproofing measures. Some easy updates are chosen for reasons of simple practicality, such as adding soffits above your wall cabinets to house new lighting or conceal ductwork from a vent fan. Replacing a plain window with a garden window is another way to make a practical improvement to your kitchen light. Whatever the purpose of your easy update, bear in mind that quick and easy should never mean sloppy. Always use caution and care when undertaking any home improvement or repair project.

This chapter shows:
- Painting
- Childproofing
- Convert a Closet to Pull-out Pantry
- New Banquette
- Garden Window
- Framed Soffits

Painting

Kitchen walls need to be washed before painting. A dirty, greasy wall will absorb paint unevenly and is more likely to cause sags or drips even in properly applied paint. Some surface dirt will even bleed through, causing staining. Use a trisodium phosphate cleaner and carefully follow the manufacturer's instructions.

Many kitchens are painted with high-gloss paint. You may need to de-gloss the old paint surface to ensure proper adhesion of the new paint. This can be done with a chemical paint de-glosser or by sanding. The de-glosser must be used with sufficient ventilation, and you should wear a respirator.

Move the stove and refrigerator if they are not built in and paint behind them. This prevents paint from dripping or spattering onto cooling fans or into vent areas. For professional results, check your walls for damage and repair the wallboard or plaster as needed. Carefully mask and tape all trim and cabinets, and cover countertops and the floor with drop cloths.

Wash kitchen walls thoroughly before painting. Grease and dirt will prevent paint from adhering fully.

Tools & Materials ▸

Putty knife	Sandpaper
Paint scraper	Spackle
Trisodium phospate	Masking tape

Surface Preparation Tips ▸

Apply lightweight spackle to holes with a putty knife or your fingertip. This keeps repair areas small. Let the spackle dry. Sand until smooth.

Water or rust stains may indicate water damage. Check for leaking pipes and soft plaster, make needed repairs, then seal the area with stain-covering sealer.

How to Patch Peeling Paint

1

Scrape away loose paint with a putty knife or paint scraper.

2

Apply spackle to the edges of the chipped paint with a putty knife or a flexible wallboard knife.

3

Sand the patch area with 150-grit production sandpaper. The patch area should feel smooth to the touch.

How to Mask Trim

Masking and draping materials include (clockwise from top left): plastic and canvas drop cloths, self-adhesive plastic, masking tape, and pregummed masking papers.

1

Use pregummed paper or wide masking tape to protect wood moldings from paint splatters. Leave the outside edge of the masking tape loose.

2

After applying the tape, run the tip of a putty knife along the inside edge of the tape to seal it against seeping paint. After painting, remove the tape as soon as the paint is too dry to run.

How to Use a Paintbrush

Dip the brush, loading one-third of its bristle length. Tap the bristles against the side of the can. Dipping deeper overloads the brush. Dragging the brush against the lip of the can causes the bristles to wear.

Cut in the edges using the narrow edge of the brush, pressing just enough to flex the bristles. Keep an eye on the paint edge, and paint with long, slow strokes. Always paint from a dry area back into wet paint to avoid lap marks.

Brush wall corners using the wide edge of the brush. Paint open areas with a brush or roller before the brushed paint dries.

How to Paint With a Paint Roller

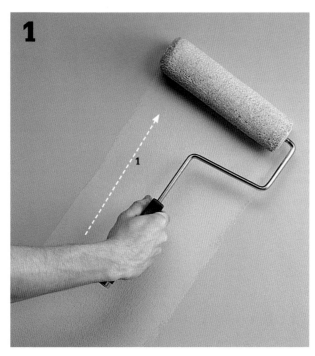

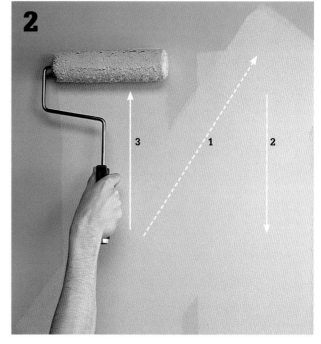

With the loaded roller, make a diagonal sweep (1) about 4 feet long on the surface. On walls, roll upward on the first stroke to avoid spilling paint. Use slow roller strokes to avoid splattering.

Draw the roller straight down (2) from the top of the diagonal sweep. Shift the roller to the beginning of the diagonal and roll up (3) to complete the unloading of the roller. Distribute paint over the rest of the section with horizontal back-and-forth strokes.

How to Paint Ceilings

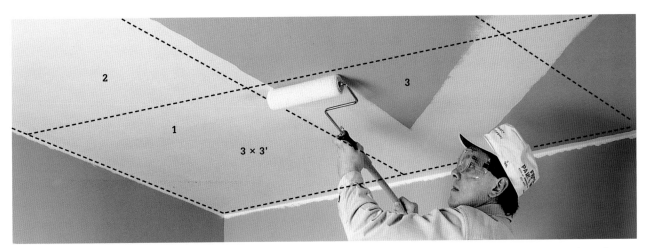

Paint ceilings with a roller handle extension. Use eye protection while painting overhead. Start at the corner farthest from the entry door. Cut in the edges with a brush, then paint the ceiling along the narrow end in 3-ft. × 3-ft. sections. Apply the paint with a diagonal stroke. Distribute the paint evenly with back-and-forth strokes. For the final smoothing strokes, roll each section toward the wall containing the entry door, lifting the roller at the end of each sweep.

How to Paint Walls

Paint walls in 2-ft. × 4-ft. sections. Start in an upper corner, cutting in the ceiling and wall corners with a brush, then rolling the section. Make the initial diagonal roller stroke from the bottom of the section upward, to avoid dripping paint. Distribute the paint evenly with horizontal strokes, then finish with downward sweeps of the roller. Next, cut in and roll the section directly underneath. Continue with adjacent areas, cutting in and rolling the top sections before the bottom sections. Roll all finish strokes toward the floor.

Childproofing

Flames, sharp knives, toxic cleaners—it's no wonder the kitchen is one of the most dangerous rooms in your house. Here, we'll present a variety of ways to childproof your kitchen. Some projects take just a few seconds. Others, like picking the right cabinet latches, require a little more planning. However, the extra effort you take to keep your child out of harm's way is time well spent.

There are many childproofing gadgets and safety devices you can buy for your kitchen that are very simple to install and use. In fact, many require no tools at all.

Poison Control ▶

According to Consumer Product Safety Commission, more than one million poisonings of children under the age of five are reported each year. In fact, about 90% of all accidental poisonings occur in the home, and the typical victim is a child under the age of six. More children die of poisoning each year than of all infectious diseases combined.

Poisons can be found all over your home, but the most dangerous poisons are generally found in the bathroom, garage, and kitchen. Almost every household cleanser is toxic to some extent. Plus, there are many other common items found in kitchens that are also poisonous. For instance, did you know vanilla extract consumed in large quantities can poison a child?

When poison-proofing your kitchen, start with the most obvious hazards. For most parents, the search begins under the kitchen sink. Next, really think about what is in your kitchen. What do you need? What do you no longer use?

Finally, be prepared. Post the number of your local poison control center near your phone. You can also receive help from the American Association of Poison Control Centers' national emergency hotline. Their number is (800) 222-1222.

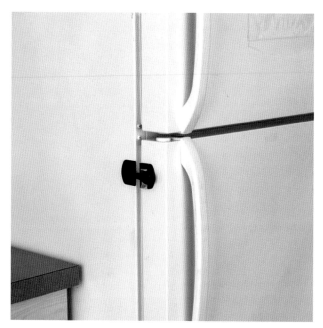

Appliance latches and straps are installed on refrigerators, freezers, microwaves, ovens, dishwashers, and display cabinets. There are many styles of latches and straps to choose from. Some hold up much better than others. Only buy latches and straps specifically designed for the type of appliance you want to secure. For instance, the latch (shown above) is designed for refrigerators and will not withstand oven heat.

Stove knob covers: These plastic covers keep the controls on an oven from being turned. They are literally a snap to install. Also consider installing stove knob covers on outdoor grills.

Kitchen Safety ▸

The main dangers in the kitchen are extreme heat, sharp objects, and poisons. You can also avert tragedy by simply being consistent about the following:

Turn pot handles: When cooking, always turn your pot and pan handles toward the back of the stove to minimize the risk of hot food pouring onto a child.

Keep cords out of reach: Children who have access to cords may pull kitchen appliances down on top of themselves. Never let cords, including telephone cords, dangle freely.

Remove tablecloths and runners: As soon as children can crawl, they start pulling on everything within reach. Anything that is sitting on a tablecloth, such as a hot cup of coffee or sharp centerpiece, is in danger of landing on a child that reaches for a tablecloth.

Guard your garbage: Put your garbage in a place your child cannot reach. Equip your garbage container with a latch and do not forget to secure it.

Skip refrigerator magnets: Small magnets on refrigerators and bulletin boards can pose a choking hazard. Magnets shaped like food are especially tempting.

Bathing Safety: Never bathe a child in the kitchen sink while the dishwasher is running. Hot water from the dishwasher may back up into the sink, scalding your baby.

Fire extinguishers: Keep a working fire extinguisher rated for kitchen use in an accessible spot. On the side of a wall cabinet near (but not directly above) the stove is a good choice. Look for an ABC extinguisher for general kitchen use.

Cabinet safety latches are one of the most important childproofing devices used in a kitchen. They effectively keep children out of drawers and cabinets, but they are not "one size fits all." In fact, many kitchens require at least two different types of latches to fit the various types of drawers and cabinets. After installing the two-part safety latches, test your work by opening and closing the drawer a few times. The two pieces should latch tightly when the drawer closes. It should not reopen without the proper pressure to unlock.

Convert a Closet to Pull-out Pantry

You can transform a small walk-in closet into a highly efficient pullout pantry by replacing ordinary shelving with slide-out drawers. This is a great way to customize your kitchen and make it more user-friendly. You can find slide-out drawers for do-it-yourself installation at online sellers. Look for shelves and rollers that are rated to 75 or 100 pounds so you don't have to worry about overload.

There are many options when planning a project such as this. You can purchase shelf rollers that mount to the back of the closet and to the doorframe, or you can purchase shelf rollers that attach to the closet walls of the pantry. Each requires some modification to the closet structure. This project uses side-mounted rollers. If you have a pantry with sides that are set back from the door to accommodate shelves along the sides as well, you will need to build out the wall surfaces of the side walls to be flush with the door frame. It is best to create a solid wall surface, rather than simply framing. A solid wall surface prevents items from falling off shelves. Closet pantries come in many shapes and sizes. The pantry we are remodeling is a 24 × 24" pantry with only a slight setback and shelves only along the back.

Tools & Materials ▸

Stud finder	2 × 4
Tape measure	Lattice trim
Level	Shelves
Table saw	Roller hardware
1 × 4	

A group of pull-out pantry trays dramatically increases the storage capabilities of the former closet.

How to Install a Pullout Pantry

1

Remove any existing shelves from the closet. Use a stud finder to locate the studs on the side walls. Mark the locations of the studs. Measure the width of the door opening. Make sure to measure at more than one location in case the door opening is not true. Use this measurement to order the sliding shelves.

2

Mark the hardware locations. First, measure the setback of the wall from the door frame on each side. Include the doorstop trim in your measurement. This depth equals the thickness of the spacers you will need for mounting the roller hardware. Mark the locations of each shelf on the side walls. Use a carpenter's level or laser level to make sure your shelf marks are level.

3

Install spacer blocks. Cut the spacers to length from material of the appropriate thickness, as determined by your measurements. If you have a table saw, you can rip spacers to thickness, otherwise use combinations of 1 x 4, 2 x 4, and lattice trim to achieve the desired depth. Mount the spacers to the studs, centered over the shelf height lines.

4

Assemble and install the shelves. Mount the roller hardware to the spacers. Check for level using a carpenter's level or torpedo level. Install the shelves on the rollers.

New Banquette

Almost everyone loves sitting in a booth at a restaurant—why not have one at home? Aside from providing an intimate, cozy setting for eating, games, or homework, a banquette or booth solves a critical space issue. An L-shaped booth eliminates the space needed to pull out chairs on two sides, plus, it allows children to sit closer together. Three kids can occupy booth space that is smaller than that required for two kids on two chairs. This project can add even more usable space by creating a roll-out storage unit under the booth seats.

This project creates an L-shaped, built-in booth in a kitchen corner. It does not show you how to redirect air vents or electrical outlets. Make sure you take into account the thickness of cushion foam if you plan on upholstering the backs. The plans assume you'll use 2" foam for seat cushions and back cushions. Thicker cushions will make the bench too shallow. Booth seating is most comfortable if the seats are 16 to 19" deep. The total height for the seat should be 18 to 19" to fit a standard 29"-tall table.

This project is designed to be painted, but if you wish to match your wood kitchen cabinets, you can use veneer plywood. Before beginning to build the

booth, carefully remove the base shoe or molding along both walls using a pry bar. Using a stud finder, mark the stud locations along both walls. Use masking tape to mark the stud locations to avoid marking on the wall surface.

Tools & Materials ▸

Tape measure	¾" paintable interior plywood
Stud finder	2 × 4 lumber
Pry bar	1 × 2 lumber
Circular saw	#8 screws (1 ⅝", 2", 2½", 3")
Cordless screwdriver	1½" finish head screws
Carpenter's square	Finish nails
Level	Edge banding
Bevel gauge	Trim molding
Compass	Painter's caulk
Jigsaw	Wood putty
Hammer	Paint
Masking tape	

How to Build a Banquette

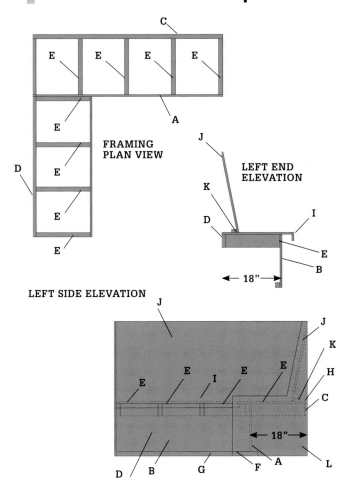

FRAMING PLAN VIEW

LEFT END ELEVATION

LEFT SIDE ELEVATION

18"

Cutting List ▶

Part	Name	Measurements	Material	Number
A	Kickboard, long	15½" × 60"	¾" plywood	1
B	Kickboard, short	15½" × 42"	¾" plywood	1
C	Ledger, long	60"	2 × 4	1
D	Ledger, short	42"	2 × 4	1
E	Braces	16½"	2 × 4	8
F	Cleat, long	60"	2 × 2	1
G	Cleat, short	42"	2 × 2	1
H	Seat, long	22" × 60"	¾" plywood	1
I	Seat, short	22" × 38"*	¾" plywood	1
J	Seat backs	60" × 24"	¾" plywood	2
K	Seat cleats	60"*	1 × 2	2
L	End pieces	20" × 40"*	¾" plywood	2

*cut to fit

Cut the kickboards, ledgers, and braces to length. Attach braces at each end of a ledger using two 2½" screws. Evenly space the other braces and attach. Attach the kickboard to the braces using 1⅝" screws. Use a carpenter's or combination square to make sure all joints are squared.

Cut the long cleat to length. Measure 18" out from the wall and draw a line parallel to the wall. Align the cleat with the inside edge of the line and attach to the floor using 2½" screws.

(continued)

Turn the brace and the kickboard assembly right side up and place against the wall and cleat. Check for level and make sure that the kickboard butts firmly against the cleat. Attach the ledger to the studs using two 3" screws per stud. Attach the kickboard to the cleat using 1⅝" screws.

Assemble the short bench and attach it to the studs and cleat following steps 1 through 3. Make sure the second bench butts firmly against the first bench.

Attach the long bench top using 1⅝" screws. Center the screws over the braces and not the kickboard. Measure from the edge of the long bench to the outside edge of the brace for the exact length of the short bench. Cut and attach the short bench top.

Lean one seat back against the wall so the bottom edge is 6" from the wall. Slide the long back cleat behind the back and mark its location. Use a bevel gauge to determine the edge bevel for the back. Remove the back and bevel the edge with a circular saw or table saw.

Attach the cleat to the seat top, using 1⅝" screws. Make sure the cleat is parallel to the wall. Apply edge banding to the top edge of the back. Replace the back and attach it to the cleat using 1⅝" screws. Attach it to the wall studs using 2" screws.

8

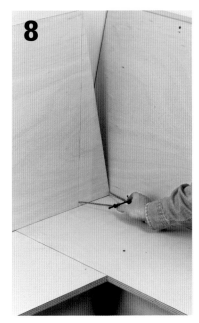

Lean the second back against the wall with its base 6" from the wall. Slide the short back cleat behind the back and mark its location. Use a compass to scribe the angle of the long back onto the short back. Cut along this mark using a circular saw. Attach the cleat and seat back as in step 7.

9

Place the end blanks against each end and trace the bench profile. Create a rounded or angular bench end that extends at least 1½" beyond the bench profile. This "lip" will prevent the cushions from slipping off the end. Cut the bench ends, using a jigsaw.

10

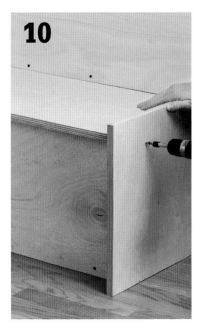

Before attaching the ends, use the jigsaw to radius the pointed bench ends to prevent bruises. Apply wood glue to the ends of the bench backs, kickboard, and bench tops. Attach the ends to the braces and bench using finish head screws every 6" to 8". Apply edge banding to the bench ends.

11

Attach the molding of your choice to the front edges of the bench with finish nails. Reattach the base molding if desired, or use trim molding to create panels, as pictured here. Fill all screw holes with wood putty, and sand smooth. Run a bead of painter's caulk along the joint between the bench top and back, the joint where the two bench backs meet, and between the bench back and wall. Smooth with a wet finger. Paint with a high-quality wood primer and satin, semigloss, or gloss paint. Make cushions, if desired.

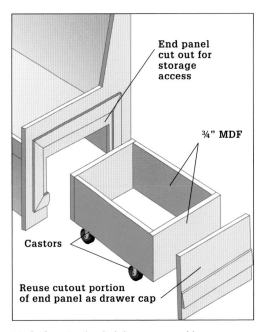

End panel cut out for storage access

¾" MDF

Castors

Reuse cutout portion of end panel as drawer cap

Variation: A wheeled drawer can add some storage space to your banquette. Before attaching the bench end, cut out an opening. Create a box with wheels and a drawer front to fit the opening.

Garden Window

Although often found in kitchens, a garden window is an attractive option for nearly any room in your home. Projecting out from the wall 16" to 24", garden windows add space to a room, making it feel larger. The glass roof and box-like design make them ideal growing environments for plants or display areas for collectibles. Garden windows also typically include front- or side-opening windows. These allow for ventilation and are usually available in either awning or casement style.

Home stores often stock garden windows in several common sizes. However, it may be difficult to locate a stock window that will fit in your existing window rough opening. In cases like this you must rebuild the rough opening to the proper size. It may be worth the added expense to custom-order your garden window to fit into the existing rough opening.

The large amount of glass in a garden window has a direct effect on the window's energy efficiency. When purchasing a garden window, as a minimum, look for double-pane glass with low-emissivity (low-E) coatings. More expensive super-efficient types of glass are available for severely cold climates.

Installation methods for garden windows vary by manufacturer. Some units include a nailing flange that attaches to the framing and holds the window against the house. Other models hang on a separate mounting frame that attaches to the outside of the house. In this project, the garden window has a built-in mounting sleeve that slides into the rough opening and is attached directly to the rough framing.

Tools & Materials ▸

Tape measure	Wood strips
Hammer	2 × 4s
Level	Shims
Framing square	Building paper
Circular saw	3" screws
Wood chisel	Drip edge
Stapler	Construction adhesive
Drill and bits	4d siding nails
Caulking gun	8d galvanized casing nails
Utility knife	Paintable silicone caulk
Garden window kit	

A garden window's glass roof makes it an ideal sunspot for houseplants, and it can also help a room feel larger.

How to Install a Garden Window

Prepare the project site and remove the interior and exterior trim, then remove the existing window.

Check the rough opening measurements to verify the correct window sizing. The rough opening should be about ½" larger than the window height and width. If necessary, attach wood strips to the rough framing as spacers to bring the opening to the required size.

Use a level to check that the sill of the rough opening is level and the side jambs are plumb. Use a framing square to make sure each corner is square. The rough framing must be in good condition in order to support the weight of the garden window. If the framing is severely deteriorated or out of plumb or square, you may need to reframe the rough opening.

Insert the garden window into the opening, pressing it tight against the framing. Support the unit with notched 2 × 4s under the bottom edge of the window until it has been fastened securely to the framing.

(continued)

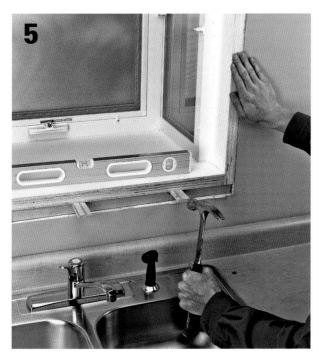

Position the inside edge of the window sleeve to be flush with the interior wall surface. Check the sill of the garden window for level. Shim beneath the lower side of the sill, if necessary, to make it level.

Make sure the garden window is level, then hold a piece of window trim in place along the exterior of the window and trace the outline onto the siding. Remove the window. Cut the siding down to the sheathing using a circular saw.

Install strips of building paper between the siding and the sheathing. Wrap them around the framing and staple them in place. On the sides, work from the bottom up so each piece overlaps the piece below. Reposition the window and reshim. Make sure the space between the window and the siding is equal to the width of the trim on all sides.

Drill countersunk pilot holes every 12" to 16" through the window sleeve into the rough header, jack studs, and sill.

9

Insert shims between the window sleeve and the rough frame at each hole location along the top and the sides to prevent bowing of the window frame. Fasten the window to the framing using 3" screws. Continue checking for level, plumb, and square as the screws are tightened.

10

Locate and mark the studs nearest the edges of the window using a stud finder. Cut two pieces of siding to fit behind the brackets, and tack them in place over the marked studs with 4d siding nails. Position the support brackets with the shorter side against the siding and the longer side beneath the window. Fasten the brackets to the window and the studs using the included screws.

11

Cut a piece of drip edge to length, apply construction adhesive to its top flange, and slide it under the siding above the window. Cut each trim piece to size. Position the trim and attach it using 8d galvanized casing nails driven through pilot holes. Seal the edges of the trim with a bead of paintable silicone caulk approximately ⅜" wide.

12

Cut all protruding shims flush with the framing using a utility knife or handsaw. Insulate or caulk the gaps between the window sleeve and the wall. Finish the installation by reinstalling the existing interior trim or installing new trim.

Framed Soffits

A soffit is a structure that hangs down from a ceiling or overhang, usually filling the cornice area where the wall meets the ceiling. You may choose to install soffits above the wall cabinets to create a solid wall surface. You may want to add a soffit to conceal the ductwork from an exhaust fan. Or, you might use a soffit to create a visual barrier (as well as a barrier to airborne food particles, odors, and grease) between the kitchen and the dining areas in an open floor plan. Soffits are also great for hiding recessed lighting fixtures if it is not possible to install recessed lighting in the existing ceiling.

If you are installing new cabinets, the soffits need to be built and installed first. This means you need to do the cabinet layout on the walls, then construct the soffits, taking care to make them level and plumb. Soffits above the cabinets may be flush with the cabinets, extend a few inches for a slight visual reveal, or extend farther (at least 8") to accommodate canister light fixtures.

You can construct soffits with 2 × 2 lumber. Size the soffit based on the size of the ductwork or the lighting that will be installed, but take care not to make them too small, as this will look unappealing.

If you are creating a soffit that will be supporting a ceiling cabinet from the soffit (there is no wall behind the cabinet), you should use 2 × 4 lumber. Build new soffits over the existing wall and ceiling surfaces. This is important because soffits create a pathway for airflow, so for insulation and fire prevention they should be separated from the wall and ceiling cavities. If your kitchen remodel is starting from stud level, install and mud the wall and ceiling surfaces before building the soffits.

Tools & Materials ▶

Tape measure	Wallboard screws
Chalkline	Cordless drill
Level	Circular saw
Stud finder	Utility knife
2 × 2 lumber	6", 8", and 10" mudding knives
2 × 4 lumber	Wallboard compound
2½" screws	Wallboard corner tape
⅝" wall board	

Build a soffit with framing lumber and drywall to open up new possibilities for installing task lighting or running ventilation ductwork.

How to Install a Soffit

1

Mark the desired outline of the soffits onto the ceiling. Use a carpenter's square to mark square corners. Use a chalk line to mark long straight sections. Use a stud finder to locate the ceiling joists and the wall studs in the area of the soffits.

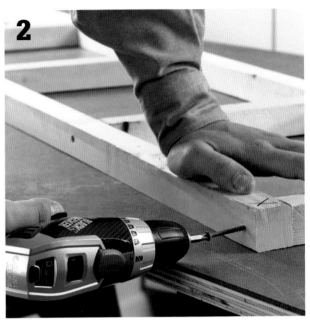

2

Build a ladderlike framework of 2 × 2s for the soffit sides. If you cannot find straight 2 × 2s, use a table saw to rip 2 × 4s in half. Attach the crossbars at regular intervals of 16" or 24" on center using 2½" screws. Create the ladder so the crossbars will not be aligned with the ceiling joists and wall studs when the framework is installed.

3

If the joists are perpendicular to the soffit, screw the soffit framework to the joists, aligned with the chalklines. If not, go to the next step.

4

If the joists are parallel to the soffit location, cut 2 × 4s to a length 1½" shorter than the width of the soffit. Screw these boards into the ceiling joists and toe-screw the ends into the ceiling wall plate.

(continued)

5

Attach the soffit framework to the ends of the 2 × 4s with drywall screws.

6

Use a level or laser level to mark the wall even with the bottom of the installed soffit framework. Cut 2 × 2s to the length of the soffit and attach this cleat to the wall aligned with the mark.

Tip ▸

If the joists are parallel to the soffit and the soffit is less than 16" wide, such as above shallow wall cabinets, you may need to remove the ceiling surface and install crossbraces between the joists. Remember that the ceiling surface must be reinstalled as a fire block before installing the soffit.

7

Cut crossmembers to fit between the bottom of the framework and the wall cleat. Attach the crossmembers by toe-screwing into the cleat and end screwing through the framework side. Place the crossmembers every 16" on center.

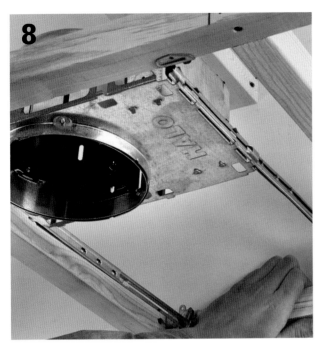

8

Install lighting or ductwork, if needed. Extend the mounting bars on recessed fixtures to reach framing members.

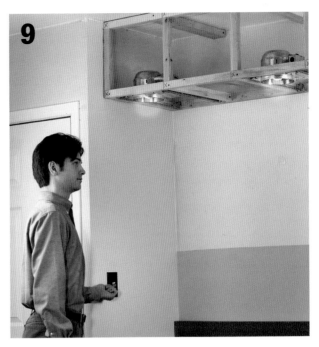

9

Finish installing lights, and then check to make sure they work. Once you've determined that the lights work properly, have the work inspected by an electrician and/or a local building inspector. With approval, you can begin to close up the soffit.

10

Cut and install ⅝" wallboard over the framework using wallboard screws. Attach the bottom sections first, then cut and attach the sides. *Note: Required minimum wallboard thickness is dictated by local building codes. Be sure to consult them before you begin installing wall coverings.*

11

Apply joint compound and tape to the wallboard. Use corner tape along all the edges. Sand smooth and finish with primer and paint.

Conversion Charts

Metric Conversions

To Convert:	To:	Multiply by:
Inches	Millimeters	25.4
Inches	Centimeters	2.54
Feet	Meters	0.305
Yards	Meters	0.914
Square inches	Square centimeters	6.45
Square feet	Square meters	0.093
Square yards	Square meters	0.836
Ounces	Milliliters	30.0
Pints (U.S.)	Liters	0.473 (Imp. 0.568)
Quarts (U.S.)	Liters	0.946 (Imp. 1.136)
Gallons (U.S.)	Liters	3.785 (Imp. 4.546)
Ounces	Grams	28.4
Pounds	Kilograms	0.454

To Convert:	To:	Multiply by:
Millimeters	Inches	0.039
Centimeters	Inches	0.394
Meters	Feet	3.28
Meters	Yards	1.09
Square centimeters	Square inches	0.155
Square meters	Square feet	10.8
Square meters	Square yards	1.2
Milliliters	Ounces	.033
Liters	Pints (U.S.)	2.114 (Imp. 1.76)
Liters	Quarts (U.S.)	1.057 (Imp. 0.88)
Liters	Gallons (U.S.)	0.264 (Imp. 0.22)
Grams	Ounces	0.035
Kilograms	Pounds	2.2

Converting Temperatures

Convert degrees Fahrenheit (F) to degrees Celsius (C) by following this simple formula: Subtract 32 from the Fahrenheit temperature reading. Then, multiply that number by $\frac{5}{9}$. For example, 77°F - 32 = 45. 45 × $\frac{5}{9}$ = 25°C.

To convert degrees Celsius to degrees Fahrenheit, multiply the Celsius temperature reading by $\frac{9}{5}$. Then, add 32. For example, 25°C × $\frac{9}{5}$ = 45. 45 + 32 = 77°F.

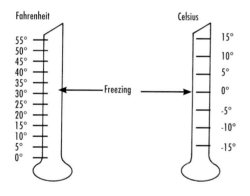

Metric Plywood Panels

Metric plywood panels are commonly available in two sizes: 1,200 mm × 2,400 mm and 1,220 mm × 2,400 mm, which is roughly equivalent to a 4 × 8-ft. sheet. Standard and Select sheathing panels come in standard thicknesses, while Sanded grade panels are available in special thicknesses.

Standard Sheathing Grade		Sanded Grade	
7.5 mm	($\frac{5}{16}$ in.)	6 mm	($\frac{4}{17}$ in.)
9.5 mm	($\frac{3}{8}$ in.)	8 mm	($\frac{5}{16}$ in.)
12.5 mm	($\frac{1}{2}$ in.)	11 mm	($\frac{7}{16}$ in.)
15.5 mm	($\frac{5}{8}$ in.)	14 mm	($\frac{9}{16}$ in.)
18.5 mm	($\frac{3}{4}$ in.)	17 mm	($\frac{2}{3}$ in.)
20.5 mm	($\frac{13}{16}$ in.)	19 mm	($\frac{3}{4}$ in.)
22.5 mm	($\frac{7}{8}$ in.)	21 mm	($\frac{13}{16}$ in.)
25.5 mm	(1 in.)	24 mm	($\frac{15}{16}$ in.)

Lumber Dimensions

Nominal - U.S.	Actual - U.S. (in inches)	Metric
1 × 2	$\frac{3}{4}$ × 1$\frac{1}{2}$	19 × 38 mm
1 × 3	$\frac{3}{4}$ × 2$\frac{1}{2}$	19 × 64 mm
1 × 4	$\frac{3}{4}$ × 3$\frac{1}{2}$	19 × 89 mm
1 × 5	$\frac{3}{4}$ × 4$\frac{1}{2}$	19 × 114 mm
1 × 6	$\frac{3}{4}$ × 5$\frac{1}{2}$	19 × 140 mm
1 × 7	$\frac{3}{4}$ × 6$\frac{1}{4}$	19 × 159 mm
1 × 8	$\frac{3}{4}$ × 7$\frac{1}{4}$	19 × 184 mm
1 × 10	$\frac{3}{4}$ × 9$\frac{1}{4}$	19 × 235 mm
1 × 12	$\frac{3}{4}$ × 11$\frac{1}{4}$	19 × 286 mm
1$\frac{1}{4}$ × 4	1 × 3$\frac{1}{2}$	25 × 89 mm
1$\frac{1}{4}$ × 6	1 × 5$\frac{1}{2}$	25 × 140 mm
1$\frac{1}{4}$ × 8	1 × 7$\frac{1}{4}$	25 × 184 mm
1$\frac{1}{4}$ × 10	1 × 9$\frac{1}{4}$	25 × 235 mm
1$\frac{1}{4}$ × 12	1 × 11$\frac{1}{4}$	25 × 286 mm
1$\frac{1}{2}$ × 4	1$\frac{1}{4}$ × 3$\frac{1}{2}$	32 × 89 mm
1$\frac{1}{2}$ × 6	1$\frac{1}{4}$ × 5$\frac{1}{2}$	32 × 140 mm
1$\frac{1}{2}$ × 8	1$\frac{1}{4}$ × 7$\frac{1}{4}$	32 × 184 mm
1$\frac{1}{2}$ × 10	1$\frac{1}{4}$ × 9$\frac{1}{4}$	32 × 235 mm
1$\frac{1}{2}$ × 12	1$\frac{1}{4}$ × 11$\frac{1}{4}$	32 × 286 mm
2 × 4	1$\frac{1}{2}$ × 3$\frac{1}{2}$	38 × 89 mm
2 × 6	1$\frac{1}{2}$ × 5$\frac{1}{2}$	38 × 140 mm
2 × 8	1$\frac{1}{2}$ × 7$\frac{1}{4}$	38 × 184 mm
2 × 10	1$\frac{1}{2}$ × 9$\frac{1}{4}$	38 × 235 mm
2 × 12	1$\frac{1}{2}$ × 11$\frac{1}{4}$	38 × 286 mm
3 × 6	2$\frac{1}{2}$ × 5$\frac{1}{2}$	64 × 140 mm
4 × 4	3$\frac{1}{2}$ × 3$\frac{1}{2}$	89 × 89 mm
4 × 6	3$\frac{1}{2}$ × 5$\frac{1}{2}$	89 × 140 mm

Liquid Measurement Equivalents

1 Pint	= 16 Fluid Ounces	= 2 Cups
1 Quart	= 32 Fluid Ounces	= 2 Pints
1 Gallon	= 128 Fluid Ounces	= 4 Quarts

Drill Bit Guide

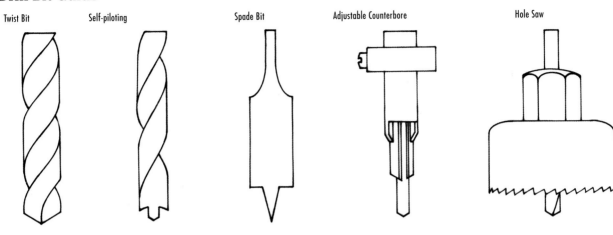

Twist Bit   Self-piloting   Spade Bit   Adjustable Counterbore   Hole Saw

Counterbore, Shank & Pilot Hole Diameters

Screw Size	Counterbore Diameter for Screw Head	Clearance Hole for Screw Shank	Pilot Hole Diameter	
			Hard Wood	Soft Wood
#1	.146 ($^9/_{64}$)	$^5/_{64}$	$^3/_{64}$	$^1/_{32}$
#2	$^1/_4$	$^3/_{32}$	$^3/_{64}$	$^1/_{32}$
#3	$^1/_4$	$^7/_{64}$	$^1/_{16}$	$^3/_{64}$
#4	$^1/_4$	$^1/_8$	$^1/_{16}$	$^3/_{64}$
#5	$^1/_4$	$^9/_{64}$	$^5/_{64}$	$^1/_{16}$
#6	$^5/_{16}$	$^5/_{32}$	$^3/_{32}$	$^5/_{64}$
#7	$^5/_{16}$	$^5/_{32}$	$^3/_{32}$	$^5/_{64}$
#8	$^3/_8$	$^{11}/_{64}$	$^1/_8$	$^3/_{32}$
#9	$^3/_8$	$^{11}/_{64}$	$^1/_8$	$^3/_{32}$
#10	$^3/_8$	$^3/_{16}$	$^1/_8$	$^7/_{64}$
#11	$^1/_2$	$^3/_{16}$	$^5/_{32}$	$^9/_{64}$
#12	$^1/_2$	$^7/_{32}$	$^9/_{64}$	$^1/_8$

Abrasive Paper Grits - (Aluminum Oxide)

Very Coarse	Coarse	Medium	Fine	Very Fine
12 - 36	40 - 60	80 - 120	150 - 180	220 - 600

Photo Resources

Aristokraft Cabinetry Styles, Solutions and More
www.aristokraft.com
p. 40 (left)

Armstrong Flooring
www.armstrong.com/flooring
p. 220, 221 (top), 230 (left)

Broan-NuTone
Bath Fans, Ventilation Fans, Range Hoods, Trash
Compactors
www.broan.com
p. 250

Cambria Natural Quartz Countertops
www.cambriausa.com
p. 88 (lower)

Julie Caruso, photographer
p. 124 (top)

Todd Caverly, architectural photographer
www.toddcaverly.com
p. 8 (top), 10 (top), 30, 130

Diamond Cabinets
www.diamondcabinets.com
p. 40 (right)

DuPont Corian
www2.Dupont.com
p. 89 (top)

Eco-Friendly
www.ecofriendlyflooring.com
p. 223 (right)

Eco-Timber
Sustainable Hardwood and Bamboo Flooring
www.ecotimber.com
p. 223 (left)

Energy Star
www.energystar.gov
p. 157 (right)

Tony Giammarino, photographer
www.tonygiammarino.com
p. 8 (lower left) design K. Kowach, 9 (lower left), 86, 131
(lower left), 154 (top)

GE Appliances (General Electric)
www.geappliances.com
p. 11 (top right), 31, 146, 178 (top left)

Green Mountain Soapstone Co.
www.greenmountainsoapstone.com
p. 90 (lower)

IKEA Home Furnishings
www.ikea.com
p. 13 (top & lower), 14 (lower right), 56, 57 (top left), 129,
131 (top right), 258

iStock Photo
www.istockphoto.com
p. 6, 11 (top left), 12 (lower), 16 (lower right), 17 (top left),
160 (lower), 228 (inset lower), 246

Kohler Plumbing
Fixtures, Faucets, Furniture, Engines, Generators
www.kohler.com
p. 16 (top left & right), 17 (lower right), 120, 196, 208, 245

LivedIn Images
www.livedinimages.com
p. 18, 85, 219, 224, 240

Karen Melvin Photography
www.karenmelvin.com
p. 243 (left)

National Kitchen & Bath Association (NKBA)
www.nkba.org
p. 10 (lower) Marcy Walls

Neil Kelly Cabinets
www.neilkelly.com
p. 16 (lower left), 242

Photolibrary
www.photolibrary.com
p. 12 (top), 14 (lower left), 15 (lower), 17 (top right)

Plato Woodwork, Inc.
www.platowoodwork.com
p. 8 (lower right)

Price Pfister
Kitchen Faucets, Bathroom Faucets, Showerheads,
Accessories
www.pricepfister.com
p. 156 (all)

Eric Roth, photographer
www.ericrothphoto.com
p. 4, 9 (top), 96 for Thomas Buekborough

Andrea Rugg, photographer
www.andrearugg.com
p. 17 (lower left)

Shutterstock
www.shutterstock.com
p. 14 (top), 15 (top), 122 (lower right), 131 (top left)

SieMatic
www.siematic.com
p. 37

Urban Homes
www.uhny.com
p. 9 (lower right), 243 (right)

Jessie Walker, photographer
www.jessiewalker.com
p. 11 (lower)

Photo Credits

p. 3 LivedIn Images

p. 4 Eric Roth

p. 6 iStock Photo

p. 8
(top) Todd Caverly
(lower left) © Giammarino/design K. Kowach
www.TonyGiammarino.com
(lower right) Plato Woodworking

p. 9
(top) Eric Roth
(lower left) © Tony Giammarino
www.TonyGiammarino.com
(lower right) Urban Homes, NY

p. 10
(top) Todd Caverly
(lower) NKBA/Marcy Walls

p. 11
(top left) iStock Photo
(top right) GE Appliances
(lower) Jessie Walker

p. 12
(top) Photolibrary
(lower) iStock Photo

p. 13
(top) IKEA
(lower) IKEA

p. 14
(top) Shutterstock
(lower left) Photolibrary
(lower right) IKEA

p. 15
(top) Shutterstock
(lower) Photolibrary

p. 16
(top left & right) Kohler
(lower left) Neil Kelley Cabinets
(lower right) iStock Photo

p. 17
(top left) iStock Photo
(top right) Photolibrary
(lower left) Andrea Rugg
(lower right) Kohler

p. 18 LivedIn Images

p. 30 Todd Caverly

p. 31 GE Appliances

p. 37 SieMatic

p. 40
(left) Aristokraft
(right) Diamond

p. 56 IKEA

p. 57
(top left) IKEA
(top right) Kohler

p. 85 LivedIn Images

p. 86 © Tony Giammarino
www.TonyGiammarino.com

p. 88 (lower) Cambria

p. 89 (top) DuPont Corian

p. 90 (lower) Green Mountain Soapstone Co.

p. 96 © Eric Roth for Thomas Buekborough

p. 124 (top) Julie Caruso

p. 129 IKEA

p. 130 Todd Caverly

p. 131
(top left) Shutterstock
(top right) IKEA
(lower left) © Tony Giammarino
www.TonyGiammarino.com
(lower right) IKEA

p. 146 GE Appliances

p. 153 (lower right) GE Appliances

p. 154
(top) © Tony Giammarino
www.TonyGiammarino.com

p. 156 Photos courtesy of Price Pfister

p. 157 (right) Energy Star / Department of Energy

p. 160 (lower) iStock Photo

p. 165 GE Appliances

p. 178 (top left) GE Appliances

p. 196 Kohler

p. 208 (top) Kohler

p. 212 General Electric

p. 219 LivedIn Images

p. 220 Armstrong Flooring

p. 221 (top) Armstrong Flooring

p. 223
(left) Eco-timber
(right) Eco-friendly

p. 224 LivedIn Images

p. 228 (inset lower) iStock Photo

p. 230 (left) Armstrong Flooring

p. 241 LivedIn Images

p. 242 Neil Kelly Cabinets

p. 243
(left) © Karen Melvin Photography
(right) Urban homes, NY

p. 245 Kohler

p. 246 iStock Photo

p. 250 (lower) Broan NuTone

p. 259 IKEA

Resources

American Institute of Architects
800-242-3837
www.aia.org

American Lighting Association
800-274-4484
www.americanlightingassoc.com

American Society of Interior Designers
202-546-3480
www.asid.org

Association of Home Appliance Manufacturers
202-872-5955
www.aham.org

Black & Decker Corp.
Power tools, home products
800-544-6986
www.blackanddecker.com

Center for Inclusive Design & Environmental Access
School of Architecture and Planning University of Buffalo
716-829-3485
www.ap.buffalo.edu

Center for Universal Design
NC State University
919-515-3082
www.design.ncsu.edu

Construction Materials Recycling Association
630-548-4510
www.cdrecycling.org

Energy & Environmental Building Association
952-881-1098
www.eeba.com

Energy Star
888-762-7937
www.energystar.gov

Kampel Enterprises
(SeamFil laminate repair compound, page 109)
800-837-4971
www.kampelent.com

Kitchen Cabinet Manufacturers Association
703-264-1690
www.kcma.org

Kohler
800-456-4537
www.kohler.com

National Kitchen & Bath Association (NKBA)
800-843-6522
www.nkba.org

National Wood Flooring Association
800-422-4556
www.woodfloors.org

Repair-It-All
(Vinyl & leather repair kits, page 109)
440-774-3900
www.repair-it-all.com

Resilient Floor Covering Institute
301-340-8580
www.rfci.com

Rockler Woodworking & Hardware
(Glass clips, page 67)
800-279-4441
www.rockler.com

The Tile Council of America
864-646-8453
www.tileusa.com

U.S. Environmental Protection Agency-Indoor Air Quality
www.epa.gov

Index

CREATIVE PUBLISHING international

NOTE TO READERS

The DVD disk included with this book is offered as a free premium to buyers of this book.

The live video demonstrations are designed to be viewed on electronic devices suitable for viewing standard DVD video discs, including most television DVD players, as well as a Mac or PC computer equipped with a DVD-compatible disc drive and standard multi-media software.

In addition, your DVD-compatible computer will allow you to read the electronic version of the book. The electronic version is provided in a standard PDF form, which is readable by any software compatible with that format, including Adobe Reader.

To access the electronic pages, open the directory of your computer's DVD drive, and click on the icon with the image of this book cover.

The electronic book carries the same copyright restrictions as the print version. You are welcome to use it in any way that is useful for you, including printing the pages for your own use. You can also loan the disc to friends or family members, much the way you would loan a printed book.

However, we do request that you respect copyright law and the integrity of this book by not attempting to make electronic copies of this disc, or by distributing the files electronically via the internet.

Creative Publishing
international

400 First Avenue North • Suite 300 • Minneapolis, MN 55401 • 800-328-0590, opt 2 • www.creativepub.com